A Practical Guide to E-commerce
and Internet Law

A Practical Guide to E-commerce and Internet Law

Osborne Clarke

 ICSA Publishing

Published by ICSA Publishing Limited
16 Park Crescent
London W1B 1AH

Typeset in Sabon and Franklin Gothic by
Hands Fotoset, Woodthorpe, Nottingham

Printed and bound in Great Britain by
TJ International Ltd, Padstow, Cornwall

British Library Cataloguing in Publication Data
A catalogue record for this book is available from the British Library.

ISBN: 1-86072-180-X

Contents

Contents

Contents

The Contributors

Maria Anassutzi – Associate Solicitor. *Date of qualification: 1995*
Maria joined Osborne Clarke in 2001 from DLA, Manchester where she advised on IP/IT law and all aspects of commercial law, including agency, distribution and franchise agreements. Maria has particular expertise in advising on software licences, software development, facilities management and outsourcing contracts. She also advises on competition law.

Amanda Clift-Matthews. *Date of admission to the Bar: 1995*
Amanda practised at the criminal law bar until 1998, whereupon she became dual qualified and moved to Lovells in order to specialise in intellectual property law. Amanda joined Osborne Clarke in December 2000 and is an experienced adviser on a full range of legal issues affecting e-commerce, in particular, online liability and cybercrime. Amanda is an active participant in the ISPA Legal Forum and is the author of a number of articles.

Laura Darby – Assistant Solicitor. *Date of qualification: 2000*
Laura joined Osborne Clarke in March 1999 as a trainee solicitor. Previously she had worked in the legal teams at ACC Telecom and Worldcom. Laura's main areas of expertise are advising on telecoms regulatory and licensing issues. She has recently set up the *TELex* regulatory service, a bespoke telecoms advisory service focusing on the regulatory issues that affect the telecoms sector. Laura also drafts, advises and negotiates a variety of commercial contracts and advises on non-contentious intellectual property matters and UK company start-ups.

Meg Francis – Tax Consultant
Meg joined Osborne Clarke in 2001, and specialises in all areas of corporate tax, particularly corporate finance, e-commerce businesses, mergers and acquisitions and international transactions. She qualified as a lawyer in Australia and practised at Ernst & Young in Melbourne Australia for two years.

Rory Graham – Partner. *Date of qualification: 1990*
Rory specialises in transactional work in the technology sector, acting for a

broad range of clients from multinational corporations to start-ups in the telecommunications, IT and digital media fields. He is recognised as an expert in technology outsourcing and acts for both users and providers of IT and telecoms services in outsourcing and managed services deals (including desktop, data centres, call centres and other voice and data services). His other work includes systems procurement and software licensing.

Lieve Jansen – Assistant Solicitor. *Date of qualification: 2000*
Lieve, a Belgium-born, English-qualified lawyer, joined Osborne Clarke in November 2000 and specialises in intellectual property, music and commercial law, particularly for the media, entertainment and advertising sectors. Her experience includes drafting agency contracts, assignments and licences of multi-media rights; advising on music management and recording contracts; providing copy clearance advice; and drafting online content and hosting agreements.

Erika Jupe – Partner. *Date of qualification: 1990*
Erika is a partner in the corporate tax unit. She advises on all aspects of corporate tax issues, including value added tax, stamp duties and SDRT, employee and cross-border tax issues. She has advised clients in a broad range of sectors, including manufacturing, venture capital, transport and IT and telecoms.

Anna Keeling – Senior Solicitor. *Date of qualification: 1998*
Before entering the legal profession, Anna worked for ten years in advertising and marketing. Since qualifying, she has specialised in intellectual property law, advising on e-commerce, trade marks, patents, research agreements and all types of rights licensing. She also advises on publishing and copyright issues, including online and electronic rights.

Lucy Lindstrom – Solicitor. *Qualified: 1998*
Lucy trained at Herbert Smith and qualified into its employment department. She joined Osborne Clarke's London employment department in March 2000 and advises on all aspects of non-contentious and contentious employment law. She has advised a number of ITTM clients, in particular drafting contractual documentation, advising on the engagement of contractors and IR35 issues, advising on termination of employment. Lucy recently spent six months on secondment to the Legal Department of British Airways Plc, advising their senior HR personnel.

James Mullock – Partner. *Date of qualification: 1996*
James specialises in content licensing agreements, e-commerce standard business contracts, telecommunications regulatory and licensing issues, encryption and data protection issues, and IT and telecoms procurement and supply contracts. He has particular experience in dealing in cross-jurisdictional transactions, especially US–UK telecoms work. James is the

co-author of a guide to the UK Data Protection Act 1998 which is published by the Stationery Office.

Emily Preston – Assistant Solicitor. *Date of qualification: 1999*

Emily has experience of a wide range of non-contentious IT and e- and m-commerce transactions, including global software development and licensing agreements, supply and installation, support and maintenance and web-based frameworks. She has advised on a range of internet issues and has been involved in the setting up Outlaw.com the web-site for e-commerce. She is also involved with the ISPA, the body concerned with issues for internet service providers.

Simon Rendell – Partner.

Simon is head of the firm's Technology, Media and Telecoms Department. He is recognised in *The Chambers Directory* and *The Legal 500* as one of the UK's leading practitioners of IT and telecommunications law. He has practised in this field for sixteen years, as well as advising on EC regulatory and competition law, intellectual property and all aspects of commercial law. Simon is also a Consultant Editor for *IT Law Today* and *International Computer Law*. He is responsible for the co-ordination of Osborne Clarke's North American business alliances and assists in the development of the firm's European Economic Interest Group.

Vincent Scheurer – Associate. *Called to the Bar: 1994*

Vincent is a barrister specialising in non-contentious intellectual property matters in the field of IT, particularly interactive entertainment and the Internet. He began working in house with an Internet Service Provider during 1996 before moving to the position of sole in house counsel with a software publisher, joining Osborne Clarke's TMT department in 1999. Vincent has extensive experience of negotiating and advising on commercial agreements for the development, distribution and other exploitation of computer software.

Paula Staunton – Partner. *Date of qualification: 1991*

Paula joined Osborne Clarke in 1996 and is now is a partner in the Technology/Media and Telecoms department, which she developed with three of her colleagues. The department is now one of the largest technology departments in the country. Paula's eleven years' experience with technology clients (both suppliers and users) has involved work ranging from intellectual property licensing to software development, advice to suppliers with their sales channels (distribution/agency) to the support and maintenance of software, data protection to the numerous legal issues surrounding e-commerce initiatives. Paula has strong links with Osborne Clarke's European Alliance and works very closely with her European colleagues while assisting clients in their expansion throughout Europe.

Claire Wagner – Partner. *Date of qualification: 1994*

Claire joined Osborne Clarke in 1996. She is head of Osborne Clarke's competition unit and specialises in advising on European and UK competition law as well as advising on other areas of European law and regulation. Following the introduction of the Competition Act 1998, Claire has worked with a number of businesses to improve and implement competition law compliance programmes.

Mark Webber – Solicitor. *Date of qualification: 1999*

Mark advises on non-contentious commercial matters in the IT, telecoms and e-commerce fields and has wide experience in transactional technology deals, service procurement, outsourcing and licensing. Mark has advised on a number of high-profile portal, MVNO, WAP and ASP ventures, as well as on numerous business-critical IT outsourcings.

Table of Cases

Table of Statutes

Trade Marks Act 1994
Unfair Contract Terms Act 1977
Value Added Tax Act 1994

Commercial Agents (Council Directive) Regulations 1993 (SI 1993 No. 3053)
Consumer Protection (Distance Selling) Regulations 2000
Control of Misleading Advertisements (Amendment) Regulations 2000
Control of Misleading Advertising (Amendment) Regulations 2000
Copyright and Rights in Databases Regulations 1997 (SI 1997/3032)
Distance Selling Regulations 2000
Electronic Commerce Directive (2000/31/EC)
Electronic Signatures Directive (1999/93/EC)
Food Labelling Regulations 1996
General Product Safety Regulations 1994
Race Equality Directive (2000/43)
Sale of Consumer Goods and Associated Guarantees (1999/44/EC)
Stop Now Orders (EC Directive) Regulations 2001
Telecommunications (Lawful Business Practice) (Interception of
    Communications) Regulations 2000
Telecommunications (Lawful Business Practice) (Interception of
    Communications) Regulations 2000
The Consumer Protection (Distance Selling) Regulations 2000
The Electronic Commerce Directive (2000/31/EC)
Transfer of Undertakings (Protection of Employment) Regulations 1984
Unfair Terms in Consumer Contracts Regulations 1999

Foreword

The internet is undoubtedly here to stay. Although the early days of rapid expansion appear over, there remains steady growth in access and usage. The internet has established itself as the medium of the third millennium and mobile connection will ensure that we are unable to live without it.

While some internet pioneers may have thought – or hoped – that the medium would remain an anarchic space beyond the bounds of law and convention, the internet has grown up. Governments and legislative bodies have been active in regulating the revolution in the last couple of years. In many areas national governments have found ways to rely on the existing law, adapting and construing it to make it applicable to the internet. In others, the legislative bodies have been obliged to create new regulations. Where Brussels considered the members of the European Union slow to act, the Commission itself took the initiative, the E-commerce Directive being a good example. If all else failed, the European courts, and in particular the English courts, have been forced to overcome the absence of new rules by slowly developing case law to fill in the gaps.

Looking back to the early days, it seems surprising that most internet companies survived without facing a major legal nightmare. It took some time for the first lawsuits to be filed, but times have changed. With fewer grey areas and increasing regulation, only the very fortunate will avoid legal exposure if companies fail to adapt to the changed environment.

Today, the primary rules for the new medium are set, but many areas are still untouched by regulation and many more remain grey. The authors of this Practical Guide, who have all developed areas of expertise at Osborne Clarke, have focused on a number of areas of the law relevant to the internet, illustrating that there is not a single area that can be called 'Internet Law'. Instead, due to the fact that the internet touches so many different aspects of our daily lives, many areas of law apply. Some are easily associated with the medium – for example, intellectual property, consumer protection and data protection. Others, like advertising rules, crime and human rights, do not so easily come to mind. But this diversity contributes to the fascination the internet offers to the legal profession.

One of the most challenging tasks for any lawyer is presenting legal content in a way that is both interesting and easy to understand. The authors of this Guide have succeeded on both counts. They have produced an accessible text, which reads almost like a novel and contains passionate contributions. It will enable you to familiarise yourself with the vital information you require for your business, job or profession. Setting up an internet business is not only challenging in terms of getting the right business plan and obtaining funding. The 'legal' requirements, making the right risk assessments for the offering of products and services and appropriate structuring of the legal relationship with the customer, can sometimes be even more demanding. You will certainly find a great deal of useful information in this book. But even if you have no professional 'obligations', you will find much of benefit. You will learn a lot about the law and also find new facets to a medium you thought you already knew.

Enjoy!

Dr Christian Keim, LL.M.
Legal Director, Yahoo! Europe

Preface and Acknowledgements

The internet is one of the most powerful tools available to modern businesses. It allows traders to advertise and sell products online. It permits customers to browse virtual shop windows from their homes, select goods and place an order at the touch of a button. If used properly, it can significantly reduce costs and increase efficiency.

However, the transition from traditional high street business to online trader is not a simple one. The infamous dot.com crash highlighted the dangers of poor planning and preparation.

The internet is not a magic formula; it is a business medium. As such, it is necessary to understand both its benefits and pitfalls. For instance, the internet offers far greater scope to marketeers, permitting them to reach a much larger audience at a significantly lower cost than traditional methods of advertising. However, as exposure to consumers is increased – often across various international borders – so are the risks.

This book targets senior business managers who want to make the quantum leap from traditional trading to e-commerce and who need to acquire a general understanding of the legal implications.

Chapter 1 provides readers with some essential background, explaining the key differences between traditional and e-commerce.

Chapter 2 aims to put the move from 'bricks to clicks' into context. Using the example of a fictional company, it creates a step-by-step scenario, walking the reader through the legal steps a traditional business might follow when preparing to trade online. It covers registering a domain name; designing a web-site; advertising; data protection; and online contracts with customers.

Most of the issues covered in chapter 2 are expanded in subsequent chapters which aim to give a broader perspective on the relevant law. These include subjects as diverse as employment, tax and competition law. The aim is to make managers who are not legally trained aware of issues that can be key to their business, but which are frequently overlooked or insufficiently understood.

For instance, why is it necessary to issue employees' with guidelines on the use of e-mail and the internet in company time? Can employers monitor their e-mail communications and internet use? How do the requirements of the EC and UK competition authorities affect e-commerce? How can a business take advantage of international tax structuring?

We would like to thank all contributors to *A Practical Guide to E-commerce and Internet Law* for their hard work and patience. These include not only the contributors, whose biographies appear at pp. xv–xviii, but also those responsible for advising, researching, proof-reading, amending and collating the book. They are: Simon Rendell (Head of the TMT Department), Paula Staunton, Nick Johnson, Andrew Braithwaite, David Cubitt, Mark Culbert, Truda Borthwick-Stevens, Anna Montes, Christina Kelly, Kumarlo Mens, Samina Khan and Samantha Griffin.

1 Introduction: The Legal Context

Introduction

This chapter seeks to introduce the reader to some of the concepts and issues relating to e-commerce that will be covered in greater depth elsewhere in this book. It starts with a review of the basic principles of contract law. While these are still relevant to modern business, the formation of contracts online has presented some interesting problems.

E-mail and click-wrap contracts, the two main methods of contracting online, are discussed; and the question of how to incorporate terms and conditions into a web-site is considered.

In addition to a brief overview of some of the relevant statutory and case law, this chapter also highlights some items of specific interest to online traders. These include: warranties; dealing with returns and refunds; consumer protection; payment and security on the internet; and law and jurisdiction.

1. Basic principles of contract

Every day, we enter into contracts without realising that we are doing so. For example, successful deals made by the sales force may comprise the 'contractual steps' set out below.

Under English law the formation of a contract requires the following elements:

- an *offer*;
- unequivocal *acceptance* of the offer, which is communicated to the person making the offer;
- *consideration*;
- an *intention to create legal relations*; and
- *capacity* in each party to be legally bound.

A contract is formed when an offer has been accepted and, following

1

acceptance, the offer cannot be withdrawn. In general, contracts may be made verbally or in writing. However, there are some exceptions; these include formal contracts made by deed and other types of contract, such as contracts for the sale of an interest in land, which must be made in writing.

It is very important to be able to identify, and control, exactly when a contract has been formed. For instance, in the case of an international contract, this will decide which country's laws will be used when interpreting and enforcing the agreement. In the context of online trading, it is crucial to control when a contract is created, to minimise business risk.

1.1 Offer

English law distinguishes between an offer and an 'invitation to treat', such as an advertisement that promotes the sale of products but is not an offer. Under traditional contract law, the display of goods in a shop is not an offer but an invitation to treat (*Pharmaceutical Society of Britain* v. *Boots Cash Chemist Ltd*. [1952] 2QB 795). Accordingly, when the purchaser asks the seller if he can buy a product, this constitutes the offer. At this point, the seller is free to accept or reject the purchaser's offer.

A business intending to trade online will be concerned to control the contract by ensuring its customers make offers, open for acceptance by the web-site owner. It should construct its web-site so that it is, in effect, a shop window. The site should carry a clear statement that the supplier will not be bound to a contract unless the supplier accepts the offer of the customer. (Statements to this effect are often seen on traditional terms and conditions and are regarded as an invitation to treat.)

The online business will also be keen to ensure it knows to whom it is making offers, and is in a position to target only those it wishes to accept. For instance, an online liquor store may target adults only; and a geographical limit on territories is often set on a retailer, who will only be able to target customers in its territory.

1.2 Acceptance

Under English law a contract is formed when the offer is accepted. Acceptance may affect both the timing of the contract and the place. In the case of timing, it may be crucial for an online auctioneer to clarify which bid was accepted first; and in the case of location, this will affect the law that governs the contract and the tax treatment of the transaction. There are two rules of acceptance:

1. The *receipt rule*: this states that a contract is formed at the time and place

when the acceptance is received by the offeror. This applies to instantaneous forms of communications such as telephone, fax and telex.
2. The *postal rule*: this applies to communications by post, according to which acceptance is effective at the time of posting of the communication. The postal rule does not apply to instantaneous communications.

Legal opinion is divided on whether the postal rule applies to e-business, that is acceptance via a web-site or via e-mail. A supplier is advised to override the postal rule by using a clear statement in its web-site terms and conditions as to how acceptance can be made, and when it becomes effective.

Acceptance of an offer is normally communicated, but can also be inferred by the conduct of the parties, which may amount to performance (for example, carrying out the service requested or paying the price for the relevant item). So it is important that the seller makes it clear which acts (if any) will amount to acceptance.

1.3 Consideration

Consideration is essential to create a contract. In simple terms it is the exchange of promises, normally for the supplier to give up something of value, in exchange for the customer making payment. The requirements are the same in online business.

Consideration need not be money. For example, an online business may offer an information service that provides information to subscribers. In return, the person receiving the service agrees to supply the provider with his or her profile and other relevant data. Such data may be valuable in itself and will therefore amount to consideration.

1.4 The intention to create legal relations

Although intention to create a binding contract is a requirement, it is generally not an issue in day-to-day business – if a party alleges a lack of intent on their part, they face a hefty burden of proof. Just consider what arguments Argos raised following a computer error, which resulted in the company advertising televisions for sale on its web-site for £3 instead of the correct price of £299.99. The intention of the parties to enter into a legally binding document can be inferred from surrounding circumstances – for example, the payment of money or compliance with certain obligations in return for goods or services.

Letters of intent (unless otherwise stated) do not create legal relations since they indicate only an intention to negotiate rather than establish contractual obligations. As we will see, the same principle applies to electronic commerce.

1.5 Capacity

A number of difficulties may arise for online suppliers over the identity of the other parties to a contract, if their details are not known. Such difficulties generally fall into two categories: legal capacity and mistake.

1. *Legal capacity*: Under English law, contracts made with minors are generally voidable at the minor's option. This means that, while not binding the minor, such contracts will be binding on the other party. However, adults who do not seek to take unfair advantage of a minor with whom they have entered into a contract are entitled to uphold a contract for certain necessary items covering a variety of goods and services excluding luxuries. Generally speaking a contract with a mental patient is valid unless the other contracting party knew of the other's disability in which case the contract is voidable.

2. *Mistake*: Under English law one party's consent to making the agreement may be void if the mistake is fundamental. It is another issue affecting online trade: purchasers seeking the goods of one company may mistakenly visit the web-site of another company with a confusingly similar domain name. Would such purchasers be entitled to return the goods or services and receive a refund once they realise their mistake? A mistake as to identity is fundamental and will therefore negate the purchaser's consent to the making of the contract. The mistake must also have induced the mistaken party to enter the contract. However, even if the mistake led a party to enter the contract, the contract will remain valid unless the mistake was operative.

   There are three general circumstances where a mistake will be operative. These are:

   a) where a reasonable person could not infer the intention of the parties from the circumstances surrounding the transaction; or
   b) where one party knew of the other's mistake; or
   c) where one party negligently induced the other's mistake.

2. Electronic negotiations

The development of e-mail and the World Wide Web has not affected the application of the current principles of contract law, nor is it expected to do so. However, there are peculiar technological issues regarding the formation of a contract online.

The supplier's web-site must act as a virtual shop window, allowing him the freedom to accept or reject the customer's offer. By this means, the supplier will have the flexibility to choose with whom to contract.

He will also be able to avoid an embarrassing and costly situation where he is contractually bound to fulfil an order but is unable to do so due to a stock shortage. For instance, the supplier may state, as a term of trading, that he will not accept an offer until payment has been taken, which, in turn, will depend on the goods being ready for despatch. In the event that the goods are not available, the supplier will not take payment and will be able to refuse the order.

2.1 Making contracts online

There are two main methods of electronic contracting, each with its own characteristics and each requiring to be treated separately. Electronic Data Interchange (EDI) has been around for a long time but is mainly used for trade between large organisations.

The first method of electronic contracting is by *electronic mail*. E-mail is considered to be the digital equivalent of a letter. It can be used to make an offer or to communicate acceptance; it can be used for advertisements and for sending unwanted communications ('spam'). If an offer and subsequent acceptance are made by e-mail, it is important to establish the point when a contract concluded by e-mail is formed. Would the postal rule or the receipt rule apply?

E-mail, although very quick, is not instantaneous and therefore it is uncertain whether the postal rule applies. If it does, the contract is formed once the customer has sent the acceptance message. It is, however, difficult for the customer to know whether or not the e-mail was ever received or, if it arrived, whether or not it was incomplete or corrupted.

If, on the other hand, the receipt rule applies, when does the actual receipt of a message occur? Is it when it arrives at the supplier's mail server or when the supplier reads it?

It may be appropriate for the supplier to specify on its web-site exactly what constitutes acceptance. For example, one suggestion has been to state that the offer is not accepted until payment has been taken from or charged to the customer.

The second method of contracting on the internet is often known as the *click-wrap contract*. The supplier will need to control both the manner in which an offer can be made and the terms on which the customer may buy from the web-site.

The way in which this can be achieved is by using standard terms and conditions for accessing the web-site and for trading, which apply to any offers made by the customer. Any invitation to treat made by the supplier must refer to the supplier's standard terms, which must be brought to the attention of the customer before the offer is made. In practical terms, the design and structure of the web-site are important, as is the navigation. Consider where the terms of contract will be displayed, whether part of them will be invisible 'below the fold', and where the 'I agree' button will be located.

2.2 Incorporation of online terms and conditions

There are a number of ways of incorporating contract terms into a web-site:

1. By referring to the terms with a hypertext link, which means that a customer can click on the link if he/she wishes to read the terms.
2. By displaying the terms on the web-site where they can be seen before entering into the contract.
3. By displaying the terms on the pre-contract web page and including a dialogue box.

The best method for ensuring the customer is aware of all the terms is the last one, which requires the customer to scroll through the terms and acknowledge acceptance by ticking a box or clicking on an icon before he/she can proceed with the transaction. As a general rule, the customer will not be bound by the terms unless they have been brought to his/her notice prior to the conclusion of the contract. Any changes to the terms must be brought to the customer's attention immediately. It is good practice to allow for a reasonable period of time to pass before the new changes become effective. The period will depend upon the seller's business.

It is important to prevent the customer from being able either to amend existing terms in the electronic form or inserting new ones.

Whether the supplier deals with consumers (business-to-consumer or B2C transaction) or with other businesses (business-to-business or B2B trans-action), he/she must consider whether the terms and conditions normally relied upon in his/her traditional commercial dealings may need to be adapted to reflect any e-commerce issues.

The following is a checklist of the terms that should be considered including those relevant to an e-seller's online trading terms:

Delivery

It is advisable to let the customer know the steps and time that will be required for the order to be dispatched. When dealing with consumers the provisions of the Distance Selling Regulations need to be taken into account (see chapter 2).

Liability

If a limitation or exclusion of liability clause has not been freely negotiated between the parties, then, depending on the details of each case, the limitation/exclusion may be regarded as unreasonable. Great care must be taken in drafting such clauses.

Under the Unfair Contract Terms Act 1977 (UCTA), whether a company is dealing with consumers or other businesses, it is impossible to exclude or limit liability for death or personal injury resulting from negligence. If the supplier is (i) contracting with a consumer or (ii) requires another business to contract on his/her standard terms of business, then the supplier must ensure that any exclusion/limitation of liability is reasonable. In order to determine what is reasonable each case must be judged on its merits. The following may provide some guidance:

- the negotiating power of the parties (inequality in the parties' bargaining positions may mean that the relevant clauses are regarded as unreasonable);
- whether the e-customer was induced to enter into the particular contract;
- having regard to standard industry practice and the parties' previous dealings, whether the e-customer ought to have known or be aware of the exclusion of liability;
- if the restriction is conditional upon the non-performance of a certain obligation, whether at the time of the conclusion of the contract it would have been reasonable to expect performance of such obligation;
- whether the goods were custom made;
- the resources of the party relying on the exclusion/limitation of liability available to meet the liability under the particular contract; and
- insurance cover for the party relying on the exclusion/limitation of liability.

At this stage, it is important to refer to a recent case (*Watford Electronics Ltd. v. Sanderson CFL Ltd.* [2001] EWCA Civ 217), which was decided in the Court of Appeal and supports the view that businesses should be free to negotiate such terms as they agree are appropriate. Three contracts were involved: a sales contract for the supply of equipment, a software licence and a separate software modification licence. The terms and conditions contained a limitation of liability clause. The supplier's liability (i) for indirect or consequential losses was excluded and (ii) for other claims was limited to the price paid by the customer. The Court of Appeal found that both exclusions were reasonable. The Court based its decision on the following issues:

- The parties had equal negotiating power.
- The key terms including the entire agreement and liability clauses were subject to negotiation.
- The parties negotiated the price and the customer received substantial reductions.
- The parties also negotiated as to which of them should bear the risk of

7

making good indirect, consequential losses and the loss of profit the customer may suffer if the product failed to perform.

■ The customer's own terms and conditions excluded liability for indirect or consequential damages. (See also *St. Albans DC* v. *ICL* [1996] 4 AII ER 481; *South West Water* v. *ICL* [1999] BLR 420; and *Pegler Limited* v. *Wang (UK) Limited* [2000] BLR 218.)

Warranties

According to the Sale of Goods Act 1979 and subsequent amendments, certain warranties will be implied in contracts unless expressly excluded. Such terms include fitness for purpose and satisfactory quality and title. As discussed in relation to exclusion/limitation of liability, attention should be paid to the provisions of UCTA. For example, while it may be reasonable to exclude all warranties in relation to software licensed free of charge, it may not be reasonable to do this in relation to software for which a licence fee is charged.

Where there are any guarantees applied to the goods, the supplier should ensure compliance with the terms of the Sale of Consumer Goods and Associated Guarantees Directive (the Guarantees Directive). Among the other requirements, the Directive provides that the consumer has statutory rights which the guarantee cannot displace.

Dealing with returns and refunds

This is an important provision especially when dealing with consumers and also in view of the latest legal developments and the E-commerce Directive. The Distance Selling Regulations (see pp. 144–5) require an online business supplying consumers to offer a minimum seven days' 'cooling-off' period, or right of cancellation. If properly handled, it could provide an excellent marketing tool for the supplier.

For instance, depending on the nature of the goods and whether the goods were faulty when dispatched or were damaged by the customer, the supplier could allow the customer to return the goods within a specified time limit with the cost of post and packaging refunded to the customer.

Law and jurisdiction

This is an important issue that requires in-depth analysis. As we have seen, the place of acceptance may govern which law will apply, and it is clearly preferable to choose the applicable law. Normally, a business in the UK will stipulate that English law governs the relevant contract and that English courts will be able to hear a dispute arising out of the subject matter of the contract. However, this may not always be the case.

In addition to reviewing their standard terms and conditions, suppliers need to consider the following:

- When information is made available via a web-site, users may try to copy and use that information; in the standard terms and conditions for accessing the web-site the supplier should restrict what users can do with such information.
- If the supplier is in the business of software licensing, as licensor he needs to ensure that the potential licensee is bound by the terms of the licensing agreement. The issues already covered in this chapter in relation to the incorporation of terms and conditions will be relevant to these circumstances.
- The consequences of collecting and using personal data need to be addressed in the terms for accessing the web-site. Adequate privacy policies need to be put in place.
- If the web-site contains third party content, the supplier will need to obtain relevant disclaimers/warranties from the content provider in relation to the content and will also need to restrict what a user can do with the content.

A US case to illustrate where the law stands

The risks to businesses of ignoring basic contractual principles in their online dealing have been brought sharply into focus in the recent US case, *Christopher Specht and others* v. *Netscape Communications Corporation and America Online Inc.* (3 July 2001, United States District Court, Southern District of New York).

Netscape allowed its users to download software electronically. To download the software, web-site users were transferred to a particular page containing a button labelled 'Download'. The only reference to a licence agreement was in a sentence, which came into view on the next screen if the user scrolled down to it, and which read: *'Please review and agree to the terms of the Netscape Smart Download software licence agreement before downloading and using the software.'*

However, before downloading the software, users were not required to read the licence agreement or even indicate that they agreed to it. The download could occur without the user even seeing a reference to the licence at all. The licence agreement contained terms indicating that by clicking the 'Accept' button or installing or using Smart Download the user accepted the terms of the licence agreement. In this case, the claimants alleged that Netscape's software Smart Download unlawfully transmitted to Netscape private information about the users' internet activity.

One of the issues before the court was whether the required arbitration clause in the licence agreement was binding on the user. Ultimately, this depended on whether or not the licence agreement itself was binding.

The judge looked at values and methods of software licensing including shrink-wrap, click-wrap and browse-wrap methods. In brief, shrink-wrap licensing is commonly used with off-the-shelf software that is in a package that advises the purchaser that use of the software is subject to a licence agreement that is contained inside the package. Click-wrap licensing is an online version of shrink-wrap. Before downloading or using software online, a message on screen requires the user to agree to the terms of the licence agreement. The user must then indicate that they agree to the terms by clicking on the 'I Agree' button (or similar) before proceeding. Browse-wrap licensing is the third method and was used by Netscape for Smart Download. The user is not required to read the terms or even acknowledge the terms exist, let alone agree to them. In the Netscape case the judge thought that the main purpose of downloading was to obtain the software rather than to indicate consent. It was also observed that the user was not made aware that he or she was entering into a contract. In order for the licensing agreement to be binding the user should have had to click on a button marked 'I Agree' before being allowed to download the software.

Netscape's failure to require its users to indicate their consent to the licence agreement before downloading the software was critical to its case. The judge concluded that the licence agreement was not binding on the users.

2.3 Contracts and place of performance

Under English law, where a contract is for delivery of physical goods the performance obligation takes place at the delivery address. However, when the delivery is electronic – for example, software sent as an e-mail attachment, or music download or streaming – the position is less clear. The place of receipt could be:

- the location of the purchaser's server;
- the purchaser's mailbox; or
- where the purchaser downloads and/or reads the e-mail.

The best tactic is to specify the place and time of performance in the agreement. If the contract is subject to English law, the usual rules concerning exclusions, limitations and standard form contracts apply. However, UCTA will not generally be applicable when one of the contracting parties is not in England.

2.4 Applicable law

Under the Contracts (Applicable Law) Act 1990 (the Act), the parties may choose their own governing law. In the absence of choice, the Act provides that the law governing the contract will be the one with which the contract was most closely connected. This will be the country where a party effects 'characteristic performance'.

The characteristic performance is the performance for which payment is made. The location of characteristic performance depends on whether the party performing it is a business or individual. For a business it will be the place of business; for an individual it will be its habitual residence. An e-seller's place of business is likely to be where physical activities are carried out – for example, from where goods are despatched or services arranged – rather than the location of the server.

However, it is possible that mandatory rules (that is, laws that cannot be contracted out of) of another country may also apply. This is particularly likely if the purchaser is a consumer. It is therefore important to take advice on the potential applicability of other laws. Consideration should also be given to refusing to supply in some jurisdictions.

3. Electronic data interchange

Businesses that trade online are relying increasingly on electronic systems and networks. This method of online trading is normally used for business-to-business trading. Trading is generally implemented by adopting an agreed method of communication, which involves defined method structures known as electronic data interchange (EDI). EDI is key to certain business methods such as just-in-time procurement where orders for the purchase of products are closely co-ordinated with suppliers. EDI is also the method used for bank automated payment systems.

EDI requires communication in a structured format, which involves significant investment in software and related hardware. It also involves modifying internal IT systems to make them compatible with the chosen format for EDI. Given the investment required, it currently tends to be adopted in trading relationships with large organisations. In an EDI transaction, the computers of the supplier and purchaser communicate using an agreed standard.

Currently, Europe and America have different technical standards, but companies and organisations are working together to develop a global unified standard.

Since EDI involves the exchange of electronic messages without human intervention, the need for a clear contractual basis is particularly important. It is usual for both parties to enter into a framework agreement governing the way in which trading contracts are formed, and their terms.

The EDI agreement normally specifies:

■ the communication protocols which are to be applied in the relevant communication;

- the procedure which is to be adopted if messages are unintelligible; and
- the time at which an electronic message is deemed to be received.

In 1998 the International Chamber of Commerce (ICC) published the Uniform Rules of Conduct for Interchange of Trade Data by Teletransmission (UNCIT Rules), which set out key principles to be addressed in interchange agreements such as storage of data.

The European Commission published a recommendation on EDI in 1994. This includes a European model EDI agreement (European Model). Also, the UK EDI Association has produced a standard electronic data interchange agreement (UK Model), which can be adopted by parties engaged in EDI. Interchange agreements do not have to follow exactly the terms of a particular standard; the parties can agree to modifications, so there is scope to take provisions from various standards. These agreements tend to be in addition to contracts setting out businesses' contractual trading terms and conditions.

The key issues addressed in an EDI agreement are as follows:

- *Technical*: The European Model requires compliance with the EU-approved version of the European technical standards (UN Edifact). Any further technical issues should be specified in the agreement.
- *Contract formation*: Where contracts are concluded using EDI, it is necessary to specify when and how the contract is formed. The European Model identifies the point of contract conclusion as the time and place where the EDI message constituting acceptance reaches the computer system of the offeror. There is no obligation to acknowledge receipt unless requested. The UK Model does not address contract formation and so this would need to be added, otherwise the formation will be determined in accordance with the governing law of the contract concluded via EDI.
- *Contract validity and admissibility*: The European Model states that the parties waive any right to contest the validity of the contract affected by use of EDI on the sole ground that it was affected by EDI. Also the parties agree that the records of EDI messages shall be admissible by the courts. Again, if EDI is used to form contracts these issues should be inserted into any agreement based on the UK model.
- *Security*: Under the European Model the parties agree to implement and maintain security procedures and measures in order to guard against unauthorised access, alteration, delay, destruction or loss of data. These procedures and measures include in particular, verification of the origin and integrity of the data. Specific procedures and measures may be set out in the technical annex to the agreement. The UK Model requires the parties to respect the integrity of messages subject to exceptions such as where an error is reasonably obvious to the recipient.

- *Confidentiality*: Both the European and the UK Models provide that the parties may agree to use a specific form of protection such as encryption for certain messages.
- *Recording and storage of EDI messages*: Both the European and UK Models require each party to store a complete and chronological record of all EDI messages in a readily accessible form. The UK Model also requires each party to designate a person to be responsible for these obligations.
- *Liability*: The European Model provides that no party is to be liable for special, indirect or consequential damages or for events beyond that party's control. The UK counterpart contains a *force majeure* clause, but does not otherwise address liability for breach on the grounds that loss is not likely to be caused by breach of the model itself. This does not preclude inclusion of such a clause.
- *Governing law and jurisdiction*: The European Model does not impose a particular European national law and gives a choice between arbitration and reference to national courts. The UK Model assumes that English law and courts will apply unless otherwise agreed by the parties.

4. Consumer protection

When a company is dealing with consumers, it needs to take into consideration consumer protection laws, such as sale of goods legislation and product safety requirements, which apply just as much offline as they do online in e-commerce. The extent to which suppliers can restrict their liability under a contract is also restricted.

An e-business will also have to take into account the Distance Selling Regulations (see chapter 2).

The nature of some e-businesses increases the likelihood of contravening laws of other jurisdictions. For example, particular care is required in relation to heavily regulated products, such as betting, alcohol and pharmaceuticals. Care is also required when dealing with products that raise safety issues such as food and motor vehicles.

5. Payment and security on the internet

Strong security mechanisms are essential for developing confidence in electronic transactions. Encryption is the process by which messages or data in readable form are encoded into unreadable cyphered data by the use of an encryption algorithm and a key, which is used to prevent others reading confidential, private or commercial data. Initially, encryption technologies were used by governments, the military and intelligence services. However, recent changes in legislation and increased use of the internet mean that there is likely to be an increase in the availability and use of strong encryption products, initially by large corporations and then by the public at large.

Encryption, of course, does not solve the problem entirely. It transfers the problem of keeping the data secret to that of keeping the key secret. The keys used to encrypt or decrypt data are essentially passwords made up of numbers. All key-based encryptions can be broken on the basis of systematic trial-and-error methods. Accordingly, the strength of a key depends on the range of numbers that can be used by the encryption algorithm. The length and strength of the key is measured by the number of the binary digits or bits. The bit length of the key used in an algorithm determines how long trial and error will take to decrypt the message and thus whether it is possible to crack a key within a practical time period.

Of course, if a sender encrypts a message, the recipient must to be able to decrypt it. The same key will be needed to encrypt and decrypt the message. This means that the parties need to agree in advance which key to use. Alternatively, they need to have some means of exchanging the keys before or after the message is sent. Since this area of the law is still evolving, the reader is advised to keep an eye on any legislative changes in this respect.

6. Electronic Signatures Directive

Under the Electronic Communications Act 2000, electronic signatures are admissible as evidence in relation to any question as to the authenticity of the communication or data or as to the integrity of the communication or data.

An electronic signature is defined as anything in electronic form that:

- is incorporated into, or otherwise logically associated with, any electronic communication or electronic data; and
- purports to be so incorporated or associated for the purpose of being used in establishing the authenticity of the communication or data, the integrity of the communication or data or both.

While electronic signatures are admissible in legal proceedings in the UK, they may not yet be afforded in all cases the same status as handwritten signatures in relation to paper-based data as they are not presumed to be legally binding. Again, the reader is advised to keep an eye on legislative changes in this respect.

7. Electronic payment systems

This is another essential development in e-commerce related to the means of ensuring payment to a supplier of goods or services on the internet. In the UK, the supplier takes most of the risk in internet credit card transactions since he will not have a credit card receipt signed by the customer on which to rely. Credit card companies may amend their rules in future so that details signed remotely with electronic signatures are treated in the same way as receipts signed with the customer present.

Other payment mechanisms and schemes have been set up but, to date, it would appear that none has really taken off. Pilot tests on the use of electronic purses (smart cards on which a cash value is held electronically) have been run with Mondex and DigiCash. However, while these products appeared to be an ideal means of payment for electronic transactions, DigiCash filed for bankruptcy in 1998 and future plans for Mondex's smart card remained unclear after the end of various pilot schemes in 2001.

In 2000, the European Council adopted a Directive on Electronic Money Institutions. This Directive introduces a special supervisory regime for issuers of electronic money. This is based on the existing prudential supervisory regime applicable to credit institutions, but certain requirements, such as adequacy requirements, are relaxed in order to reflect the specific risks associated with the issuance of electronic money.

The Directive defined electronic money as monetary value as represented by a claim on the issuer which is:

- stored on an electronic device;
- issued on receipt of funds of an amount not less in value than the monetary value issued; and
- accepted as a means of payment by undertakings other than the issuer.

Under the Directive only regulated credit institutions may issue electronic money and their activities are to be limited to financial and non-financial services which are closely related to the issuing of electronic money.

The Directive has been implemented in the United Kingdom by the Financial Services and Markets Act (2000) (Regulated Activities) (Amendment) Order 2002. Its effectiveness will be reviewed by the Commission by 27 April 2005.

Getting Down to the Business of Going Online

Introduction

This chapter takes the approach of a case study, by providing a step-by step example of how a fictitious traditional, 'bricks-and-mortar' company goes about developing its business online. The subject of this case study, Traditional Company Limited, typifies many other companies interested in using the internet to improve their competitive edge.

The types of concerns and issues raised by Traditional Company's directors regarding such issues as domain name registration, data protection and liability for web-site content are likely to be shared by directors and managers of actual companies. It is therefore hoped that the solutions and action points offered to Traditional Company Limited will be of value and relevance to other companies and organisations as they make the transition from traditional business to e-business.

The main issues for Traditional Company Limited are set out below:

1. Obtaining a domain name
2. Signing up with an ISP
3. Setting up a web-site
4. Protecting trade marks
5. Advertising online
6. Web linking
7. Selling online
8. Defective goods
9. Data protection
10. Employment
11. Tax
12. Competition law

Cross-references appear throughout this chapter to other areas of the book in which particular legal issues are dealt with in more depth.

Meet Traditional Company Limited

In 1990 Traditional Company Limited was incorporated in the UK. Since that time the company has been successfully selling widgets through its twenty UK retail outlets.

Despite the fact that the widget industry is thriving, Traditional Company Limited has experienced a reduction in turnover during the past twelve months. It is therefore prompted to conduct a customer survey to ascertain the reasons for that downturn.

The results of the survey reveal that the way the market operates has changed. Many of Traditional Company's competitors now operate web-sites, selling their widgets online. Unfortunately for Traditional Company, many of its previous customers have been lost to such competitors, as they find it less expensive and more convenient to shop online.

Traditional Company Limited's board meet to discuss the survey results and come up with a plan to become more competitive and to recoup lost sales. After much discussion, the board decided on a web strategy, which will involve it setting up a web-site to promote its products and sell its widgets. Additionally, it decided that advertising on its new site might be a good way to generate additional revenue for the online business. However, the board was not sure of the best way to proceed. This chapter charts their progress.

1. Obtaining a domain name

1.1 Some domain name basics

What is a domain name?

A domain name is a unique Internet Protocol (IP) address in an easy-to-remember alphabetical form. IP addresses are individual 32-bit numbers used to identify computers connected to the internet. A computer user will type a domain name into a web browser to locate a particular web-site (the domain name should always appear in the browser preceded by the letters http://www.). The computer will translate the domain name into the IP address, retrieve the data (text and pictures, etc.) forming the web-site from the computer on which it is stored and display it on the user's own computer.

How are domain names constructed?

[name]	*'dot'*	[second-level domain if relevant]	*'dot'*	[generic or country-code top-level domain]

For example:

osborneclarke Traditionalcompany			'dot'	com net org ie (for Ireland)
bbc	'dot'	co	'dot'	uk ltd plc net org

Why should I register a domain name?

The ideal domain name provides an address for a company's web-site, which is easy for its customers to remember. Domain names are typically allocated by the domain name registrars on a first come, first served basis, and currently over 850,000 are being registered world-wide each week. At the time of writing a total of 36,278,755 .com, .org and .net domain names have been registered.

Like company names and logos, domain names can be effective marketing tools and become valuable assets in themselves. This is particularly the case where the company is, or becomes, synonymous with the domain, e.g. scoot.co.uk, or lastminute.com. More generic domains can also be valuable: cinema.com recently fetched $700,000, if.com $1,000,000 and business.com $7,500,000.

How do I choose a domain name?

- You cannot register a domain name if it has already been registered. To find out which domain names have been taken and by whom you can do a 'whois' search. See: http://www.whois.net. Alternatively, an Internet Service Provider (ISP) might be able to suggest some appropriate domain names that are available. See http://www.whois.net/suggest.cgi; and
- you should not register a domain name in bad faith (see chapter 7) or in order to 'cyber squat'.

Are there any restrictions over the choice of domain name?

There are various restrictions. For example:

- domain names can contain letters, numbers and a hyphen only;
- domain names cannot contain spaces or begin or end with a hyphen;
- .com, .net, and .org domain names cannot be more than 63 characters long in total (including the .com, .net, .org or other extension);

- .uk domain names cannot be more than 64 characters long in total (including the .co.uk, .org.uk or other extension);
- .uk domain names must be longer than two 'letters' (although a letter and a number are allowable);
- .uk domain names and top level domains are not allowed as third level names. For example net.co.uk would not be allowed;
- only UK limited companies may register .ltd.uk domains and only UK public limited companies may register .plc.uk domains; and
- only UK Internet Service Providers may register .net.uk domains.

1.2 How do I register a domain name?

ISPs

You can register a domain name online through an accredited ISP, who will deal with the registration requirements on your behalf, and will often provide domain name hosting services. See http://www.icann.org/registrars/accredited-list.html and http://www.nic.uk/members.html. It is important to remember that an ISP will act as agent between you and the relevant registrar. Therefore, in registering a domain name, you will, in effect, be entering into two contracts: between you and the registrar in respect of the registration of the domain name, and between you and the ISP in respect of any additional services provided by the ISP (such as e-mail). The registrar is not a party to the second contract and therefore has no power over these provisions.

The following details are required to register a domain name:

- name, address and contact details of the person or company the domain name is to be registered to;
- name, address and contact details for any queries, etc.;
- name, address and contact details for billing details:
  a) payment details; and
  b) company registration number for .ltd.uk or .plc.uk domain names.

It is important to ensure that the details submitted are accurate, as any inaccuracies will delay or invalidate the registration process.

Costs

Registration charges vary between ISPs. Typically, for a two-year registration, you could expect to pay approximately £30 for a .co.uk and £60–70 for a .com.

Time

It usually takes between 24 and 48 hours, although a .com can take up to five days. Once registered, it can take up to 36 hours before your domain name is fully visible across the internet.

1.3 Someone has already registered my choice of domain name – what can I do?

How do I find out who has registered my choice of domain name?

You can perform a 'Whois search' to discover the contact details of the registrant. This search is not reliant on whether a web-site has been constructed at the domain name in question.

First come, first served

Traditionally, domain names are registered on a first come, first served basis. However, this has meant that some companies have discovered that they have been too late to register their name as a domain name. Unlike trade marks, where the same mark can be owned by two or more people in any of 45 different classes, there is no equivalent system for domain names. Therefore, where a domain name has been registered and is being used in good faith, a complainant is unlikely to be able to force a transfer of that name.

Obviously, as a first step, it is important to work out to what use the domain name is being put. This is simply a matter of viewing the web-site through a browser.

Buy the domain name

You could investigate the possibility of buying the name from the registrant. Domain name transfers are discussed in more detail in chapter 7.

The courts

If you have enforceable trade mark rights that pre-date the registration of the domain name, you may be able to sue the registrant to achieve a transfer of a domain name that is identical or similar to your trade mark. If you are unsure of the existence or scope of your trade marks, you should perform a trade mark search. If you do not have registered trade mark rights, it may be possible to rely on unregistered rights. However, in a situation where you do not have a well-known mark or a reputation in the UK, the courts are more likely to apply the first come, first served rule.

Dispute resolution procedures

Alternatively, you may decide to follow the dispute resolution procedures of the relevant authorities, which are incorporated into the agreements with the registrants. This can be cheaper and quicker than going to court. Dispute resolution and the relevant procedures are discussed in more detail in chapter 7.

2. Signing up with an ISP

2.1 What is an ISP?

An ISP is a company that provides third party access to the internet. It is front-end access to all that the internet offers and is made up of a network of servers, routers and modems attached to a permanent high-speed internet 'backbone' connection. Businesses can simply use their modem to connect to the ISP, which then links them to the internet automatically.

Although the prices and facilities of ISPs differ, they should all offer some standard services such as 24-hour internet access, a unique e-mail address for your company, storage space for your own web-site and basic software programs for browsing the internet.

ISPs (also called online information providers) can potentially provide extra services such as access to databases of business information.

2.2 What should you look for in selecting a particular ISP?

The choice and number of ISPs is immense. It is recommended that businesses choose an ISP that is a member of an industry association, for example, an organisation such as the ISPA (Internet Service Providers Association http://www.ispa.org.uk/). This is because ISPA members sign up to a code of conduct, which is intended to ensure that they will provide a certain level of service and abide by an industry-approved set of standards as well as providing for a standard complaints procedure.

Such industry associations are useful if you have a complaint against your ISP as they have a high rate of success in solving any problems between customers and ISPA members without the need to enter into any official legal proceedings. If your ISP is not a member of an industry association, although it is possible to refer any problems to the local Trading Standards office, this is likely to be a more time-consuming process and more expensive since in all probability legal advice will be required.

Since ISPs offer different services it will depend on your business requirements which of these you most want to take advantage of. As a general rule, almost all ISPs act as e-mail hosts and allow access to the internet (see below on what to look for in an agreement with your ISP for hosting and access). Some also act as content providers and gather together useful information, which can be accessed by their subscribers only.

The larger ISPs have their own high-speed leased lines so that they are less dependent on the telecommunications providers in order to provide a better service to their customers.

2.3 What to look for in an ISP agreement

The following checklist sets out some of the key factors to consider before signing an ISP agreement:

 CHECKLIST

→ *Price*: What set-up/on-going fees are payable? Do you get unlimited access for your price?

→ *Reliability and service availability*: Is it a well-established and well-regarded ISP? Is its size or quality of service offered appropriate for your business? Does it offer guarantees of availability of access or connectivity that will be sufficient for your business requirements?

→ *What security measures are in place*? An ISP should at the very least have secure servers and encryption technology for transmission of your information to ensure it is safeguarded.

→ *Features*: Do you have sufficient available bandwidth and web space for your business purposes? Check any restrictions on storage space for web-sites or e-mails. What is the user-to-modem ratio and what type of connection does the ISP use to the internet?

→ *Support, service levels and response times*: You should ensure that there is 24-hour support service with sufficient response and repair targets. Check if the ISP has included any permitted downtime, and if so, whether the times are acceptable.

→ *Cancellation*: If you are unhappy with the service, are there any cancellation charges or options for a refund?

→ *Law enforcement requirements*: Given the current climate, it is likely that an ISP will reserve the right to forward your user details to the police or regulatory authorities when requested for law enforcement or compliance purposes.

→ *Content*: Where you are providing content for your business site, it is likely that a contract will include restrictions/exclude liability for your content.

→ *Web-site development*: You can either use your ISP or a specialist developer to develop your web-site to your specification. Web-site development is detailed in section 3 below.

2.4 Acceptable use policies

An ISP contract will normally incorporate an acceptable use policy. This consists of guidelines relating to misuse of the service by anyone other than the ISP. Typically, this will include any online behaviour of a criminal, libellous, defamatory, obscene, pornographic, threatening, abusive or illegal nature, as well as the use of the service to spread unsolicited e-mail ('spam'). It will generally exclude all liability on behalf of the ISP for such behaviour and will explicitly state that you should comply with its acceptable use policy.

You should pass these requirements on to your users, especially as there may be ISP sanctions associated with a breach of the guidelines, for example, suspension or termination of the service, or compensation or an 'indemnity' may also be payable for any loss suffered by the ISP associated with such breach of the guidelines.

2.5 Use of web-site 'chat rooms'

If your ISP hosts a chat room or bulletin board for use by your staff or external partners, you must be prepared to accept responsibility for illegal or offensive material. This is unlikely to be the ISP's responsibility (see chapter 4). You should, therefore, make sure your employees or any other users of your web-site who are posting information in the 'chat room' are aware of these restrictions and comply with them. This can be achieved by including specific terms of use and disclaimer statements on the web-site – these terms must be clearly visible to users and must be in plain English.

3. Setting up a web-site

Traditional Company Limited now has a domain name and an agreement with an ISP. Before it can trade online it will need to design and create its web-site, taking into account at all times its web strategy and any legal requirements associated with the operation of the web-site.

Unless a business has its own skilled IT personnel, it will usually outsource the development work to a web-site developer, who will design, build and possibly host the web-site. Traditional Company Limited does not have the internal skills to develop its own site so is looking to an external developer to carry out the design and development work.

3.1 What type of web-site?

First impressions are very important. 'Glossy' web-sites are attractive, but too many graphics and video footage and sound may use too much bandwidth and result in the site being slow to navigate. Internet users are easily put off by web-sites that are slow or difficult to navigate and it is crucial when creating its web-site that Traditional Company Limited bears in mind the needs of the likely user (e.g. its customers). It can be difficult for a business to know what it wants its web-site to do and what is achievable technically and financially.

Traditional Company Limited must ensure it selects the correct developer to assist with these decisions. Practically, Traditional Company Limited should meet several developers before selecting one that it feels it can work with closely. It should also ask to see examples of the developers' work and obtain references from past clients.

Traditional Company Limited wishes to maximise its potential customer base by ensuring that its online information is accessible to visually impaired people. Traditional Company Limited's HR director is also keen to comply with The Disability Discrimination Act 1995, which places duties on those providing goods, facilities and services not to discriminate against people with disabilities. Traditional Company Limited's HR director is familiar with the Royal National Institute of the Blind's (RNIB) 'See it Right' campaign (http://www.rnib.org.uk/digital), and is keen for the chosen web-site designer to follow the RNIB's recommended content accessibility guidelines (see http://www.w3.org/WAI/).

3.2 Is an agreement necessary?

It is tempting for both parties to start work on the web-site design and development without signing a written contract. However, this is ill advised. Once work has begun it will become increasingly difficult for Traditional Company Limited to extricate itself from working with the developer if the web-site specification is not met.

Traditional Company Limited should be wary of signing the developer's standard terms and conditions which will be favourable to the developer. These can be reviewed and amended, or alternatively Traditional Company Limited may prepare its own terms and conditions based on its requirements, which will then be ready for negotiation with the developer. This may appear to be holding up the progress of the web-site development, but ultimately will be worth it.

3.3 Will Traditional Company Limited need a detailed web-site specification?

Traditional Company Limited will need to develop a web-site specification, which will set out what it wants the web-site to do and how it will do it. This may include how it wants the web-site to look and feel, so if particular colours and fonts are required, these should be stated in the specification. In addition, since Traditional Company Limited will be selling over the internet, security of the web-site, importantly keeping the financially sensitive material of its customers secure, will be need to be addressed.

The specification is a key document – it is against this that the performance of the developer is measured.

3.4 How much will it cost?

The price may include not only the web-site development work but also any charges for future hosting and support and maintenance, if these are to be provided. Where possible Traditional Company Limited will wish to ensure that the price is payable only on the web-site meeting the requirements set out in the specification. Alternatively, part-payment can be made against achieved milestones set out in the contract.

Judging whether the specification has been met can be achieved by means of a clear acceptance testing procedure. Failure to meet the acceptance tests can lead to a variety of remedies:

- the developer is usually given a grace period within which to make any necessary changes to meet the specification;
- liquidated damages (usually either payment or service credits) may be payable for delays to the 'go live' date – please note that these damages will only be enforceable if they are a genuine pre-estimate of Traditional Company Limited's losses; and
- repeated failure of the acceptance tests may result in termination of the contract.

3.5 IPR ownership

The development agreement must clarify who owns the intellectual property rights (IPRs) in the web-site. This will be the main area of value in the web-site and is certainly central to the ability of Traditional Company Limited to exploit fully its use of the web-site both now and in the future.

It is a common misconception that when a party has paid for an external consultant to design and build a web-site, or even to create a piece of bespoke software, that all the IPRs in the web-site or software automatically belong to the commissioning party. This is not accurate, since under the Copyright, Designs and Patent Act 1988 (CDPA), the IPRs in the commissioned work will belong to the creator of the work (subject to trusts and equities) unless they are assigned (i.e. transferred) to the commissioning party by the developer in writing.

Unless there are some underlying IPRs of the developer/third party in the web-site (use of which should be licensed indefinitely to Traditional Company Limited – see below), an assignment of all IPRs in the web-site from the developer to Traditional Company Limited must be included in the web-site development agreement.

Below is a more detailed analysis of the possible IPRs associated with the development of the web-site.

Copyright
The main IPR which arises in the development of a web-site is copyright.

Separate copyright will arise in the following: written text of the web-site; photographs and graphics; sound recordings and musical works; animation and film footage; and the computer program which runs the web-site. In each case the work must be original work if it is to be copyright protected. In fact, a copy of an existing work will not be granted copyright protection and is likely to infringe another party's copyright.

Trade marks

Please refer to section 4 below, which discusses trade marks in more detail.

Patents

Although computer software is not patentable in the UK, an invention implemented by means of a computer program is patentable so long as the technical aspect of the invention represents an inventive step previously unknown.

Database rights

Database rights were introduced by the Database Directive. A database can attract copyright protection where the selection and arrangement of content is the result of 'personal intellectual creativity'. In addition, or alternatively, if the database does not attract copyright protection, there may be available a database right, which is not linked to creativity but requires substantial investment in obtaining, verifying or presenting the content.

Background IPR and foreground IPR

A further complication is that IPR in a web-site can be divided into two elements: pre-existing IPR and new IPR, known also as background and foreground IPR.

Background IPR: The pre-existing or background IPR will usually be made up of content which is owned by Traditional Company Limited, or licensed to it by a third party and pre-existing software and tools which are owned by the developer, or licensed to it from a third party, and used in the development and operation of the web-site.

Foreground IPR: The new IPR will usually be made up of the software, tools and content that the developer creates specifically for Traditional Company Limited, either at its request or in the course of developing the web-site in accordance with the specification.

Ownership of background and foreground IPRs

Clearly, Traditional Company Limited will want to obtain ownership of all the IPRs associated with the development and operation of its new web-site, but in practice this may not happen for the simple reason that the developer's own business is built around the use and re-use of elements of its background IPR. In addition, where any third party software or content is included in the web-site, the third party owner will not want to transfer ownership of its 'crown jewels' to the web-site operator.

In this instance, Traditional Company Limited should secure a non-exclusive, world-wide, royalty-free, perpetual licence from the developer (or possibly the third party owner) to use its and the third party's background IPR.

Traditional Company Limited will, however, require an assignment to it of the foreground IPR in the development agreement.

Where Traditional Company Limited already owns any background IPR (e.g. its content, logos, etc.), it must ensure that it does not unwittingly assign these rights to the developer in the agreement. The developer can be licensed to use Traditional Company Limited's background IPR solely in connection with the development work.

Warranties in respect of the background/foreground IPR

In the development agreement Traditional Company Limited will need to protect itself as fully as possible against possible infringement of the IPRs of a third party through its operation of the web-site. This can be achieved in the agreement by securing warranties from the developer that the use by Traditional Company Limited of the background and foreground IPRs will not infringe the IPRs of any third party and that if Traditional Company Limited suffers any loss in respect of any alleged or actual infringement, the developer will indemnify Traditional Company Limited against such loss.

Moral rights

In addition, the development agreement should include an express waiver of the developer's moral rights in respect of any copyright (but excluding copyright in any computer programs since it is not applicable) assigned under the agreement.

Escrow

Where any background software of the developer or any specialist third party software is licensed to Traditional Company, it is advisable to enter into an escrow agreement, to enable Traditional Company to access the source code in certain key circumstances, e.g. the insolvency or failure of the developer to maintain and support the software. An escrow agreement is usually between the licensor, the licensee and a third party (e.g. The National Computing Centre: http://www.ncc.co.uk).

Additional costs will have to be borne by Traditional Company Limited to set up and maintain the escrow agreement but where non-proprietary software is fundamental to the operations of a business, it is money well spent!

4. Trade marks

In addition to its existing marks, Traditional Company Limited wishes to use a new trade mark specifically for its web-site.

There are a number of issues it will need to consider before doing so.

4.1 What is a trade mark?

A trade mark is any sign that can distinguish the goods and services of one trader from those of another and be represented graphically. It includes words, logos, slogans, three-dimensional shapes and sometimes sounds and smells. It is used as a marketing tool so that customers can recognise the product of a particular trader. Trade marks are divided into 45 internationally agreed classes of goods and services (see http://patent.gov.uk/tm/reference/&search/index.htm). It may be necessary to obtain a registration for one or more classes depending upon the goods and services which it covers.

National trade marks

Each country has its own national trade mark registry. In general, a national trade mark registration is only valid in that particular country. Before applying for or using its new trade mark, Traditional Company Limited should carry out a search in all the countries in which it intends to trade. Details of searches are detailed below.

Community trade marks (CTM)

The European Union operates an EU-wide trade mark system: this means that a CTM is valid across all fifteen member states (however, Monaco is excluded). A CTM is competitively priced when compared to filing fifteen separate applications in the national registries.

International trade marks

The World Intellectual Property Organisation operates an international trade mark system. Such a trade mark will be valid in certain countries which can be nominated, including the UK, Monaco and France (although, notably the US is not a member of this system). This can be cheaper than applying for individual trade marks. However, an international mark can be filed only once a national application has been made.

What is a good trade mark?

Invented words or arbitrary use of words, which are not descriptive or suggestive of the goods or services they cover are the best trade marks.

What is a bad trade mark?

A 'bad' trade mark is one which cannot be registered, e.g.

- A mark that is the same or similar to a trade mark that someone else uses with similar goods or services.

Traditional Company Limited should try to avoid adopting a mark like this. This is because, unless it is able to show that it is using the mark honestly and concurrently with the other trader, not only will it be prevented from registering that word as a trade mark, but it may also be sued for trade mark infringement by the other trader.

In some situations it may be possible to obtain consent from the owner of the other mark to defeat an objection from the Trade Marks Registry to register the mark. However, consents are often not given, are sometimes offered at a very high price, and generally take a long time to secure.

- A mark that is not capable of distinguishing goods or services from those of your competitors.
- A mark that is devoid of any distinctive character.
- A mark that is descriptive of the kind, quality, quantity, intended purpose, value, geographical origin or other characteristics of the goods or services.
- A mark that is in customary usage (i.e. generic).
- A mark that is contrary to public policy.
- A mark that is made up of descriptive words.
- A mark that is made up of laudatory words, that is, expressing or containing praise, e.g. 'The Best of . . .'.
- A mark that is made up of words in common usage, e.g. 'war', 'car'.

Traditional Company Limited should try to avoid choosing these words as trade marks. This is because, until that word becomes synonymous with its goods through *use*, the protection that will be afforded to this mark will be weak: it will not be granted a trade mark registration; and will not acquire exclusive rights in the mark. (This means that it will not be able to prevent its competitors from using the same mark.)

4.2 Trade mark registration

Searches

Before applying for or using its new mark, Traditional Company Limited should carry out a trade mark search to determine whether a third party has already registered an identical or similar mark for the same or similar goods or services. The types of search available are:

Identical-only search

This will identify registered marks only or pending applications that are identical to Traditional Company Limited's chosen mark for identical goods or services. It will not identify similar marks for similar goods or services. However, this provides a relatively quick and inexpensive method of determining whether its chosen mark has already been registered.

Full search

This will identify all marks that are identical and similar to its chosen mark for goods and services in all classes. Ideally, a full search should be carried out prior to any application.

Common law search

Neither an identical-only search nor a full search will identify any marks which have not been registered, but which are nevertheless being used. The owner of such a mark may have 'common law rights' and therefore may be able to prevent Traditional Company Limited from using its chosen mark. Although it is possible to perform a 'common law search', it is not possible to search all sources cost-effectively.

4.3 Registration procedures

Registration procedures vary from country to country. However, as a general guide once a trade mark application has been submitted to the relevant registry it will be examined by that registry to determine whether the mark is capable of registration (e.g. whether it is descriptive and whether there is a prior mark which is identical or confusingly similar to the proposed mark for identical or similar goods or services). If the application is accepted by the registry, the mark is published in a trade mark journal and interested third parties will have a period of time (three months in the UK) to oppose the application. If there are no oppositions, the mark will become registered.

4.4 Using trade marks

Trade marks can be a very valuable asset. A trade mark can distinguish Traditional Company Limited's goods from those of its competitors. It is vital, therefore, that it uses its trade marks correctly to ensure that they receive the maximum protection possible.

Traditional Company Limited should remember the following:

■ Ensure the trade mark is continually used.
■ Always use the trade marks in the same format.

31

■ Use the appropriate trade mark symbol in each country where the trade mark is used/registered. For example:

® if the trade mark is registered;

™ if the trade mark is not registered.

However, if its web-site is available in many different territories, Traditional Company Limited should list those countries it is registered in and those where it is not.

4.5 Protection of trade marks

An unregistered trade mark can be protected by the law of 'passing off' in the UK, or the laws of 'unfair competition' in other jurisdictions. In its most simple form, these laws mean that a trader may be able to prevent the same or similar mark (or 'get-up') which he uses on his goods or services from being used on the same or similar goods or services by another trader. However, an action for passing off or unfair competition can be expensive and time-consuming as there are various evidential hurdles which have to be jumped.

By contrast, obtaining a registration of a trade mark and protecting that trade mark once registered can be relatively simple and cheap. For example, a trade mark owner does not have to prove that it owns the trade mark as it can rely on the entry in a relevant national Trade Marks Register as proof of ownership. Furthermore, the complainant does not need to prove confusion where there is 'classic' trade mark infringement, that is, where an identical mark is affixed to identical goods or services.

Trade mark registration is purely territorial and in order to obtain maximum protection a registration must be obtained in each territory in which the goods and services are used. In the European Union a trader can apply for a 'Community Trade Mark' (see above). In the US, it is possible to obtain one or more State registrations providing protection in those States, or a Federal trade mark which provides protection in all States.

4.6 How else can Traditional Company Limited stop infringements of its trade mark rights?

Traditional Company Limited should stop infringement of its trade mark rights as quickly as possible. The longer an infringement is allowed to continue, the more damage will be done to its trade mark rights.

Traditional Company Limited should also consider using a trade mark watch service. A trade mark agent will usually provide this service by reviewing the trade mark journals and looking out for applications to register identical or similar marks in the UK and overseas. This will give it the opportunity to try to prevent the registration of similar marks.

5. Advertising online

5.1 Deciding to introduce advertising

Allowing other companies, individuals, clubs or groups to advertise their products or services on your site can generate revenue for your business. When setting up and maintaining your web-site this revenue can contribute towards the costs of running and development. It should be noted however that few sites rely solely on the income generated from advertising to fund their entire online business.

5.2 First step

Once the decision to introduce advertising is made, the first step you need to take is to communicate the decision. Just because you have decided to make advertisement space available on your site doesn't mean that people will automatically know that your site sells advertising space. Therefore, you need to do some advertising of your own. Prominently display the advertising opportunities available on your site, and until your advertisement programme takes off, use the spaces designated for advertisements for the advertising of your own services or products.

In order to attract advertisers to your site you should work towards:

- standing out from other sites;
- offering advertising space that meets the needs of advertisers;
- building relationships with potential advertisers;
- developing a pricing structure and terms that work for you and your potential advertisers; and
- keeping up-to-date with technological developments so that your site can carry all types of advertisements.

5.3 Advertising agreements

For any advertising that you attract to your site, an agreement should be signed by the parties involved to cover the terms under which the advertisement appears. The agreement should cover such things as how the advertisement is to be paid for, practicalities such as the size of the advertisement, where it is to be positioned and whose responsibility it should be to ensure compliance with the relevant laws governing the advertisement.

This section looks at the clauses that should be included in the terms and conditions of an online advertising agreement. The terms look at the best position for the owner of the web-site as opposed to that of a potential advertiser.

5.4 Terms of payment

The terms of payment clause will be one of the most important in the agreement as it will set out how you are to be paid for the advertising that appears on your site.

There are a variety of ways in which payment for advertisements can be structured. These include:

Flat fee	a set amount charged either monthly or yearly for advertisement placement on a site
Cost per click (CPC)	the price of placing an advertisement on a site is determined by how many times the advertisement is clicked on by users
Cost per lead (CPL)	the price of placing an advertisement on a site is based on how many leads the advertisement generates for the advertiser
Cost per sale (CPS)	the price of placing an advertisement on a site is determined according to how many sales result from the advertisement
Costs per thousand (CPM)	advertiser is charged a set fee for every 1,000 impressions of their advertisement delivered on a site

To decide which method is best for you and appropriate for your site, you need to take a realistic look at the value of the advertising you are offering.

To do this you should consider the following:

Site audience

Most sites cater for an identifiable group, for example, teens, people with an interest in a certain hobby, people of a particular profession, and so on. Such targeted sites create access to niche markets for advertisers. It may therefore be possible to charge a higher rate if your site is the best opportunity for advertisers to reach a particular audience.

Types of advertising offered

Advertising on sites can appear in a number of different formats, for example through sponsorship of a site or the more traditional form of banner advertisements. The vast majority of sites use a form of banner advertisement. Banners vary in size and style and can be, for instance, full banners, half banners, vertical banners, buttons or micro buttons. Full banners obviously tend to be charged at a higher rate than buttons or micro buttons.

Positioning and number of advertisements

If an advertisement is to be prominently displayed, or is to be the only adver-tisement to appear on the page, its impact will be greater and subsequently its worth to the advertiser greater.

It is more common for high traffic sites to sell their advertising packages on a CPM basis, whereas lower traffic sites tend to price using the flat rate.

For sites in the process of being developed or updated that require adver-tisers to provide some of the working capital for their site building, a flat rate has some advantages. In particular, it allows for earlier invoicing for the relevant advertisement than the calculation of methods such as CPC and CPL allow.

As with agreements for other services, the payment clause should include details of when you are to invoice, whether VAT is included in the price quoted, and whether interest is to be charged for late payment.

Whichever method is chosen, it is recommended that as much detail of the pay structure is provided in the agreement so as to avoid uncertainty.

5.5 Licensing

Intellectual property rights

Intellectual property rights (IPRs) in any advertisement will (usually) be owned by the advertiser or by its creative agency, and it will usually incorporate specific items that are the advertiser's intellectual property, for example their trade mark. Under the agreement you will be required to carry the advertisement and therefore it is likely that you have an implied licence to display the trade mark on the site. However, it is also common in online advertising agreements to expressly state that you have a licence giving you permission to display the trade mark and other intellectual property in the advertisement. This acts as an added protection for you as the site owner, and clarifies the extent of your licence.

Type of licence required to reproduce and display the advertisement

The licence referred to should be a world-wide licence as access to your site can be achieved through a computer with internet access in any country in the world.

The license should also be non-exclusive as you do not want, or need, to prevent the advertiser from using their own trade mark elsewhere, for whatever means they choose.

Screen shots

Once you have developed your web-site you may choose to publicise its existence through reproducing in paper format, for example, pages from the site, or incorporating images from the site in advertising for your own business. In order to reproduce the page ('screenshot') as it appears on the site, the licence you obtain from the advertiser needs to cover your use of screen shots. Without such a licence you will need to edit the printed page so as not to infringe the advertiser's IPRs.

Trade marks and copyright are more specifically dealt with above.

5.6 Data protection

Depending on the type of advertisement (e.g. interactive or html banners which allow for the input of data) it may be possible for personal data to be collected about visitors and customers. If this is the case, the agreement should deal with the obligations of the parties concerning data protection and privacy to ensure compliance with the Data Protection Act 1998. Data protection is discussed more fully in chapter 3.

5.7 Legislation

There is no single statute that codifies the laws applying to advertising. There are, however, numerous legislative provisions that impact on this area that online advertisers need to comply with. Relevant legislation is discussed in chapter 6.

Similarly, codes governing industry best practice need to be considered. The Advertising Standards Authority (ASA) has confirmed that its codes of practice apply to some forms of advertising and promotion on the internet, and in particular to banner advertisements. See chapter 6 for further details of the codes and how they apply.

As part of the terms and conditions, the parties should state who is responsible for compliance with these laws and codes, so that both parties are aware of whose obligation this is.

5.8 Advertisers' obligations under the agreement

Applicable law/regulations
The advertiser should be required to give assurances regarding the advertisement it has produced. It should be asked to warrant that:

■ the advertisement does not violate any applicable law or regulation; and
■ it has complied with the codes of practice issued by the Committee of Advertising Practice in the UK in respect of electronic and online advertising and all other relevant industry codes of practice.

Third parties' rights

As noted above, it is common for the advertiser to grant a licence for intellectual property use. In order to ensure you have some right of redress in the event of third party claims, the advertiser should be required to warrant that it has the right to publish all of the contents of the advertisement and can lawfully grant you such a right. The advertiser should also confirm that the advertisement does not infringe any other rights of third parties including all IPRs and rights of privacy.

Financial promotions

In the UK, a person is prohibited from communicating an invitation or induce-ment to engage in investment activity unless that person is an authorised person or the communication has been approved by an authorised person (as defined by the Financial Services and Markets Act 2000 (the Act)). Failure to comply with this provision is a criminal offence. It is therefore important to have the advertiser warrant that the advertisement either:

- does not constitute a financial promotion under the Act; or
- has been approved by an authorised person or is otherwise permitted under the Act.

Where financial services advertisements are carried, it is also prudent to put in place compliance systems to ensure that all advertisements are properly signed off by the relevant compliance officer(s) within the advertiser's business.

Indemnity

To give additional teeth to the warranties that the advertisement does not breach relevant laws or codes, does not infringe any third party rights and does not breach the Act, advertisers should also be required to indemnify you against any claim resulting from the advertisement. This should ideally extend to holding you harmless against any expenses (including legal costs), damages or losses (including loss of profit) in connection with any claims arising from the advertisement.

5.9 Limitation of liability

Having covered the advertiser's obligations and duties, you should state in the agreement what your liability to the advertiser will be. In particular, you should state what the consequences will be if you fail to publish an advertise-ment or deliver the advertisement for the required amount of time. You should aim to limit your liability as you would not wish to be responsible for the costs of a whole advertising campaign or any indirect or consequential loss that the advertiser claims. It is common to find terms providing that liability is expressly limited to publishing the advertisement or a replacement advertisement, or refunding the advertising fee. While one cannot say with certainty that it would always satisfy the requirement of reasonableness in UCTA 1977, it is probably not a bad position for most web-site owners to adopt in practice.

5.10 Usage statistics

In return for paying to advertise on the site, the advertiser may typically want assurance on a range of issues, in particular the number of visitors to the site. However, it can be difficult to measure the exact number of visitors to a site due to such practices as the creation of web caches (whereby ISPs store copies of popular sites for access by their customers) and mirror sites around the internet to improve access times. It is also an issue over which the host party has no control. It is therefore advisable to note in the terms and conditions that any usage statistics referred to or discussed are estimates only, and that no guarantee is given with regard to usage.

5.11 Format of advertisement, etc.

The terms and conditions should set out practical considerations such as the format in which the advertiser should provide the advertisement. This can help avoid situations where you may have to reject the advertisement (if the agreement allows) or spend time converting it into the correct format in order to carry the advertisement. Provisions dealing with operational requirements should ideally deal with format, file size, manner of transmission between the parties, lead-time prior to publication and any other relevant technical or operational specifications.

From the point of view of the web-site owner, it is advisable to allow for rejections of the advertisement if the advertiser does not comply with the relevant requirements (see below).

5.12 Positioning

Discretion as to positioning of advertisement
It is usual for the web-site owner to retain the right to decide where to position an advert within their site. However, as with all agreements, this will be open to negotiation depending on the bargaining power of the parties.

Competitors' advertisements
The agreement terms may also include a provision dealing with the placement or inclusion of advertisements for an advertiser's competitor. As a site owner your main aim is to attract as many advertisers as possible and not limit

opportunities. Advertisers, on the other hand, may not want their advertisements displayed alongside their competitors. The standard position in your advertising terms should be that no exclusivity is granted and that competitors' advertisements may be displayed. However, in certain cases, this position may be varied by express written terms

Any agreed restriction should be limited. It could be stipulated as being, for example, for the length of the agreement or the time during which your site is carrying a particular advertisement. It should also clearly define the categories of competitors who are covered.

5.13 Assignment or resale of advertisement space

In order to maintain control of the advertisements carried on a site, it is possible to include in the agreement a clause that restricts the advertiser from assigning, transferring or reselling any of their rights under the agreement to another party. Without this clause, you may be obliged under contract to carry advertisements that are inappropriate for your site.

This term could also be used to prevent an advertiser with whom you have an agreement making a profit from the sale of advertising space on your site by reselling for more than you charged.

5.14 Right to reject advertisement

As with preventing the right to resell the advertising space, you should keep ultimate control of your web-site content by retaining a right to reject an advertisement or remove it from the site at any time. The right should not be unreasonably used, but having it will clarify from the beginning the conditions under which an advertisement may be rejected or removed, helping to prevent problems later on.

5.15 Other things to consider

The terms outlined above would be suitable for use in most online advertising agreements. However, when accepting advertisements for your site, special care and consideration should be given to advertisements for products and services that attract specific legislation or codes of conducts. Such products and services include:

- tobacco advertising;
- alcohol advertising;
- advertising aimed at children;
- advertising for medicines and medical products; and
- financial services.

In some cases, such products may not be advertised or are subject to restrictions. Even where an advertisement is permitted, additional terms may have to be incorporated into the agreement.

Further details regarding the advertising of specific products and services is dealt with in chapter 6.

Lastly, when considering the content of an online advertising agreement, reference should be made to chapter 1 which deals with contract formation and other relevant clauses, such as jurisdiction and governing law, that need to be included to complete the agreement.

6. Web linking

6.1 Web link – friend or parasite?

Links are vital to the interaction between your site and others. Internet users use links frequently to access both other web-sites and to move around a single site. A link will build brand awareness and drive users and potential revenue to your site. But care needs to be taken in implementing and using links.

How links work

A link, at its simplest and most straightforward, is an embedded electronic address, or hypertext link, that points to another web location. The link stores the electronic address of the destination site or page, and clicking on the link sends the address to the browser, which then moves the user to the new destination. The new web-site is shown in its entirety on the screen, usually with the full web address.

A simple hypertext link, while it has some potential problems, is relatively straightforward. The use of an embedded address is usually viewed as part of the intrinsic structure of the Web. Legal rights to link are granted by way of an implied licence to link to the second site and reproduce and distribute the material contained on that site. It is only where use of the link creates difficulties for the linked site – for example, by driving so many users to the site that its infrastructure cannot cope, or by encouraging users to copy third party material – that the linked party will want to regulate more formally or prohibit this type of link.

A second type of link is more complex. This link acts as a 'pointer' to a document, image or audio clip (or other content) contained in another web-site, which 'pulls' in the image, text or audio clip from the other web page into the current web page for display. The user's browser still points to the original site.

It is possible for the material from this form of link to be displayed within the frame or border of a page on the linking web-site. This type of use is known as 'framing', and content from a number of sites may be pooled on one web page. A banner containing the original site's branding is likely to be viewed along the top and down the side of one or both sides of the linked page. In some cases, all of the linked site's branding is obscured. This category of link can create obvious difficulties for a web-site owner, as material may be pulled to a third party 'parasite' web-site without his knowledge. A connection is likely to be created in the mind of the user between the framed material and the parasitic web-site, which may dilute or damage the goodwill or branding of the originating business. Use of third party marks or advertising ('ambush marketing') to boost the profile of one site can impact on advertising strategy or contractual commitments, for example, exclusivity agreements.

Action may be taken to prevent this type of link on grounds of passing off (trading on another's goodwill so as to create confusion between businesses), copyright or database infringement. No cases have been finally decided in the English courts but the general weight of legal opinion is that a passing off action may be successful.

In January 2001, Haymarket issued proceedings against Castrol Burmah for passing off, when Castrol framed links from the Haymarket sites, autosport.com and whatcar.com within a Castrol site, without Haymarket's permission. Castrol has since dropped the links (see *Financial Times*, 10 January 2001).

A related category of link that has been in the forefront of recent disputes is the 'deep link'. This is a type of link which links to material contained on another web-site, but bypasses its homepage and other proprietary pages, depriving that web-site of brand recognition. Material accessed by a deep link may be framed with a bundle of other content within a third party web-site.

In March 2000, Ticketmaster Corp (Corp) bought an action in the US against Tickets.com for deep linking to Corp's web-site, Ticketmaster Online (*Ticketmaster Corp* v. *Tickets.com*, US District Court, Central District of California, 10 August 2000). Tickets.com had created thousands of links, which led users to Ticketmaster online web pages. Corp claimed unfair competition, breach of terms and conditions, unlawful interference (as the linking prevented its web-site from operating commercially), and passing off (as the user would be confused as to the relationship between the two sites). The judge to date has allowed the claims of passing off and unlawful interference to remain, although he did not allow the claim of unfair competition. He did, however, not exclude the possibility that deep linking could amount to unfair competition in particular circumstances.

The Stepstone case (*Stepstone* v. *Ofir*, 28 February 2001) highlights the possible danger of a claim for database rights infringement.

Other sub-categories of link include 'page jacking' when users believe they are going to a particular web-site and are diverted to a pornographic web-site;

and 'mouse trapping', when users close a page and it takes them to another page, which they cannot exit.

'Namestuffing' and 'metatagging' are also types of hidden and potentially misleading links.

6.2 Practicalities

Linking, even at the simplest level, can create risk for a web-site owner. The cases demonstrate that there is no clear guidance (as elsewhere on the internet) on the legal and commercial parameters governing their use.

Some businesses have taken the view that the benefits of deep-linking outweigh the risks, but any links should be implemented only with an understanding of the potential liabilities. Preferably sites should play safe and avoid accusations of passing off, unfair competition and trade mark, copyright or database infringement by following basic guidelines.

6.3 Think before you link

If linking:

- Check the sites you are linking to. Are there online terms regulating or restricting links? Has the site owner taken action against third parties before?
- Are you intending to frame or deeplink to material and in what context?
- If framing or deeplinking, minimise risk by:
  a) notifying visitors of the relationship between your site and the linked sites;
  b) identifying third-party trade marks and copyright ownership;
  c) including disclaimers of liability for content and make sure that they are brought to the attention of the user; and
  d) ideally, agreeing a proper linking agreement (see below).

If linked to:

- Place notices on your site restricting links. Specify that any links can only be made with prior approval and include an e-mail address for approvals.
- Monitor links to your site.
- Evaluate links. Has any material or trade mark been copied? Is there any possible passing off? Take professional advice if necessary.
- Implement a common gateway interface to encourage linkers to go to an agreed home page.
- Preferably, regulate all deep or framed links with a proper linking agreement.

Example: Site disclaimer

[We] *do not represent or warrant that any information which may be obtained* [on this site] *or through any link to or from this site is accurate, complete or current. We do not accept any responsibility for any loss that may arise as a result of relying upon such information. Material contained in any third party site or web page accessed from this site is outside our control and will be subject to third party intellectual property rights, separate terms of use and policies covering data use and privacy. You are advised to read applicable terms and policies before use of this web-site or any other.*

If you wish to link to this site please send an e-mail to [e-mail address] *for express authorisation.*

6.4 Linking agreement

A properly drafted linking or framing agreement is the most secure way of lessening risks in linking content in or to your site where content is intended to be incorporated within another web page. It is also likely to be operative in establishing partnership relationships and driving and creating revenues.

From the framer's viewpoint, the agreement should include service levels to ensure that the framed site will be available to the framer's users. Content may be specified, or certain types of content excluded. The display of both parties' branding will need to be considered. If the framed content is to appear as the content of the framer's site, it may be appropriate for the provider to use 'mirror' or 'white-labelled' web pages with a different URL, stripped of all provider branding or other identifiers.

It may be necessary to include development provisions and acceptance procedures if, for example, bespoke web pages are being created.

There may in addition be e-commerce add-ons, enabling users of one site to order from the other, possibly with commission payments.

Framing agreements may of course, also be two-way.

6.5 Key provisions for a linking or framing agreement – where one party is framing content taken from another's web-site

- Include as a schedule a detailed specification of the type of link required and associated service level agreements (SLAs). You may also need to schedule development milestones. The following points are key:
  a) Specify the relevant URLs of the sites. What are the visual requirements? What constitutes the frame (e.g. this may be as simple as a branded banner across the top of the screen)? What URLs are to be visible? Where on the web page is the link to appear? Above the fold (i.e. on the

visible screen) or below the fold? Where are scroll bars to appear? Is there to be a menu down one side of the framed material?

b) If it is necessary to create specially developed web pages or content, who will be responsible for development? Who is paying for development? Set out a timetable for development and acceptance.

- SLAs should specify who has responsibility for maintenance, response times and security provisions, including possibly password access to specific areas of the other's sites.
- The SLAs should also set standard web performance targets for uptime, response times for maintenance, and so on.
- If possible, agree detailed specifications and SLAs before entering into the agreement. It is these areas that are most likely to give rise to a dispute later – and signing an agreement where these issues are 'to be agreed' will weaken its effectiveness.

Branding

- What use is to be made of the other party's trade marks? Specify what trade marks or logos are to be used.
- Where are these to appear? Are all trade marks cleared for use? Potential infringement liabilities may be lessened by obtaining warranties and indemnities from the other party, but it is also sensible to ask the question at the start.
- Are there to be express acknowledgements of trade mark ownership on the web page incorporating the link?
- From the point of view of the trade mark owner, an acknowledgement of trade mark ownership should be included, either on the page or by a further hypertext link.

Intellectual property right licences

- Has each party reserved rights in their own intellectual property rights and granted a licence of copyright or trade marks to the other party, for the purposes of the link?
- An express grant of rights is important in defining the scope of use that the other party is entitled to make.
- Ensure that suitable copyright notifications appear in any content provided or on linked web pages.

Controls and approvals

- What control is each party to have over the other party's site or content?
- Is one party allowed to veto certain types of content or third party links?

- What practical arrangements are needed to approve content? Copy may be submitted by e-mail 24 hours before posting, possibly combined with an editorial right to amend copy when posted. Include a right to amend if either party is made aware of any infringement or regulatory breach.
- If links to third party sites (or corporate intranets of either party) are envisaged, where are the links to be held?
- Is the linking arrangement to be exclusive between the parties in relation to a particular area of trade? This type of provision may at first sight be attractive, but may limit the potential usefulness of a site to users, who wish to see a wide range of links.

Data use and protection

- What use is either party to be allowed to make of the other party's data? Is particular use of data to be prohibited? For example, it may be preferable for data to be used on an aggregated basis within either party's entire database, not targeted as a specific visitor sector.
- Provisions should cover compliance with data protection legislation, ensuring, for example, that both parties have a full online privacy policy and that all necessary consents are obtained from users to transfer of data.

Advertising

- Are the parties to be given access to the other's advertising? If so, ensure that any third party terms are not breached.

Payment

- If commission is being paid, does the party paying have full audit rights? Include detailed provisions for the calculation of commission, payment terms and review clauses.

Term

- What is the term of the agreement? In general, short-term agreements are preferable, to give the parties scope to re-evaluate.
- Is there a right to terminate on notice? Make sure termination rights also include a right to terminate in the event of insolvency or breach of warranty.
- Include a right to remove the link immediately on termination or if the other party is in breach.

Consequences of termination

- How are the parties to deal with post-termination issues, such as transferring data to the other party? Provide that all data are returned or deleted as soon as possible and that all licences to use intellectual property rights terminate.

- If one party is paying commission to the other, the Commercial Agents (Council Directive) Regulations 1993 (SI 1993 No. 3053) may apply. If so, have measures been taken to ameliorate their effect, such as express indemnity payments? The regulations also set minimum notice periods that must be observed.

Liability

- Include limitations on liability, bearing in mind the provisions of the Unfair Contract Terms Act 1977 that such limitations must be reasonable. Other statutory legislation will apply if the parties are dealing with consumers, such as the Unfair Terms in Consumer Contracts Regulations 1999.
- Include disclaimers of liability, particularly in relation to the provision of professional advice by the content provider.

Warranties

- It is normal practice for both parties to warrant ownership of their own intellectual property rights, and that all content provided will comply with relevant legislation and not be defamatory or negligent.
- Warranties are particularly important if content may be relied on by the user. The framer will wish to see a warranty that the content is in accordance with best professional practice, while the provider will want to disclaim responsibility for reliance (to the greatest extent possible).
- Warranties may need to exclude content provided by third parties or be made subject to a specific disclaimer or online terms and conditions.

Insurance and disaster recovery

- If the provision of the link requires substantial investment or carries any unusual risk or high value transactions, have the parties considered insurance for downtime or other loss? What disaster recovery mechanisms are in place?

Confidentiality

- Mutual confidentiality provisions should be included.
- Specify governing law but bear in mind the problems of enforcing these types of clauses.

6.6 How to prevent unwanted linking

Discourage parasites by stating on your web-site that:

- any link can only be made with approval and provide an e-mail link via which approvals may be sought;
- links are to be made only through a designated home page; and
- material on the web-site is subject to trade mark, copyright and database right and any unauthorised reproduction of this material is prohibited.

If troublesome illegal links are made to your site, notify the third party as soon as possible that the link is unauthorised and ask for it to be removed. Do not threaten trade mark or copyright infringement without taking legal advice as making groundless threats of infringement may result in a claim being made against you.

If possible, avoid taking legal action by negotiating a properly regulated linking arrangement that will benefit both parties, but if there is no option, take legal advice. It may be possible to claim passing off or trade mark, copyright or database infringement. You will also need advice on the most appropriate jurisdiction. Bear in mind that any legal claim is, as a general rule, only worth doing if you are suffering or are likely to suffer measurable damage.

7. Selling online

Traditional Company Limited will need to ensure that its online contracts for the sale of its widgets are legally binding.

The development and operation of Traditional Company Limited's web-site needs to take into account the processes and legislation governing e-commerce sales to consumers in the UK and Europe including, but not limited to, the Unfair Contract Terms Act 1977 (UCTA), the Unfair Terms in Consumer Contracts Regulations 1999 (the Regulations), The Consumer Protection (Distance Selling) Regulations 2000 (the Distance Selling Regulations) and The Electronic Commerce Directive (2000/31/EC) (the E-commerce Directive).

Traditional Company Limited also needs advice on its obligations under the Data Protection Act 1998 and what it should do if its widgets are defective. These issues are addressed in section 8 below and in chapter 3. (Chapter 1 provides an overview of the basic rules of contract.)

7.1 Terms and conditions

Traditional Company Limited will need to publish online terms and conditions for the sale of the widgets on its web-site. As Traditional Company Limited will be selling widgets to consumers, under the Regulations it must ensure that its terms are fair and reasonable or they will not be enforceable.

If Traditional Company Limited uses terms that are deemed unfair pursuant to the Regulations, the Director General of Fair Trading can investigate the terms and conditions and request that the unfair term and any similar term is removed.

If necessary, the Director General can seek an injunction from the courts to prevent the unfair term being used. In addition, bad publicity can result from any involvement of the Office of Fair Trading (OFT). The findings of the OFT are published and are available to the public and will be highly damaging to the reputation of a company.

What does 'fair' mean?

The following list sets out some examples of what may constitute unfair terms under the Regulations:

General

- Terms that are misleading.
- Terms that are not in plain English.
- Terms that use legal terms or other terms that are not generally understood by the public.
- Terms that exclude or limit any terms implied by law (e.g. that the company owns the goods they are selling).
- Stating that the written terms incorporate the whole agreement (i.e. do not include pre-sales discussions).

Liability

- Terms where the parties have different liability levels.
- Terms that exclude or limit liability for personal injury or death caused by negligence (such a term would also be prohibited under UCTA).
- Terms that exclude or limit liability if the goods do not match their description, are not of satisfactory quality or are not fit for the purpose for which they are usually used.
- Terms that exclude or limit the buyer's statutory rights.
- Terms that limit the types of redress that are available to the buyer.
- Terms that limit or exclude loss which the parties could have been expected to foresee at the time they entered into the contract.
- Terms that state that the goods are sold as seen or disclaim responsibility for failure to meet any reasonable standard.

Delivery

- Terms that do not state a delivery time.
- Terms that exclude or limit liability for non-delivery/delay.
- Terms that pass risk before delivery.
- Terms that deem that the goods are accepted on delivery.

Payment/Cancellation

- Terms that request full payment in advance.
- Terms that give the supplier the right to vary the price after the contract has been concluded.
- Terms that place excessive penalty/compensation obligations on the buyer.
- Terms that give the buyer unequal/inadequate cancellation rights.
- Terms that allow the supplier to cancel the contract without refund/notice.

The E-commerce Directive was adopted on 8 June 2000 and published in the Official Journal of the European Communities on 17 July 2000. It was due to be implemented in the UK by 17 January 2002, but this deadline has not been met. The UK published draft Regulations in March 2002 and the DTI's public consultation process on the draft Regulations finished on 2 May 2002. The E-commerce Directive provides that, except when otherwise agreed and except for contracts concluded exclusively by exchange of e-mail messages, the service provider should communicate 'comprehensively and unambiguously' prior to the placement of the customer's order at least the following information:

- the different technical steps needed to conclude the contract;
- the language available for the conclusion of the contract;
- the technical means for identifying and correcting input errors; and
- whether the contract will be archived and be accessible.

The service provider must also provide the customer with details of any relevant codes of conduct and details of how these can be accessed.

7.2 Governing law/jurisdiction

Traditional Company Limited is keen for English law to apply to its online contracts. As discussed in chapter 1, Traditional Company Limited should make it clear in its terms and conditions of sale that the sale of the widgets is subject to English law.

However, since Traditional Company Limited is dealing with consumers, potentially in many jurisdictions, the choice of law clause will not be able to override any mandatory rules of law in the consumer's home state.

In addition to the EEA countries, Traditional Company Limited has four or five key countries to target for the sale of its widgets and so decides to take local legal advice in respect of these countries.

If it has been decided that because of the laws which apply in those countries, Traditional Company Limited does not wish to sell widgets there, then the web-site should make it clear that it is not targeting customers within those states.

To minimise its risk, the practical solution for Traditional Company Limited is to limit sales of the widgets to consumers in countries whose laws have been checked. This may, for example, be achieved by requiring the consumer to select a delivery address from a drop-down list of acceptable countries. In addition, the site can include protective mechanisms such as requiring all visitors to state the jurisdiction in which they are based before allowing further access or including a statement on the web-site that buyers in certain states are precluded from purchasing the widgets.

As well as expressing a choice of law in the contracts with its customers, Traditional Company Limited may wish to increase the chance of the English courts having jurisdiction to hear any dispute. If so, it would be well advised to specifically state in its terms and conditions that the English courts will have exclusive jurisdiction.

7.3 Easy access

The terms and conditions may not be enforceable unless they are easily accessible and specifically brought to the consumer's attention. Practically, users of Traditional Company Limited's web-site should be able to 'click through' to the terms and conditions from each page of the web-site and must 'click to agree' to them before using services or ordering goods available from the site.

7.4 Information

Information on the web-site

By law, all companies must include the following information on their company web-site:

- company name;
- company number;
- registered office address;
- where the company was registered; and
- VAT number.

This is often included in a 'Contact Us' page on the web-site.

Information to be provided to the consumer

The Distance Selling Regulations and the E-commerce Directive aim to enhance web-site transparency and Traditional Company Limited must provide the following information in an easy, direct and permanently accessible form to its customers before they make a purchase:

- identity of supplier;
- supplier's geographical address;
- supplier's e-mail address;
- supplier's company registration number;
- VAT number;
- authorisation by or membership of any professional bodies;
- main characteristics of goods;
- price of goods (including all taxes) and payment arrangements;
- where applicable, the period for which the offer or price remains valid;
- arrangements for payment, delivery or performance, including any delivery costs;
- the existence of the consumer's right to cancel the contract (including cancellation procedures and conditions);
- whether the supplier may provide substitute goods if the requested goods are unavailable, and if so, that the cost of the consumer returning such substitute goods in the event of cancellation will be borne by the supplier;
- the cost of ordering the goods via the web-site where this is other than the basic rate;
- the cost of using the means of distance communications where it is calculated other than at the basic rate;
- where appropriate, the minimum duration of the contract, in the case of contracts for the supply of goods or services to be performed permanently or recurrently;
- information about any after sales service and guarantees.

Accurate and up-to-date information

It is important that any information published on Traditional Company Limited's web-site is accurate and kept up-to-date (e.g. catalogues or price lists).

If at any time information is not up-to-date, the site should clearly say this. A phrase commonly used on web-sites is *'Prices are valid at the time of posting'*, but this is not recommended as the customer will not necessarily know the date that the information was published on the site. *'Prices are valid up and until 5 pm on 25 December 2001. For a free price list after this date please call [0800 XXX XXX]'* may be used as an alternative.

7.5 Sales process

Traditional Company Limited needs a clear sales process and has suggested that the developer takes into account the following process whilst carrying out the development work:

The consumer is provided with the information set out above and access to the terms and conditions of sale and privacy policy.

Consumer completes order form following a clear and easy to follow step-by-step guide, which enables him/her to change items in the order at any time.

Consumer is obliged to view and click to accept the terms and conditions of sale before submitting order.

Consumer submits order form.

Traditional Company Limited sends consumer a return e-mail confirming receipt and the details of the order and highlighting any returns policy/cancellation rights (the consumer will have seen these already in the information provided during the ordering process) and gives the consumer a second chance to check that details are correct.

Consumer confirms details are correct.

Traditional Company Limited despatches goods to consumer and notifies consumer of despatch date.

7.6 Delivery of goods

Unless the parties agree otherwise, Traditional Company Limited must deliver the goods within a maximum period of thirty days from the day after the day on which the consumer sent his order. If Traditional Company Limited cannot do so, it must inform the consumer and reimburse any sum paid as soon as possible or, at the latest within thirty days beginning with the day after the day on which the period for performance expired.

7.7 Cancellation

Right to cancel

Under the Distance Selling Regulations, subject to a few exceptions a consumer has the right to serve a *notice of cancellation* to cancel the online contract within a cancellation period, usually within a period of seven working days following delivery of the goods. (See chapter 6.)

Consequences of cancellation

If a consumer does cancel an order, Traditional Company Limited must refund any sum paid by him as soon as possible and, in any case, within thirty days from the day on which the notice of cancellation was given. Traditional Company Limited may charge for the direct cost of recovering any goods supplied where a term of the contract provides for the consumer to return goods if he cancels and the consumer does not comply with this provision or returns the goods at the expense of the supplier. However, this right may not apply if the consumer has the contractual right to reject the goods, or has the right to reject under a term implied by law or if such a term is 'unfair'.

Following cancellation, where a consumer does have goods in his possession, he has a duty to retain them and take reasonable care of them and either make them available for collection or deliver or send the goods to Traditional Company Limited.

Cancellation of the contract also has the effect of automatically cancelling any related credit agreements.

Please note that the information and cancellation period will differ if Traditional Company Limited provides services rather than goods.

8. Defective goods

Traditional Company Limited also needs a refresher on where it stands if the widgets are defective.

8.1 Sale of Goods Act 1979

Under the Sale of Goods Act 1979 (the Act), the widgets must be of 'satisfactory quality'. This means that whilst the widgets do not need to be perfect, they should be of a standard that a reasonable person would regard as satisfactory in all the circumstances, such as concerning the price and any description of the widgets.

Quality means appearance, safety, freedom from defects, durability and fitness for their purpose. The widgets will need to be of a satisfactory quality for a reasonable amount of time. The exact amount of time will depend on the type of goods and their usual life expectancy. For example, food will not be expected to last as long as a car.

Under the Act, if Traditional Company Limited's widgets are not of satisfactory quality (e.g. if they do not work), the customer can reject them and claim a refund and/or compensation provided the widgets have not been 'accepted' by the customer (see later). There is no legal right to have the goods repaired or replaced under the Act (but see below on the Directive on the Sale of Goods and Associated Guarantees) and Traditional Company Limited cannot repair, replace or provide a credit note instead of allowing the customer to reject the widgets unless the customer agrees. There is no need for a customer to prove that Traditional Company Limited is at fault.

The liability is based on the fact that Traditional Company Limited has breached an implied term that the widgets will be of a quality and/or safety that could reasonably be expected. It is important to note that the customer can only claim a remedy under this Act from the seller. Unless the manufacturer and seller is the same entity, the customer cannot claim redress from the manufacturer.

Traditional Company Limited will not have to provide a refund under the Act if the customer accepts the widgets (however, please refer to the consumer's right to cancel under the Distance Selling Regulations, which are discussed in section 2 above). Acceptance can be as follows. When the customer intimates to the seller that he accepts the goods; when the goods have been delivered to the customer and he does an act in relation to them which is inconsistent with the ownership of the seller, and when the customer retains the goods after a lapse of reasonable time without intimating to the seller that he has rejected them.

8.2 Consumer Protection Act 1987

In addition to the above, Traditional Company Limited may be liable as the manufacturer of the widgets under the Consumer Protection Act 1987 if the widgets are defective and cause damage.

The Act imposes direct liability upon manufacturers, own branders and importers of products in favour of anyone injured and in respect of any damage above £275 caused to private property as a result of the defects.

If Traditional Company Limited is sued under the Consumer Protection Act 1987, there are a number of defences it can rely on including if:

- the defect is attributable to compliance with a statutory or EU requirement;
- the defect did not exist at the relevant time ie when the widgets were supplied by one producer to another; and/or
- the state of scientific/technical knowledge at the relevant time was not such that a producer of products of the same description as the product in question might be expected to have discovered.

8.3 The General Product Safety Regulations 1994

The General Product Safety Regulations 1994 apply to new and second hand (but not antiques) consumer products, except products covered by specific

European legislation. They place a duty on all producers of consumer goods to supply safe products. There is a lesser duty in the Regulations for distributors (ie someone whose activities do not affect the product's safety).

Safety takes into account factors such as the product's characteristics, instructions and warnings and the categories of consumer at risk when using the product, particularly children. Any relevant British or European standards may be taken into account in assessing safety.

A breach of this legislation can result in fines, imprisonment or prohibition and suspension orders.

A revised General Product Safety Directive was adopted by the Council on 27 September 2001 and will be implemented into UK law within two years of the date of its publication in the Official Journal (15 January 2002).

8.4 Liability in tort

Under the law of tort, those who use a defective widget may be able to claim damages for personal injury, death and/or damage to property. This may arise where injury or property damage is caused as a result of Traditional Company Limited's negligence in designing or manufacturing the widgets.

8.5 Guarantees

Many manufacturers provide guarantees to their customers in which they agree to replace or repair defective products for a specified period of time, usually for a year.

Under the Directive on the Sale of Consumer Goods and Associated Guarantees (1999/44/EC, L171), consumers will be entitled to bring a claim against the seller of the goods if the goods do not conform with the contractual specifications. This right will be for a period of two years from the time of delivery of the goods.

This right means that, where the goods are faulty/defective, the consumer/purchaser will be entitled to their repair or replacement free of charge unless this is impossible or disproportionate to do.

The consumer may be entitled to a reduction in price or refund if:

- he is not entitled to repair or replacement; or
- the supplier has not completed the remedy within a reasonable time; or
- the supplier has not completed the remedy without significant inconvenience to the consumer.

The consumer is not entitled to have the contract terminated if the defect is minor. The Directive also ensures that any guarantees given by the manufacturer/seller are legally binding and must be clear to understand.

Whilst the Directive was due to be implemented into English law by 1 January 2002 this deadline was not met and the DTI has indicated that it is likely to be delayed until late 2002. A second document (with draft Regulations) was released in February 2002, with a deadline of 23 May 2002 for responses.

8.6 What steps can Traditional Company Limited take to minimise its risks for defective products?

Product safety bureaucracy
A robust, paper-based monitoring system will enable it to demonstrate compliance with its legal duties. Procedures also need to be put in place so that any necessary product recall can be carried out slickly and with the minimum of economic and commercial damage.

Quality control, warnings and instructions
It should ensure there are pre-delivery checks to ensure compliance with the various product safety requirements. Instructions and other customer literature should contain appropriate warnings as to possible safety dangers. The bodies who enforce safety legislation are also often willing to give guidance as to the adequacy of safety procedures.

Purchase of raw materials
Where possible appropriate indemnities should be sought from component or raw material suppliers.

Insurance
Take out appropriate product liability insurance.

9. Data protection

Once up and running, Traditional Company Limited's online activities will mean that it will be processing many more details about individuals and in many different ways than was the case when it was purely operating off line. For instance:

- Online customers will be likely to register their names and addresses and pass credit card details for payment of products bought off the web-site.
- The company's sales and marketing department may want to analyse the business's customer base as part of its schemes and wheezes which seek to squeeze greater sales from the company's existing clientele.

- If the company wants to learn more about those who use its web-site (including those who do not necessarily buy its products), it may well ask visitors to register further details about themselves so that it can inform them of new product lines or offers that may be of specific interest to them.
- Potentially, the company may want to exchange these details with another business in return for details about that other business's customers – the question of using another business's customer data is dealt with in chapters 3 and 6.
- Customer information may need to be passed to third parties to whom the company outsources elements of its operations (e.g. those who run call centres which are established to answer customer enquiries).
- The company may want to advertise job vacancies and accept applications for those vacancies on line.
- Cookie technology may well be used on the company's servers to make the process of using its web-site more convenient (a cookie is the name given to technology which enables a web-site to remember information given by individual visitors who have previously used that site).
- Finally, it may well be that the company needs or wants to transfer customer details abroad, perhaps because it has overseas operations or because a partner with whom it wishes to share the details is based overseas.

In chapter 3 we introduce the subject of data protection laws and explain the likely consequences of not complying with those laws and some of the specific obligations imposed by them that an online business should consider in relation to its operations.

The obligations apply to any use that is made of information from which it is possible to identify a living individual. They apply not only to computerised data, but also to many paper-held records. Therefore, Traditional Company Limited should not assume that data protection compliance is a new issue. The company is always likely to have processed a great deal of information about individuals, be they its employees (current or past), contractors, suppliers, customers or potential customers, and all of these uses will continue to be bound by the obligations of data protection laws. However, the dramatic increase in the amount of additional processing of information about individuals which will take place once the company's web-site is operational means that now is a good time to review whether the business's operations as a whole put it in danger of breaching data protection laws. A full data protection audit of the company's on- and offline operations should be considered.

Many of the data protection law obligations detailed in chapter 3 will require Traditional Company Limited to inform users fully of its web-site as to what information the company uses which identifies them, and how that information will be used. Some of the obligations will also require Traditional

Company Limited to obtain consent from its web-site's users for these uses to be made. Such consents generally have to be obtained from users at the point when their information is acquired by the company, or as soon as possible after that time.

This means that it is very important that the company include a detailed privacy policy on its web-site in which it comes clean about what and when user information will be obtained and how it will be used. The policy should be prominently positioned on the web-site and should be cross-referenced in opt-in consent wording at any point on the site where information is obtained from users (a fuller commentary on tick box wording is included in chapter 3).

The details which Traditional Company Limited should include in its privacy policy will depend on what information about its users it plans to obtain and what uses it intends to make of that information. The box below illustrates some general categories of use which an online business should consider including in a web-site privacy policy. These are not intended to provide a definitive privacy policy.

For a list of the other steps that an online business should take before its web-site goes live, see chapter 3.

Issues to consider in an on-line privacy policy

1. Details of when information contained in the policy was last updated.
2. Full details of the web-site operator and other group companies that will be given user details – including the companies' full names and addresses.
3. Contact details of the online business for users who have enquiries about how their data are used, and to correct out of date information held by the online business.
4. A general introduction as to how user data are collected.
5. Details of whether and how cookie technology is used by the web-site.
6. A general description of security measures taken in connection with user details.
7. Details of how user data are used to supply products/services.
8. Details of situations in which users may be contacted .
9. Details of marketing activities for which user data will be used.
10. A description of data which may be passed to third parties and such details as are possible about likely third parties: e.g. a) data processors (e.g. call centre operators, billing system operators, hosting providers, customer support services, etc.); b) business partners; c) law enforcement agencies or other third parties authorised by law to access the data; and d) future owners of the business.
11. Details of non-European Economic Area countries to which user data will be transferred. Specific countries should be named.
12. Details of how information supplied pursuant to a job application will be used (to the extent not covered by the above points).

---

10. Employment

A number of employment issues arise from the decision by Traditional Company Limited to provide e-mail and internet access to its employees. These issues need to be addressed at an early stage and the requisite policies and procedures put in place to minimise the risk of claims against Traditional Company Limited which may be as diverse as libel, sex or race discrimination or breach of copyright. In chapter 8, we discuss the misuse of e-mail and the internet by employees and how the liability for such misuse may rest with Traditional Company Limited. We consider the rights of Traditional Company Limited to monitor its employees' e-mail and internet activities, taking into account the protection afforded to employees by the human rights and data protection legislation. We advise on the benefits of drafting and implementing an effective e-mail and internet policy and how to manage employees who breach the policy.

11. Tax

Traditional Company Limited will need to consider some of the taxation implications that may arise when it sets up a web-site and begins to trade online. The tax considerations hinge largely on the structure that Traditional Company Limited adopts and the manner in which it trades over the internet.

If, by way of example, the following structure was adopted (and please seek advice before automatically adopting this structure for your own business):

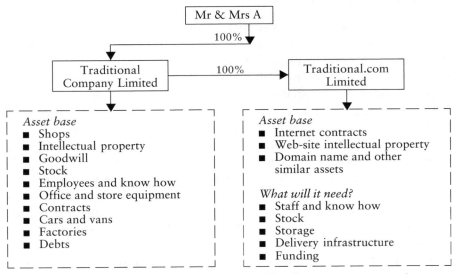

Nb: these lists are not exhaustive – they are intended for illustration purposes only.

Then the following considerations will need to be addressed:

- How will Traditional.com access the 'items' that it needs to run its business?
- How will Traditional.com account for income and capital gains tax?
- How will Traditional.com account for VAT?
- What reliefs are available?
- How will Traditional.com access funding?

11.1 How will Traditional.com access the items that it needs to run its business?

One of the more common and easier ways to allow the internet arm of a business to access the assets, etc. belonging to the physical arm of the business is to put a management agreement in place.

The management agreement would, in its generic form, ensure that Traditional Company Limited is able to provide know-how, other intellectual property, staff and the physical resources (such as computers and offices) etc. to Traditional.com as and when required.

The domain names and other web-related assets including the customer contracts could likely be purchased or effected in the name of Traditional.com.

The fee arrangements contained in the agreement would need to be determined on a case-by-case basis and the taxation implications of each arrangement would then need to be considered.

11.2 How will Traditional.com account for income and capital gains tax?

If a management agreement was effected and we assumed that Traditional Company Limited and Traditional.com are in the same group for corporation tax and VAT purposes (explained in chapter 9) then the imposition of any fees is tax-'neutral'. It is 'tax-neutral' because the fee payer (Traditional.com) is usually entitled to a deduction and the recipient (Traditional Company Limited) must account for the receipt of that fee as income and in this way the expense and the income are offset against each other within the group.

Easier compliance with Inland Revenue requirements is certainly one example of the benefits of running the Traditional.com business through a separate business vehicle, such as a company, as it becomes easy to identify any income or capital gains attributable to Traditional.com. It is relatively easy to trace any gains or losses incurred in Traditional.com as it will have its own accounts, asset sheets, company number and the like as distinct from its parent, Traditional Company Limited.

Traditional.com should state the net of its gains and losses from trans-actions occurring over the internet in its tax returns for the year. We can also assume that the entire group are UK residents for taxation purposes which means that Traditional.com will be liable for tax on income, profits and gains that it derives in the UK and abroad (subject to Double Tax Agreements which seek to reduce or eliminate double taxation).

11.3 How will Traditional.com account for VAT?

The VAT treatment in our above example is relatively straightforward.

As far as VAT is concerned, any transactions arising under the management agreement are 'ignored' provided both parties are in the same VAT group and are registered as a group with HM Customs & Excise (Customs and Excise). This means that Traditional Company Limited need not impose VAT on the services/goods provided to Traditional.com under the agreement (but it may need to impose VAT on goods or services provided to third parties). Traditional Company Limited remains the head entity and must account to Customs and Excise for the VAT liability of the whole group (including vatable transactions made by other group members). Specific advice should be sought in all circumstances.

For transactions occurring outside the group – such as with customers introduced over the Internet and even customers outside the UK, the VAT position becomes slightly more clouded. It would be wise for Traditional.com to request that Internet customers inform them as to which country they are transacting from and their VAT (or consumption tax) number if relevant. The acquisition (or import) in the United Kingdom of goods from a member of the European Union will be subject to VAT. However, VAT is generally not charged on exports of goods or services made by a UK company but there are exceptions depending on country of destination.

For transactions occurring over the Internet but within the UK, VAT is still due (but there is some debate about how Customs & Excise will be able to determine what transactions have occurred (and therefore collect the revenue) if there are no invoices). We recommend that VAT is paid and that full VAT invoices are issued as if the transaction was occurring in paper format.

There is also some scope in the very near future for digital invoicing.

11.4 What relief is available for intra-group transactions?

Assuming that Traditional.com and Traditional Company Limited are within the same group for VAT and corporation tax purposes (and are registered as such). Very broadly, for VAT purposes, any intra-group transactions are ignored and Traditional Company Limited assumes the VAT liability for the whole group as the head company.

For the purposes of corporation tax on chargeable gains and stamp duty, any transfer of assets between group members is not subject to tax until such time as the company leaves the group or other events happen. However, for both corporation tax on chargeable gains and stamp duty, the Inland Revenue has the power to retract any relief claimed in certain circumstances. For example, in the 2002 Budget, the Government announced that Inland Revenue may retract group stamp duty relief where a UK property has been transferred from one company (for example, Traditional Company Limited) to another company in the group (for example, Traditional.com), and within two years the company in receipt of the property (Traditional.com) leaves the group.

11.5 How will Traditional.com access funding?

The range of funding options available to Traditional Company Limited, Mr and Mrs A and even Traditional.com itself is broad and beyond the scope of this chapter. It is raised in this forum as a pointer and something that should not be forgotten when contemplating the transaction as a whole. There is a matrix of funding options – such as third party loans, Enterprise Investment Schemes (EIS), debt, management agreements and the like – each of which have their own tax consequences, some of which are discussed in greater detail in chapter 9. Regard should also be had to the Government's new Investment Readiness Programme announced in the 2002 Budget.

✳

As you can see there is a myriad of options, considerations and taxation consequences, which may arise from the decision to move from bricks to clicks. Each of these will vary depending on the individual circumstances of the business and indeed, the nature of the business moving from bricks to clicks.

We cannot reiterate enough the importance of seeking specific taxation advice. Automatically adopting the structure as discussed above would rarely be appropriate.

12. Competition law

In deciding how to conduct its business in the market place, Traditional Company Limited should not overlook its duties and rights under both domestic and European competition law. The basic theme is that the company should not behave in a manner that is anti-competitive towards other competing companies or consumers. Likewise, other companies are prevented from acting in a way that is anti-competitive towards Traditional Company Limited.

Broadly speaking, in order to comply with these rules, Traditional Company Limited must not enter into any agreements, take any decisions or adopt any practices that may prevent, restrict or distort competition in the UK or the EC. For example, fixing prices or market sharing is strictly forbidden. If, later on, Traditional Company Limited performs well and gains a significantly high market share, it may occupy a dominant position in the market and should be careful not to abuse its dominance, as this constitutes unlawful behaviour. Examples of abuse include discriminatory or excessive pricing, or refusing to supply.

Traditional Company Limited should also be aware of the laws relating to merger control. If it decides to merge with another company, depending on the size of the transaction, the merger may be subject to an investigation at either domestic or European level to ensure that it will not damage competition. Competition law may, at first, seem rather draconian, but it is designed as much to protect Traditional Company Limited as to control it. It is, therefore, in Traditional Company Limited's interest to be able to recognise where other companies may be acting in an anti-competitive fashion or abusing a dominant position and to report such behaviour to the competition authorities for investigation.

Chapter 10 discusses these issues in more depth.

3

Data Protection and E-business

Introduction

Data protection laws impose obligations governing the way in which information about living individuals is processed. They also give rights to individuals in relation to how third parties use their data. This chapter is an introduction to the data protection laws most relevant to an online business and suggests the steps that should be taken to reduce the risk of an online business's operations not complying with obligations imposed by those laws.

Data protection laws have been passed in the UK since 1984, but as the internet and online trade have developed, so has the scope of the laws passed. Having initially permitted a rather *laissez-faire* approach to e-commerce privacy and encryption, the UK – along with its fellow EU member states – is now probably the most highly regulated jurisdiction when it comes to laws governing the use of information about living individuals, in terms of both the scope of the activities regulated and the number of regulations imposed. At the time of writing, there is no sign of any respite from either the introduction of new data protection laws or from the tweaks made to existing obligations which have been a feature of this area of e-commerce law since the first of the current generation of privacy regulations was introduced in May 1999. For these reasons, anyone taking advantage of the edge which technology gives their business would be well advised to consider seriously how data protection laws impact on that business. The days of *laissez-faire* data regulation are over and the consequences of non-compliance with the rules and regulations (criminal liability, fines and bad publicity) are distinctly unattractive.

UK law has been driven by Directives of the European Parliament. Like all EU member states, the UK is obliged to implement such Directives. Unfortunately for anyone wishing to initiate any element of electronic trade in its business today, the core European Directive which began the most recent wave of European data protection regulations was finalised in 1995 before use of the internet had developed in any meaningful way. Although it was not implemented in the UK for four and a half years, the Directive in question was not passed into law in an e-commerce-friendly way. As a result, subsequent data protection laws, while well intended, have been somewhat reactive to the rapid technology developments made since 1995 and the ways in which businesses take advantage of them. The laws have not always kept pace with these developments. Further, while EU-led laws have ensured a degree of harmonisation of data protection laws across Europe, certain key issues are dealt with differently by different European countries. For any business, but particularly a non-European-based business which is considering establishing operations in Europe, the vast array of regulations and the subtle differences adopted by different European countries can make data protection law compliance a seemingly daunting task.

This chapter provides guidance on data protection isues by:

- explaining why compliance with data protection laws is an important issue for an online businesses;
- explaining what activities of an online business are likely to be regulated by data protection laws;
- summarising the major obligations which the laws impose upon an online business; and
- identifying the areas of an online business's operations that should be considered in light of the UK's data protection laws and suggesting steps which can be taken to assist compliance with them.

The laws and regulations of certain other jurisdictions are referred to below, however, this chapter should be used only as a guide to UK laws and regulations. In general terms, it is safe to assume that the UK's data protection laws are very similar to those passed by the other EU member states (some of the key differences are identified below). Similarly – and this is another generalisation – if a business complies with the European data protection laws, then it is likely to comply with the spirit of the laws of many other countries, such is the far-reaching nature of the effect of Europe's data protection laws. Where what from a legal point of view is likely to be a controversial e-commerce activity, it is advisable to take advice on a country-by-country basis in jurisdictions that are important to a business.

1. Why compliance with data protection laws is an issue – fines, enforcement and bad publicity

The key questions a business is likely to want answered when being given an explanation of what an area of legal regulation means for it are: What are the consequences if we get caught for non-compliance? And, what are the chances of our getting caught?

A number of laws, regulations and codes of practice govern the processing of information about living individuals, but the starting point in answering these questions is the provisions of the Data Protection Act 1998. Failure to comply with this Act's obligations can be punished by the imposition of fines and, in certain instances, criminal liability, both of which may be imposed on directors, managers or other officers of a company who consent to or negligently permit the non-compliance. At the time of writing, in respect of breaches of the Act, Magistrates' courts can impose fines of up to £5,000 and Crown courts unlimited fines where serious offences have been committed. Individuals are also empowered to take action to prevent use of data that are likely to cause damage or distress. They may also obtain court orders to require inaccurate information about them to be destroyed or corrected, or to require its use to be blocked. There is also scope for private actions being taken if an individual suffers damage or distress (providing that it has led to quantifiable damage) following a breach of the Act.

The government body empowered to enforce the provisions of the Data Protection Act (and certain other data protection laws) is the Office of the Information Commissioner (OIC). Provided that an appropriate warrant is obtained, these powers include a right to enter a business's premises to seize evidence that a breach of the Act has taken place. Given that the OIC's resources are limited, to date enforcement actions under the Data Protection Act 1998 have been relatively rare. In the twelve months to 31 March 2001, 8,875 requests for assessment and enquiries were handled by the OIC, 715 premises were visited by its staff and 23 cases were taken to court (Annual Report of the Information Commissioner 2001, available at http://www. dataprotection.gov.uk/ar2001/annrep/index.htm).

Of more concern to any business should be the bad publicity that could result from an alleged failure to comply with data protection laws. This is particularly true for businesses whose products or services rely on the provision by its customers of sensitive information, or for businesses that are sensitive about protecting the goodwill in their brand. Most online businesses or departments consider customer trust in using technology to buy its products or services as key to their development. As certain banks and major retailers have discovered, publicity surrounding alleged breaches of the Data Protection Act's provisions relating to system security or marketing activities can be particularly unwelcome.

Also worth considering are public and business expectations when it comes to giving personal details to another party, particularly over the internet. It is fair to say that the growth of web-site privacy policies and tick box consent statements mean that many internet users expect, as a matter of course, to be told how information about them will be obtained and used, and look for an opportunity to consent or opt out of such uses. The inclusion of such policies and tick box wording are required by a number of provisions of the Data Protection Act (see section 5.3 below). Those not complying with the law by including them on their web-sites should consider whether public reaction to their sites will be affected regardless of whether they are accused of breaching data protection laws.

Similarly, most businesses tendering for suppliers to assist them by carrying out activities which involve the processing of their customers' information do so by requiring a high level of data protection law compliance. Those suppliers may not win business if they cannot show that they operate in accordance with data protection laws. They are certainly likely to be asked to give undertakings and warranties against the Data Protection Act by any well-advised customer. To turn the above points on their head, an e-business should ask itself: Can we turn data protection compliance into a selling point?

Finally, the reactions of a potential investor in or purchaser of an e-commerce business to risks taken by a business in relation to data protection regulation compliance should be considered. Data Protection compliance audits have become an increasingly important part of the due diligence which investors and purchasers conduct on targets before committing their money to a project.

2. Who enforces data protection laws?

The OIC is the principal enforcer of data protection laws. At the time of writing, the Information Commissioner is Elizabeth France and therefore all references in this book to the Commissioner are in the feminine. The major data protection obligations which the OIC enforce are those deriving under the Data Protection Acts, those specifically introduced by parliament to regulate the operations of communications providers (in particular telecommunications companies) and those falling under the Freedom of Information Act which governs public authorities.

However, the powers of other regulators are also likely to be relevant to an e-business's activities. For instance, the Advertising Standards Authority's (ASA) Codes of Practice which govern a large number of different forms of UK advertising and promotional activities contain obligations relevant to how personal data can be used for marketing purposes. As these rules supplement provisions included in other marketing-focused data protection legislation, it is possible that a business could be challenged by both the OIC and the ASA for the same marketing activity. Similarly, the Direct Marketing Association (DMA) issues Codes of Practice which bind its members. These Codes are generally regarded as a good indicator of what is deemed accepted practice in the marketing services sector. It is also the DMA that operates the various Preference Service lists to which individuals and companies can enter their telephone, fax, e-mail and address details to signify that they do not consent to marketing materials being sent to those numbers/addresses. (For fuller details of this obligation see point 5.5 of this chapter.) Accordingly, even if an online business does not consider itself to be a marketing business it would be wise for it to make itself aware of the ASA's and the DMA's respective Codes of Practice. Links to the ASA's, the DMA's and the Preference Services' web-sites are all included in the Appendix to this book.

Financial Services regulators also have powers relevant to the use of personal data. For instance, the Financial Services Authority can enforce regulations in respect of the use of personal data in marketing communications sent by financial promotions companies, under the Business Standards section of the Conduct of Business Sourcebook introduced under the Financial Services and Markets Act 2000.

3. What activities of an online business are likely to be regulated by data protection laws?

Before this chapter covers details of the data protection obligations with which an e-business must comply and suggests measures that can be adopted to ensure compliance, it is worth clarifying what activities are regulated by data protection laws.

The UK's data protection laws apply to '*processing*' of information conducted within the UK from which it is '*possible to identify a living individual*'. We will provide more detail below on what the law deems to be covered by the terms 'processing' and 'possible to identify a living individual', but it can be assumed that both cover a very broad range of an online business's activities indeed.

That leaves the question: When is an online business likely to be deemed to be processing information *within the UK*? Where the e-business's servers or other processing equipment are located is a good starting point, as a UK location will immediately qualify that country's laws as governing activities carried out using those servers. Even if its servers are located outside the UK, it is very likely that an e-business whose operations are targeted at a UK audience will involve some use of information in the UK. This is particularly the case if the business has or establishes a UK operation or if it employs staff in the UK. If that operation or those employees conduct activities such as processing online customer orders or providing customer support by viewing on-line customer information, then UK data protection laws (and the obligations and rights detailed in this chapter) will apply to those activities. Conceivably, third parties may be engaged in the UK to run the business's day-to-day operations, in which case those third parties will be obliged to meet the UK's laws although the e-business will be held ultimately responsible for their actions (see engaging third parties below for further details).

Of course, if an online business is planning to house its servers or run any element of its operations from any EU country other than the UK which has adopted data protection laws, then obligations broadly similar to the UK's will have to be met.

As EU data protection laws are seen as onerous when compared to the laws of other jurisdictions, conceivably a global business may benefit from locating elements of its operations, such as its servers, outside the European Union. The likely affect of the data protection laws of the country in which those operations are based, and the obligations detailed later in this chapter relating to overseas data transfers, should first be considered before a decision to avoid the UK on these grounds is taken. As many other jurisdictions are following the example of the European Union by introducing stringent data protection laws, the likelihood of benefits arising in this way are likely to diminish.

The obligations apply to the *processing* of any information from which it is *possible to identify a living individual*. These terms are defined very broadly indeed and the result is that it is inconceivable that the operations of an online business located in the UK will not be affected. 'Processing' covers just about any use of information imaginable. Everything from viewing information on a screen, storing it on a back-up server or printing the information would be deemed to be processing under the Data Protection Act. Even the act of destroying data will be deemed to be processing. Likewise, it will be deemed possible to identify a living individual from information even if such an individual is not directly named in that information. The Data Protection Act says that information is regulated by its provisions if it is possible to identify someone:

- directly from the information in question;
- from the information when it is combined with other data in its possession; or
- from the information when it is combined with other data which is likely to come into the processor's possession.

This means that processing information such as a post code, an e-mail address, a telephone number or a customer reference number could be deemed to be covered by the Data Protection Act's obligations. In each situation it is possible that the user of the data could combine the data with other data and as a result identify a living individual.

Whether an e-mail address is sufficient to identify a living individual will depend on the information contained in that address. For example, james.mullock@osborneclarke.com is more likely to identify an individual than james@oc.com (which is perhaps why Osborne Clarke have chosen the former and not the latter style of e-mail address). Businesses that operate a web-site from which they obtain user information such as their names and addresses (for instance, via a registration page or order forms) should be aware that as a result they will likely be deemed to hold information sufficient to identify an individual when those details are combined with other apparently harmless information in their possession. The e-mail address james@oc.com may not be sufficient to identify James Mullock on its own, but if James Mullock is a registered user of a web-site and recorded this address along with his full name at any time when using the site, then, in processing his e-mail address and any information connected to it, the web-site owner must comply with data protection law obligations.

It is also worth mentioning that the Information Commissioner has indicated that she interprets the Data Protection Act's provisions to mean that where a business's name includes the name of a living individual, processing that name constitutes processing information about a living individual. Hence use of the name Paul Smith Limited (in relation to the clothes designer) would be deemed covered by the Data Protection Act's obligations, while use of the name WH Smith (in relation to the well-known UK retailer) would not as Mr W. H. Smith, after whom that business is named, is no longer alive.

There is a common misconception that data protection law obligations apply only to computerised data. This is not the case. The obligations govern the use of information which is processed on any automised equipment or which is filed in a way that it is easily to reference a living individual. In plain English, in addition to computerised information, data protection obligations could cover the use of information about individuals recorded on paper or captured on film (including CCTV), audio tape, microfiche, CD-ROM or other disks. This means that use by a business of information relating to its customers, suppliers, agents or distributors, its business contacts, employees or contractors could be all regulated.

Departments of a business which will be affected are likely to include its marketing and promotions, IT, customer support, human resources, accounts and customer relations departments.

4. An overview of the major obligations imposed by data protection laws

If one major misconception made in relation to data protection laws is that they apply to computerised information only, another potentially more significant misconception is that compliance with data protection laws entails only registering a business with what used to be called the Data Protection Registrar (now the OIC).

Set out below is a brief summary of the major obligations imposed on anyone processing information about individuals and the rights which UK law gives those individuals. These lists do not offer an exhaustive list of relevant obligations and rights, but they provide a useful point of reference for a business when it is considering specifics as to how it should comply with data protection laws.

Data protection obligations and rights were originally written before use of the internet had taken off and the wording of the obligations is rather non-specific. As a result, the steps recommended here, which an e-business should take to seek compliance with these obligations, are intended to provide broad guidance. An online business that is serious about full compliance with data protection laws should audit its operations to ensure that the risk of not complying with the legal requirements which it faces are minimised. How such a risk assessment might be carried out are also set out in brief in the final section of this chapter.

1. Summary of obligations imposed by data protection laws	2. Summary of rights given to individuals in respect of their data
(a) *Unsolicited junk faxes and cold calls* – both are prohibited where recipients (be they companies or individuals) have either previously notified the party contacting them that they do not wish to receive unsolicited marketing communications or have registered with the Fax or Telephone Preference Service.	(a) *Right to rectify, block, erase or destroy inaccurate information –* subject to certain exemptions, anyone who is the subject of inaccurate information can apply for a court order to enforce this right in respect of inaccurate information or any expression of opinion based upon it.
(b) *Fair and lawful processing –* an obligation that on obtaining data (or as soon as possible thereafter) to fully inform individuals how and by whom their data will be used, and an obligation which is likely to require those individuals to consent to their data being processed.	(b) *Right of information and access –* individuals can demand details of: any data held about them; the purposes for which the data are held and the source of the data. A copy of the data must also be supplied. In certain cases exemptions apply.
(c) *Adequate, relevant and non-excessive use –* following on from (b), data must be processed in a way which is adequate, relevant and not excessive given the purposes for which they were obtained.	(c) *Right to prevent processing likely to cause unwarranted damage or distress –* individuals can write to anyone processing their data to demand compliance with this right.

1. Summary of obligations imposed by data protection laws – *continued*	2. Summary of rights given to individuals in respect of their data – *continued*
(d) *Data accuracy* – data must be kept accurate and, where necessary, up-to-date.	(d) *Compensation* – can be claimed for breaches of the Data Protection Act which cause damage and distress.
(e) *How long data should be kept* – data should only be kept for as long as is necessary given the purposes for which they were obtained.	(e) *Right to prevent use of data for direct marketing* – individuals can write to anyone processing their data to demand compliance with this right.
(f) *Security* – data must be kept using appropriate techniques and technology to prevent unauthorised or unlawful use of the data and their accidental loss or destruction.	(f) *Automated decisions* – decisions taken about individuals without human input which significantly affect them can be challenged.
(g) *Using third party data processors* – where information or access to information about individuals are given to third parties (e.g. a call centre operator or a hosting services provider) a written undertaking must be obtained from the third party that it will only use the data as instructed to do so and that it will meet the obligations of (f) above.	
(h) *Transfers abroad* – data must only be transferred from the United Kingdom to a non-European Economic Area[a] country if that destination country offers data protection rights equivalent to those of the United Kingdom. Transfers are permitted if (amongst other situations) the individual whose data is being sent abroad consents to his or her data being sent to the specific country concerned or if the transfer is necessary for a contractual obligation to be provided to that individual.	
(i) *Notification* – details of all purposes for which data are processed must annually be notified to the OIC.	

Note:
a. The European Economic Area comprises the fifteen European Union members states plus Iceland, Liechtenstein and Norway.

5. Specific data protection issues to consider

5.1 Where to locate servers, call centres, billing operations, etc.

Not all businesses can choose where to locate different parts of their operations. Those considering expanding from the UK (perhaps amongst other European territories) for the first time clearly can. Similarly, a multinational business which includea a UK branch and which is looking at adding an online operation for the first time could base staff and equipment for that operation in one of a number of locations.

Issues other than data protection law compliance will probably be high on the list of factors that determine how a business chooses where to locate the assets which are behind its online operations, such as its servers, call centres or billing centres. The likely cost of each different location option is likely to be top of the list. However, as the physical location of equipment and people which are used to process information about a business's customers, suppliers and employees will determine which jurisdictions' data protection laws govern those operations, legal factors should also be considered. If an area of a business's operations is likely to process a great deal of data about individuals, it makes sense to locate it in an area which will give the business fewest compliance headaches.

Basically, an online business would be well advised to assess:

- The data protection laws of a country in which it plans to base any part of its operations which will process large amounts of information about individuals; and
- The data protection laws of other countries where it has subsidiaries in respect of what they say about transferring data to the country where it plans to base its heavy processing operations.

For instance, USA Co. is considering establishing a European operation, which will include USA Co. Ltd in the UK. It is trying to decide between locating its European billing processing operations in the UK, the Netherlands or India (the latter offering a set-up and running cost saving). From a data protection compliance law point of view, USA Co. needs to consider the following issues:

a) Are India's data protection laws dramatically more or less onerous than those of the UK or the Netherlands? (These are likely to be similar as both are EU member states and so are obliged to introduce the same data protection laws.)

b) The obligation imposed by UK law on those who transfer data from the UK to non-European Economic Area countries (see obligation 1 (h) in the table). If India is selected as the processing site's location, then this obligation will apply to any customer data sent to it by USA Co. Ltd, as India is not in the

European Economic Area. Indeed the local law of each of USA Co.'s other European subsidiaries will very likely impose an identical obligation.

5.2 Transferring data outside the European Economic Area

Like the question of where to locate overseas processing operations, this will not be an issue for all online businesses. However, any UK business which has operations outside the European Economic Area must consider obligation 1(h) in the table carefully.

The obligation is perhaps the best example of a data protection law which was dreamt up before the internet became a major force, but which nevertheless must now be complied with. Its origin was the European Union's desire to introduce laws that protect its citizens and give them rights in respect of how their data are used both in and outside Europe. Hence the requirement imposed on anyone transferring data outside the European Economic Area that they should only transfer data to a country whose laws offer adequate rights and protection to the person identified in the data as compared to the data protection laws of the European Union.

Online businesses can meet this obligation owed to their subscribers in one of a number of ways. These include the following:

a) *Fulfilling a contractual obligation*: If the transfer is made in order that a contractual obligation owed to a subscriber be fulfilled, then the obligation is deemed met (e.g. if the data are sent to enable a service to be provided to the subscriber).

b) *Consent*: If the subscriber consents to his/her data being sent to a specifically named non-European Economic Area country, then the obligations will be deemed to have been complied with. Hence, listing the specific countries to which subscriber information will be sent in a web-site privacy policy to which subscribers then consent via opt in tick box wording, is likely to be the best means of meeting this obligation.

c) *Approved destination country/Safe harbour*: If the subscriber data are sent to a country whose data protection laws the OIC has identified as offering adequate protection, then all transfers of data to that country will meet this obligation. At the time of writing the only non-European Economic Area countries identified are Canada, Hungary and Switzerland and transfers of not every type of data to those countries have been approved. However twelve other countries or territories (Australia, Guernsey, Hong Kong, Isle of Man, Israel, Japan, Jersey, New Zealand, Poland, the Slovak Republic, Slovenia and Taiwan) have been identified by the OIC as having laws likely to offer adequate protection for these purposes. Controversially, the US has not been named, but following protracted negotiations between the

European Union and the FCC it was agreed that where American entities entered into a so-called safe harbour scheme, transfers of data to those entities would be deemed to comply with this obligation.

d) *Model contract*: If the online business which is transferring the data to an non-European Economic Area country signs a contract with the recipient of the information which has been issued or approved by the OIC, then adequate protection will be deemed to have been ensured. To date, only two model contracts have been approved and it is likely that they will be seen by many non-European businesses as containing onerous provisions. Signing a model contract is only likely to be a reasonable route to complying with this obligation where data are transferred to a group company.

5.3 Web-site privacy policies

Informing individuals what uses will be made of their data and obtaining their consent for these uses to be made are common features of the obligations listed in column 1 of the table (pp. 72–3) (in particular they are relevant to obligations 1(a), (b), (c) and (h)). For this reason a clearly worded privacy policy should be included on any web-site from which information about individuals is either overtly or covertly obtained. The policy should detail what information is obtained by the online business about those who use its web-site, and what uses will be made of those data or any other data relating to those individuals which come into the business's possession. Some suggested uses that might be included in a privacy policy are set out in chapter 2.

Of key importance is that the policy details as many possible future purposes for which user data may be used as possible. An online business that uses its subscriber's data for a new purpose for which it has not obtained their consent will have to re-contact its users to obtain their permission before it can proceed with a new use. The policy should also be linked to opt in consent wording so that users have an opportunity to give their approval for their data to be used as is detailed in the web-site's privacy policy. Points to note in relation to such consent wording are set out at the next section.

5.4 Online forms

For an e-business to obtain the consents which it will need to comply with the obligations set out in the table above, the details set out in its privacy policy need to be linked to a statement via which users consent to those uses being made of their information. The most frequently asked question about what are commonly known as tick boxes is: Do they have to be worded so that a user gives 'opt-in' consent as opposed to 'opting out' of giving his/her consent? In other words, does the user have to give a positive indication that he/she consents by clicking a tick into a box? To date, data protection laws have been drafted in a way that does not provide a clear answer to this question in all scenarios. Explicit consent definitely has to be obtained in any situation where what the Data Protection Act defines as sensitive data are obtained.

Sensitive data is any information about an individual's:

- racial or ethnic origin;
- political opinions;
- religious or other similar beliefs;
- membership of a trade union;
- physical or mental health or condition;
- sexual life; and
- criminal record or offences committed or alleged to have been committed.

Web-sites that obtain or deal in any of these types of information should definitely include opt in consent wording linked to their privacy policies.

Web-sites that obtain or deal in other types of information would be well advised to obtain opt-in consent too. The law does not state this as a requirement, but the OIC has stated her opinion that consent must be freely given.

Legislation is currently being considered by the European Parliament and could oblige opt-in consent to be obtained before direct marketing e-mails are sent to individuals or businesses. It is likely that such obligations will make their way into the UK's laws in 2003, if not before. Many other European countries have already introduced this obligation (see section 5.5). Somewhat controversially, the possibility of requiring opt-in consent on every occasion that a web-site uses cookies is also being considered as part of the same legislation. Any business that seeks to rely on opt-out tick box consent to permit it to e-mail marketing information to its users or to use cookies on its web-site therefore runs the risk that when this legislation is finalised, if it chooses to comply with the new laws, it will have to re-contact its entire subscriber database to re-request permission to use their data for e-mail marketing.

An opt-in consent tick box like the following should be included on any part of a web-site from which user information is obtained:

By ticking this box I confirm that I have read and understood your Privacy Policy [include link to policy] *and that I consent to the activities detailed in it.*

An alternative approach would be to link the submitting of a registration form with the giving of consent, for example, by prominently including the following wording on a registration page's submit button:

By submitting this form I confirm that I have read and understood your Privacy Policy [include link to policy] *and that I consent to the activities detailed in it.*

A golden rule in respect of tick box wording – whether opt-in or opt-out – is that they should always be clearly visible.

5.5 Marketing with user details

The obligation to inform individuals (about whom information is obtained via a web-site) how that information will be used (obligation 1(b) in the table) is probably most significant when it comes to a business's planned marketing activities. This is because the scope for user complaints is perhaps at its greatest when unsolicited marketing communications are involved. For this reason, before contacting an individual with any marketing information, an online business should consider what that person has been told his or her details will be used for and whether he/she has consented to those uses.

If the user's details have been taken from the online business's database of its registered users, this will be likely to boil down to what details about marketing activities were included in its web-site's privacy policy when the user's details were obtained and whether the user consented to those uses. Although the UK's data protection laws do not contain an explicit requirement for opt-in consent (other than where sensitive data are being processed), the laws of some European countries do require such consent to be obtained before unsolicited marketing e-mails are sent. Austria, Finland and Germany have all passed legislation to this effect. Also, at the time of writing, the European Parliament is considering a draft Directive which would oblige member states of the European Union to implement laws to explicitly require opt-in consent to be obtained before spam e-mails are sent to individuals or companies. Any pan-European e-mail marketing campaign should bear these differences in mind.

If the user's details have been obtained from a third party (for example, if a database of the third party's customers has been purchased), the online business should ask the third party to guarantee that contacting those named on the database will not land it in hot water. If the third party has neither informed its customers nor obtained their permission to pass on their details to other businesses to enable them to send marketing communications to those customers, then both the third party and the online business will be in breach of their respective obligations under data protection laws. To say the least, this could affect the value of its database to the online business.

Similarly, before passing a customer database to a third party, an online business should bear in mind that it is obliged to have informed the individuals named in that list that their details will be passed on to other businesses and to have obtained their consent for this to happen.

Data protection marketing obligations have an additional layer in that both individuals and companies have a right to register details of their telephone and fax numbers with a registry run by the Preference Service to record the fact that they do not consent to receiving unsolicited marketing details at those contact details (see obligation 1(a) in the table). The Preference Service is run by the DMA. Details of the web-site addresses of each of the different divisions of the Preference Service which control the databases of telephone, fax and e-mail addresses registrations are included in the Appendix at the end of this book. It would be wise for any business that acquires marketing database lists from third parties to check those lists against the relevant Preference Service register before using it. Similarly, businesses should regularly clean from their own marketing databases the names of individuals and companies named on a Preference Service register and who have not consented to their contact details being used for marketing purposes. The Preference Service and a number of companies currently offer a list cleaning service. Businesses with pan-European operations should bear in mind that most EU member states also operate equivalent registries to those run by the Preference Service, all of which should be checked before pan-European marketing activities are commenced.

5.6 Security

As one might expect, data protection laws include obligations that require any-one processing information about living individuals to do so in a secure way. The wording of the relevant obligation is not specific. It refers to a requirement to use *appropriate techniques and technology* to prevent unauthorised or unlawful use or accidental loss of that data (see obligation 1(f) in the table). The OIC has said in its guidance notes to the Data Protection Act that compliance with this requirement will be judged against what technology is available at any time and what it would cost to take advantage of that security. The reliability of staff who have access to data will also be considered.

It is difficult to generalise about what steps an online business should take to seek to ensure that its data processing activities are deemed to be secure given the above obligation. Common sense will provide a useful guide and the opinion of expert security consultants should be sought where specific knowledge is lacking within a business's internal technology departments. Businesses should bear in mind that, as with other data protection law obligations, security obligations will potentially apply to its use of paper information as well as to its processing of machine-readable data. As mentioned above, the Data Protection Act regulates any structured collection of information that identifies a living individual. Therefore, the security under which files of customer records and accounts information are held should be reviewed just as carefully as the firewall and virus alert technology used by the business's technology systems.

5.7 Engaging third parties – call centre providers, billing processors, hosting services technical support

With the security requirements detailed above in mind, an online business should also consider the circumstances under which it engages third parties to process data about its customers, suppliers, distributors, contractors, employees or any other individuals involved in its operations. The Data Protection Act contains specific requirements that oblige anyone who shares such information with a data processor to take responsibility for the processor's actions by requiring them to:

- Choose a data processor which gives sufficient guarantees in respect of the security measures which it will use in processing data; and
- Enter a written contract with the processor obliging it to:
  - use their data as instructed to do so; and
  - hold the data at all times using appropriate techniques and technology to prevent unauthorised or unlawful use or accidental loss of that data.

A business whose data processors cause a security breach can be held liable for that breach. Therefore, the contractual terms agreed by an online business with any third parties to whom it outsources (say) its call centre operations, its invoice processing, its hosting operations or the technical support of its equipment, its goods or its services should all be reviewed carefully. In each of these scenarios the third party outsourcer is likely to be given personal data about the online business's customers. Accordingly, the online business needs to enter a written agreement with each under which strict security undertakings are given to it.

5.8 Notification (or registering under the Data Protection Act)

All businesses which process information about individuals are required to have pre-notified to the OIC via a standard form details of the types of data it will process and the purposes for which processing will take place. Notifications must be updated annually and a fee (currently £35) must be paid to the OIC for it to process the notification. Some data do not need to be notified, for example uses made of most non-computerised data need not be included and details of data used for staff administration, advertising and marketing or accounting purposes are also exempted from this obligation. Notifications can be made online at the OIC's web-site (details are included in the Appendix to this book). It is not possible to make a group-wide notification with the OIC. Individual company details are required to be submitted seperately.

It would be wise for an online business to appoint an individual within its organisation to take responsibility for ensuring that its data protection notification is up-to-date and accurate. This individual could also take responsibility for dealing with other data protection issues, such as ensuring that a prompt response is given to requests from individuals for information about or access to data which is processed by the business.

5.9 Privacy audits

The list of issues relevant to online businesses set out in this chapter demonstrates the quantity of regulations that potentially could affect a business's e-commerce activities. While the establishment of a new online trading activity will provide a business with a good opportunity to assess the extent to which those activities could potentially give rise to a data protection issue and the extent to which it is worried about that fact, many businesses will already have online activities underway. Any business concerned about the bad publicity or the fines that could result from a breach of data protection laws being uncovered should audit its activities to assess:

- where risks arise;
- where those risks are business critical; and
- what changes can be made to reduce those risks.

It is difficult to draw up a definitive list of actions for every type of business, setting out how such a privacy audit should be carried out, but the following points may be of assistance:

- The business activities which should be audited for compliance with the obligations of data protection laws are those that involve the use of any information from which it is possible to identify a living individual. Departments whose activities are therefore likely to be relevant are: personnel, marketing, customer relations, IT/technology support and accounts/billing.
- In introducing the audit to staff, involve senior management. If changes to procedures need to be made to reduce the risk of non-compliance with data protection laws, these changes will then be easier to implement. Senior management have a vested interested in ensuring data protection compliance as they potentially can be held personally liable for certain breaches of the Data Protection Act.
- Bring together the heads of the departments most likely to be audited to explain why the audit is necessary (emphasising the consequences of serious non-compliance), what areas of their activities are regulated and how they will be audited.
- Prepare a questionnaire to circulate within the departments to assess what information about individuals is processed by that department and the purposes for which it is used or could be used in the future. This

information-gathering process could be supplemented with a round of interviews with staff in relevant departments. In particular consider:

- how information is obtained;
- how information is used;
- what individuals are told when their data are obtained;
- what consents are obtained from individuals;
- whether the information is sent abroad and if so where;
- how long information is kept and how it is kept accurate and up to date;
- security measures taken to safeguard the information;
- whether third parties are engaged to process the information and if they are what contracts have been entered with those third parties;
- the business's ability to retrieve information if requested to do so; and
- the business's notification to the OIC – i.e. does it include all information processed and all purposes for which processing is taking place?

■ Assess the results for compliance with the obligations of data protection laws detailed above and the extent to which it is desirable to change current policies and procedures to reduce the risk of non-compliance.

Web-site Content – Whose Responsibility?

CHAPTER

4

Introduction

A business operating online will necessarily publish large amounts of content on its web-site. To a large degree, the business will be able to exercise control over this content (for example, the business's own content relating to its services); however, there may be content on the site which a business could have difficulty controlling. Such instances usually occur where a business allows a user to post material on its site, such as by operating a bulletin board, where users can post comments or exchange information with other users.

Who is responsible for this content if an aggrieved person presents a legal claim? Can the business point the aggrieved person in the direction of the user making the posting? Or can the internet services provider hosting the business's web-site be held responsible?

This chapter highlights some of the claims that can arise from web-site content. In particular, it seeks to show how far a web-site operator (e.g. a business operating online) or an internet services provider can be held responsible for content on web-sites which they either operate or host. Businesses that are aware of the potential liability attached to content will be better placed to judge the content that it intends to display on its web-site. Where material has been posted by a third party, businesses that are aware of the potential liability attached to content will be better placed to determine what practices should be implemented to minimise the risk of claims.

1. Intermediary services providers – publisher or carrier?

A business operating online or a web-site operator, which allows unknown third party material to be posted on its site, faces similar considerations, in terms of legal liability, to internet services providers on account of its reduced ability to control what might end up being displayed. Some might argue that an internet services provider should receive greater immunity from liability because of the sheer volume of content in which it must deal, in contrast to a web-site operator, who would be responsible for vetting its own site only. Such argument is beyond the scope of this chapter. Thus this chapter adopts the terminology of the E-commerce Directive (Directive on Legal Aspects of Information Society Services (The Electronic Commerce Directive) 2000/3P/EC; further discussion as to how it will affect ISPs is discussed at the end of this chapter), which, generally speaking, refers to both internet services providers and web-site operators collectively as intermediary services providers (ISPs).

Central to the debate on the extent of ISP liability at both civil and criminal law has been the issue as to whether an ISP is a 'publisher' like a newspaper, or a 'carrier' such as a telecommunications service provider. If an ISP is a publisher, then it is more likely to be found liable for content 'published'. Alternatively, where it is viewed as a carrier, it is less likely to be held liable for the content it permits users to access. As yet, there is no general principle under English law on the exact status of an ISP. The E-commerce Directive aims to rectify the uncertainty. However at present, whether an ISP is publisher or carrier, or indeed neither, is decided by reference to each specific piece of legislation under which the potential liability falls. Therefore, in order to assess fully the risks associated with web-site content it is still necessary to consider separately actions under English law, both civil and criminal, commonly perceived to give rise to ISP liability, some of which are set out below.

2. Civil liability

2.1 Defamation

Defamation claims have, perhaps, attracted more publicity than any other civil right of action. This section concentrates on what constitutes defamation under English law and whether or not an ISP or web-site operator might become liable under English defamation legislation.

What is defamation?
An action in defamation requires a statement to have been published that harms a person's reputation. Written or other 'tangible' defamatory statements are known as libel, whereas spoken defamatory statements are known as slander. A defamatory statement must be a false statement, so that a defence to a defamation claim is truth. In other words, even if a statement harms another's reputation, it is not defamatory if it is true. Other defences include

'absolute' or 'qualified' privilege and 'fair comment'. However, the defences that are likely to be relevant to an ISP which is not the maker of a statement are not so much to do with the content of the statement and the motivations for making it, but the manner in which such statement was made available to the public.

When is an ISP liable?

Whether an ISP is liable for defamatory statement on its servers or its web-site, or whether it is the author who is solely liable, will depend on whether the ISP can be classed as a 'publisher' under the Defamation Act 1996. Under the Defamation Act a person will not be classed as an author, editor or publisher if he is involved only:

- in printing, producing, distributing or selling printed material containing the statement; or
- in (i) processing, making copies of, distributing or selling any electronic medium in or on which the statement is recorded, or (ii) operating or providing any equipment, system or service from which the statement is retrieved, copied, distributed or made available in electronic form; or
- as the operator of or provider of access to a communications system by means of which the statement is transmitted, or made available, by a person over whom he has no effective control.

The courts have indicated expressly or impliedly that the third category set out above can exempt internet services providers from being classed as publishers. Logically one would also expect a web-site operator to be exempt under the second category. *Totalise plc* v. *Motley Fool Ltd* ([2001] All ER 213) appears to confirm such expectation by finding that the web-site operator, Motley Fool, was not a responsible for publications under section 10 of the Contempt of Court Act 1981 as there was no editorial control.

The most recent case confirming this approach with respect to internet services providers concerned an injunction preventing the publication of the identities of the two young men convicted of murdering James Bulger (*Thompson and Venables* v. *Newsgroup Newspapers*, Order of Dame Elizabeth Butler-Schloss in the Family Division of the High Court, 10 July 2001, unreported). Certain campaigners intended to publish recent photographs of one of them on the internet. Although not a defamation case, the High Court agreed to grant special dispensation to internet services providers. It was decided that, unlike the general press, for the lifespan of this injunction, internet services providers will be liable only if they know that prohibited material has been or is likely to be placed on their servers or accessed via their services and they have failed to take *all reasonable steps* to prevent this publication or to block access to it.

The proviso that internet services providers must take all reasonable steps to prevent publication or to block access is important, as the same is expressly set out under the Defamation Act. For the Act states that where a person is not the author, editor or publisher of a defamatory statement, in order to avoid liability, he must also show that:

- he took reasonable care in relation to the statement's publication; and
- he did not know, and had no reason to believe, that what he did caused or contributed to the publication of a defamatory statement.

In the case of *Godfrey* v. *Demon Internet Ltd* ([1999] 4 All ER 342), Demon Internet faced liability for defamation for material posted by an unidentified third party about Dr Godfrey, but did not take any action to remove the offending posting for ten days following complaint by Dr Godfrey. The judge concluded that, although an internet services provider may not be a publisher within the meaning of the Defamation Act, because it (i) chose to store postings, and (ii) could edit or delete the postings, it could none the less be held responsible for causing or contributing to that publication. The court was of the view that Demon Internet could not show that it had taken 'reasonable care' in relation to the publication needed under the Act to exempt it from liability.

The conclusion to be drawn is that providing an ISP does not exercise any 'editorial control' over the information published, and takes reasonable steps to remove any defamatory material brought to its attention, then it is unlikely to be held responsible for that defamatory material. Therefore, an ISP needs to have procedures in place to react quickly to any complaint about material posted to a site. Ways in which an ISP might best avoid liability are discussed at the end of this chapter. However, there is still much scope for debate on how ISPs can minimise risks since, as in the Bulger case, the courts have so far declined to give guidance on what are the reasonable steps an ISP must take to prevent publication of, or block access to, offending material.

Likewise, the E-commerce Directive is silent on the requirements for an adequate notice and takedown procedure following complaint relating to offending material, for the European Commission has made it clear that it favours voluntary self-regulation in the industry, with self-regulatory bodies devising their own codes of practice (although the Directive does not prevent member states imposing formal legislation).

2.2 Intellectual property

Intellectual property rights are rights that subsist in intangible property. The scope of intangible property protected is very broad and could take the form of a song, a play, a computer program, a compilation or some form of distinctive branding. Intellectual property rights most relevant to the content of web-sites are copyright, database rights, trade marks and passing off. Some intellectual property rights, namely trade marks and passing off, are also relevant to the subject of domain names (not themselves intellectual property rights). Trade marks and passing off in the context of domain name disputes are discussed in detail in chapter 7.

Copyright infringement

Copyright is the term given to certain legal rights that protect the *expression* of ideas (but not the ideas themselves). Copyright arises automatically when a work is created without the need for registration and can take many forms: literary, musical or dramatic works. In addition, the fixation of works into other mediums can themselves attract copyright such as sound recordings, films or broadcasts. Text, images, music and video footage therefore are all usually 'works' for the purposes of copyright, as are computer programs which are considered to be 'literary works'.

The Copyright Designs and Patents Act 1988 (CPDA) gives the owner of copyright the right to control the manner or extent to which a work is exploited and covers, for example:

- copying – such as simply reproducing a literary work onto a web-site ('copying' under the CPDA includes storing material in electronic form);
- issuing copies to the public – such as allowing an unpublished work to be downloaded via a web-site;
- performing, showing or playing in public – such as making concerts or films available to the public via a web-site;
- broadcasting – such as live concerts broadcasted over the internet; and
- adapting – extracts of a work used or manipulated for use in some way, such as song lyrics modified for the purposes of an advertising campaign.

When displaying another's content (which usually amounts to copying or issuing copies to the public) an ISP must take care not to infringe another's copyright. No knowledge element is required for copyright infringement, thus it is irrelevant whether an ISP is ignorant as to whether or not a third party's copyright exists in a work. Furthermore, copyright infringement can occur even if just part of a work is used, if that part is a substantial part. Whether that particular part used is a substantial part of the work is judged qualitatively and is not solely based on how much of a work has been reproduced, so that, for example, the reproduction of a few distinctive bars of a song could sustain a claim for copyright infringement. Hence, an ISP may not avoid copyright infringement by simply using small extracts of another's work.

An ISP should therefore attempt to limit the risk of copyright infringement by ensuring it has the consent of the copyright owner to its material for the activities for which it intends to use it. Alternatively, the CDPA does permit certain activities and it is possible an ISP may be able to bring itself within the permitted exceptions. The exceptions include use of the material for research, education, the reporting of current events and for the purposes of criticism or review. However, in all cases where there is a risk of infringement, ISPs should err on the side of caution and obtain a licence from the copyright owner which permits the ISP to make the content available via its site to users.

Databases

Some databases will be protected by copyright as original compilations, however most databases will be protected by the Copyright and Rights in Databases Regulations 1997 (SI 1997/3032). Under the regulations, a database is defined as a collection of independent data arranged in a systematic and methodical way individually accessible by electronic or other means. Due to the way in which web-sites are constructed, a web-site will generally fall within the definition of a database, as it is a collection of data files stored in a systematic way which allows for the formation of individual web pages.

The 'database right' is granted to a person who takes the initiative or invests in the obtaining, verifying or presenting of the contents of the database. The owner of a database right can prevent the extraction of all or a substantial part of the database, or the repeated systematic extraction of insubstantial parts if such repeated extraction in itself amounts to an extraction of a substantial part. Reproducing the content of another's web-site (a database in itself) could give rise to a claim for infringement of database rights. The full extent of the database right is, however, uncertain, pending consideration of its scope by the European Court of Justice (Referral by the Court of Appeal of *British Horseracing Board* v. *William Hill Organisation Ltd* to the ECJ, 31 July 2001).

Trade marks

A trade mark is some form of graphical representation which is capable of distinguishing the source of a product or service. Trade marks can therefore be words, images, shapes and, in some cases, a mere combination of letters, numbers or colours. They are valuable tools used by businesses to differentiate their brand or product line to generate repeat business. The Trade Marks Act 1994 gives certain monopoly rights to use a trade mark to the owner of that mark where it has been registered with the UK Trade Marks Agency (or the European Union trade marks registry, the Office for Harmonisation in the Internal Market or OHIM).

Furthermore, a trade mark owner can sue for damages for loss sustained through any unauthorised use of his or her mark, or for use of a mark which is similar to his or her registered mark and is being used in association with the same or similar goods or services, providing customers are likely to be confused by the use of the similar mark.

An ISP might find itself infringing the trade mark rights of another person if it displays a trade mark on a web-site without that person's consent to do so. Thus, using the trade mark to advertise or offer goods or services for sale under that mark will infringe a trade mark owner's rights if it done without his or her consent. This fact is important to bear in mind where an ISP is offering second-hand goods for sale on its site, or operating an online auction for the sale of goods between users, where it is unlikely that there is a reseller arrangement in place between the ISP and the trade mark owner under which one would ordinarily expect re-seller to have been given the right to use the mark.

One exception under the Trade Marks Act to the restriction on usage is the permission to use another's mark for the purposes of comparative advertising. An ISP may wish to refer to the products or services of others in its advertisements in order to show its own goods or services in a favourable light. Providing it is done in accordance with honest commercial practices and providing use does not take 'unfair advantage' of the mark or is detrimental to its distinctive character or reputation, such advertising may involve the use of the other parties' trade marks.

What constitutes the 'unfair advantage' of a mark has been much debated with no firm conclusions, as by its very nature, comparative advertising shows another's goods or services to be inferior, which could take unfair advantage of a mark or be detrimental to its reputation. The Control of Misleading Advertisements (Amendment) Regulations 2000 attempts to address the problem by setting out certain conditions that a comparative advertisement should meet. By adhering to these Regulations, the ISP at least limits the risk that it will be infringing trade marks or acting illegally in advertising campaigns that compare the goods or services of another to its own.

Passing off

Passing off is an area of law that protects the goodwill of business and seeks to restrain one business from passing off its goods or services as being those of another. Although much of a business's goodwill is concerned with its name, so that a claim for passing off will often overlap with trade mark infringement actions, passing off is wide in scope and is capable of protecting names, logos, materials, advertising themes and any other part of a business's general 'get-up' that distinguishes its goods or services from those of others. There is no requirement for registration in order to invoke the law of passing off, but a business must first have a reputation, in other words some goodwill, to protect.

Essentially, a claim for passing off will be made out if a misrepresentation is made by a business to potential customers which causes confusion as to the origin or association of its goods/services, and it is reasonably foreseeable that the goodwill of another business will be injured by this confusion and is likely to suffer loss as a result. A fraudulent motive is not necessary for a claim of passing off and relief may be granted even where the passing off was unintentional. ISPs may find that passing off is particularly relevant in cases of 'deep linking' and 'framing'.

Deep linking and framing

'Deep linking' is the linking of a user from one web-site to another in such a way so as to bypass the homepage of the second site. Bypassing a homepage can be objectionable as it may enable a user to bypass registration or log in procedures, terms and conditions of use, or revenue generating advertising.

'Framing' is the linking of one web-site with another in a manner that presents the content of one or more pages from a linked web-site within the frame of the original web-site, sometimes even removing all distinguishing features of the linked site so that the user is deceived into believing that that he or she is still viewing content from the original site.

Potentially, copying (by downloading or storing) text as a result of a link could give rise to a claim for infringement of copyright or database rights. Framing another's text or otherwise embellishing material taken from a third party's site could lead to a claim for passing off. Using a trade mark as a link button could give rise to a claim of passing off or for trade mark infringement. However, the status of deep linking and framing and to what extent such practices will be caught by copyright, database and trade mark legislation or the law of passing off is still untested in the UK and it thus remains unclear whether the consent of the owner of a web-site is required before a link can be provided to his or her site. In view of the uncertainty, some practical guidance is given at the end of this chapter to assist with minimising the risks of infringing another's intellectual property rights by linking or framing.

Metatags

Metatags are words or a series of words embedded in a web-site's HMTL (Hypertext Mark Up Language, the language used to create internet documents) which are descriptive of the site and enable search engines to pick out relevant sites in response to a user request. Some web-site operators have used another's trade marks as metatags as a means of diverting users to their sites. Use of another's trade marks in this way may amount to trade mark infringement (*Roadtech Computer System Ltd* v. *Mandata (Management and Data Services) Ltd* [2000] EMTR 97, where Mandata admitted trade mark infringement and the Court awarded damages to Roadtech).

2.3 Confidential information

The law of confidence protects confidential information from disclosure to parties to whom the owner of that information has not authorised disclosure.

Information protected can be personal, commercial, industrial, state – in fact information of almost any character, providing:

- it is specific;
- is of limited availability;
- has a quality of confidence;
- has been disclosed to another in circumstances containing an obligation of confidence; and
- unauthorised use of that information has caused harm to the person who imparted it.

Specific
For material to be protected as confidential it must be possible to point to a piece or collection of material that is not so entwined with publicly available material that it is impossible to isolate and identify.

Limited availability
In the context of confidential information, limited availability does not necessarily mean that the authorised user group is narrow, but could include any material that is communicated to recipients on the understanding that it is for their use alone. In fact, the action could be made out if all the individual items of information constituting the material were publicly available, but if others would need to expend effort or money collating the information in the form in which it was communicated deems the material of limited availability.

Quality of confidence
Material having the quality of confidence is material that is not a matter of general public knowledge.

Obligation of confidence
Examples of relationships that confer an obligation of confidence include an employment relationship, or a customer's relationship with its bank, confidence imposed under a contract, or any information that is disclosed to another marked 'confidential'.

Unauthorised use has caused harm
Material that has no value is not protected. The value need not be commercial, but trivial information such as gossip is not protected.

Breach of confidence
A breach of confidence is committed when a recipient:

- discloses or uses information; or
- receives information

when he or she knows, or ought to know, that its disclosure, use or receipt is unauthorised. Even if the material was initially obtained innocently, a breach of confidence can be committed if the recipient realises or ought to realise that the material is confidential and retains or uses the material improperly.

The recent case of *Sir Elton John* v. *Countess Joulebine* (QBD, 26 January 2001, unreported) demonstrates how the law of confidence is relevant to ISPs. Countess Joulebine failed to defend an action brought by Elton John and his solicitors for breach of confidence, in respect of the display on the Countess's web-site of a legal opinion of Elton John's legal counsel concerning Elton John's ongoing legal action against his accountants. It was accepted that she was not initially aware that the information had been posted, however she was deemed to have 'received' the information once she became aware that it was on the site. Although the Countess also claimed that she did not realise that the legal opinion was confidential, the court found that she *should* have realised that the information was confidential and consequently ensured its removal from her site.

It is perhaps noteworthy that Countess Joulebine claimed not to have received (and on this point was not challenged) any complaints about the posting of counsel's legal opinion on the site and yet remained liable. Thus, it is clear that ISPs will need to exercise their own judgement as to the confidential nature of any material posted and take appropriate action at their own accord in order to escape liability.

3. Criminal liability

Certain web-site content can lead to prosecution for a criminal offence. Some of the most topical forms of criminal liability that can arise are discussed below.

Offences can be committed by individuals and by companies. Usually, if a company acts upon a decision made by its board and thereby commits an offence, then it is the company that is prosecuted. Penalty on conviction is a fine. However, in certain circumstances, and notably for the offences of obscene publications, indecent child photographs and racial hatred set out below, the legislation permits officers of a company to be charged for the offences personally in addition to the company. When charged personally with some of the offences described below, officers of a company could face imprisonment on conviction.

ISPs should also bear in mind that, providing a magistrate agrees that there are reasonable grounds, the police possess powers of entry and seizure to confiscate hardware and other equipment on which offending material is suspected to be stored. Powers of search and seizure can be exercised prior to the commencement of any prosecution and regardless as to whether or not a prosecution is subsequently launched. Quite apart from any damage that might result form seizure of equipment, the police may remove documents and other information relating to the trade carried out by the ISP, which can exacerbate the disruption to a business.

3.1 Obscene publications

Under the Obscene Publications Act 1959 it is an offence to 'publish an obscene article for gain'. The maximum penalty is three years' imprisonment and/or a fine. There are three elements to the offence that must be fulfilled. An ISP must have:

- published;
- an article;
- which is obscene.

Publishing

By making material available to be downloaded from a web-site an ISP will, on the face of it, 'publish' that material under this legislation. Further, the Act itself expressly states that publishing includes transmitting electronically stored data. Clearly, ISPs could find themselves liable as a publisher for material they make available to the public.

Article

An article under the Obscene Publications Act can be in the form of text, an image or even information on a computer disc. Material found on a web-site hosted on ISP servers is likely to be construed as an 'article'.

Obscene

An article is considered obscene if it tends to 'deprave and corrupt' persons likely to see it. The material covered includes not just pornographic materials as are commonly associated with the concept of obscene materials, but also material relating to explosives, violence or perhaps even illicit drugs.

Defences

It is a defence to offences under this Act for a person to show that they had not examined the article in question, and they had no reasonable cause to suspect that their publication of the article would lead to liability for such an offence.

Since, on the face of it, by making obscene material available via a web-site an ISP is likely to be guilty of the offence, it must therefore ensure that it is in a position to be able to rely on one of the defences available and that its business practice facilitates such reliance. For example, an ISP may decide not monitor the content hosted on its servers or posted to its web-site so that it can prove that it had not examined the obscene article. (Admittedly a refusal to monitor is perhaps more difficult to justify when a web-site operator is merely operating a single site.) Or, if the material concerned is only available on a section of the ISP's site that is not accessible to children, then it may be more difficult for the prosecution to prove that material has a tendency to deprave and corrupt those likely to view it.

3.2 Indecent images of children

The Protection of Children Act 1978 contains a variety of offences relating to indecent images of children. The offence most relevant to ISPs concerns: (i) making such images; and (ii) distributing or showing such images. The maximum penalty is three years' imprisonment and/or a fine.

For an ISP to be convicted, the elements therefore are as follows:

- an image;
- must have been made, distributed or shown;
- of a child;
- which is indecent.

Image
An image includes a photograph and a pseudo-photograph (such as a computer-generated graphic image) and any material stored on a computer, disk or other electronic means that can be converted into a photograph.

Making, distributing or showing
In theory, ISPs can actually be convicted of 'making' an indecent image as the technological process of a user uploading such an image onto its servers involves the copying of the image by the ISP's server. Easier to prove is the distribution and/or displaying of such images. An ISP can be deemed to 'distribute' images by the fact they are stored on its servers and then made accessible to internet users with or without the use of a password.

Child
A child is defined as a person under the age of sixteen.

Indecent
Whether a photograph is indecent is a matter for a jury or magistrate trying the case to decide.

Defence
Falling within a defence is clearly important for an ISP. The legislation provides a defence to the acts of displaying an indecent image for those that

can show that they had had not seen the image and therefore did not know or have any cause to suspect that such image would be indecent. If the presence of an indecent photograph is brought to the attention of ISP staff, such as through a user complaint, then the ISP must ensure that the material is deleted or handed over to a law enforcement agency immediately, or the ISP runs the risk of not being able to rely on the defence.

3.3 Racial hatred

The Public Order Act 1986 prohibits (i) the display of written material which is threatening, abusive or insulting; and (ii) the publishing or distributing of written material where the material is intended to encourage racial hatred or such racial hared is likely to result. The maximum penalty is two years' imprisonment and/or a fine.

Therefore, to be convicted of an offence, an ISP must have:

- displayed, published or distributed;
- written material;
- which is threatening, abusive or insulting; and
- where the material is intended to encourage racial hatred or such racial hared is likely to result.

Displaying, publishing or distributing
What constitutes the display, publication or distribution of offending material under this Act is likely to entail the same analysis as discussed for previous criminal offences. An ISP can be deemed to fulfil one or more activities by the fact that images are either displayed on a web-site, or stored on its servers and made accessible to internet users.

Written material
Written material includes any sign or visual representation.

Threatening, abusive or insulting
Whether the material is 'threatening, abusive or insulting' must be determined by reference to the ordinary dictionary meanings of such words.

Intended or likely to encourage racial hatred
This aspect makes plain that even if an ISP did not intend to stir up racial hatred by any such display or publication or distribution, it can still be convicted of the offence if a jury or magistrate considers that racial hatred would be likely to result from the material. (Racial hatred under the Act is hatred against a group of persons in Great Britain defined by reference to

colour, race, nationality, or ethnic or national origins – examples of ethnic groups that are not a race or nationality are Sikhs and Jews.)

Defence

The Act provides a defence to ISPs that can prove that they were unaware of the content of the material and that they did not suspect and had no reason to suspect that the material concerned was threatening, abusive or insulting. Again, as with other offences under the Act, the ISP could argue that in not vetting content on its servers prior to their availability to the public, they are not aware of the nature of the content. But the ISP must be aware that the availability of such a defence will greatly decrease once material has been brought to its attention by means of a complaint from a user or member of the public. Once again, therefore, careful attention to the ISP's internal procedures dealing with complaints is critical.

The Public Order Act 1986 contains a number of additional offences that could apply to ISPs, such as the offence of distributing or showing a recording of visual images or sounds which, in the circumstances, is likely to incite racial hatred, and the possession of racially inflammatory material with a view to it being displayed, published, distributed, shown or played. Each offence contains a defence in similar terms to that already outlined above.

3.4 Financial services

The Financial Services and Markets Act 2000 (FSMA) prohibits a person from communicating an invitation or inducement to engage in investment activity unless either the person communicating the inducement is authorised under the Act to do so, or if the communication is approved by an authorised person. Therefore, an ISP communicating such invitations must comply with the requirement set out in the Act. Failure to do so leaves an ISP open to a maximum penalty of two years' imprisonment and/or a fine.

Where an internet services provider transmits an advertisement acting as a mere conduit, it should be exempted from the Act by virtue of the Financial Promotions Order (SI 2001/1335). Hence internet services providers when hosting web-sites are likely to fall within this exemption, however the position is not quite so clear in respect of web-site operators. If a web-site operator allows investment advertisements to be carried on its site (e.g. in the form of a banner or hyperlink, or by operating a chat room in which financial investments are discussed), it may not be able to abdicate responsibility fully for such promotions. In such circumstances, the legislation may require that web-site operator to either become FSA-authorised, or as is sometimes possible, obtain a certificate confirming that it is exempt from the need to be FSA-authorised, or have promotions approved by an authorised person. Plainly, whichever legal requirement is applicable, a web-site operator should be cautious when allowing others to advertise financial services material on his or her site, or indeed linking to web-sites displaying financial services material.

Defence
A defence exists for a web-site operator who, on reasonable grounds, believed an advertisement to have been prepared or approved by an authorised person, or if he took all reasonable precautions to avoid committing such an offence. There is currently no indication that a web-site operator has any special obligation under financial services legislation to monitor web-sites for unauthorised investment business, but clearly the obligation to take 'all reasonable precautions' to avoid committing the offence could require him or her to do so.

Civil liability
The FSMA also gives customers who suffer loss as the result of an illegal promotion the right to bring a civil action against the person communicating the advertisement.

3.5 Regulation of Investigatory Powers Act 2000

In some circumstances and notwithstanding that an ISP itself might have no liability at either civil or criminal law for the content of a web-site, an ISP can become liable to disclose information about the user who is responsible.

Regulation of Investigatory Powers Act 2000 (RIPA) came into force on 28 July 2000. The basic premise of the Act is that it is a criminal offence for a person (including an ISP) to intercept, at any place in the UK, any communication in the course of its transmission.

Exceptions are permitted primarily related to law enforcement and, therefore, a business sending data over the internet or vial e-mail, whether or not this is part of its operation of a web-site, should be aware that it is forbidden to intercept third party data (unless consent has been obtained), although that data (including its own data and not just third party data) are liable to interception by enforcement agencies and other government bodies.

Under RIPA, disclosure of traffic data (such as to whom and from whom the communication is being transmitted) or the disclosure of the contents of the communication, can be ordered even where additional methods of confidentiality have been used, such as a password, access code or from of encryption needed to unlock the data into a readable form. In all cases it is a criminal offence not to comply, and can result in a maximum penalty of two years' imprisonment and/or a fine.

Data intercepted under this Act which is encrypted will need to be decrypted. Any person reasonably believed to be in possession of the key, or in possession of information which might facilitate the discovery of the encryption key, can be required to disclose the facilitating information or use the key to produce the intercepted data in intelligible form. Sometimes disclosure of the encryption key itself can be ordered. Failure to comply can result in a criminal prosecution for an offence carrying a maximum penalty of two years' imprisonment and/or a fine. It is also a criminal offence for a person to tip off any party that disclosure relating to the encryption key has taken place. The maximum penalty in such circumstances is five years' imprisonment and/or a fine.

Human rights implications

Where the interception relates to traffic data, the Act permits, for example, the police or Customs and Excise to require an internet services provider to intercept data for a number of reasons including *'the economic well-being of the UK, public safety, preventing or detecting crime or preventing disorder, collecting any tax, duty or levy'*. It has, therefore, been argued that the government will invariably be able to justify almost all cases of interception when RIPA has been drafted in such wide terms.

Interception of data inevitably makes the government vulnerable to claims of unlawful interference with human rights and rights to privacy in particular the right to respect for private and family life, home and correspondence enshrined in Article 8 of the European Convention on Human Rights and implemented into UK law in the Human Rights Act 1998. The Convention imposes a positive obligation on the UK government to take measures which actively promote and safeguard the rights enshrined within it and makes it unlawful for a public authority to act in a way incompatible with a Convention right.

At the time of going to press, a joint complaint has been lodged by Liberty, the Irish Council for Civil Liberties and British-Irish Rights Watch against the British government for the alleged unlawful interception of communications from Ireland between 1990 and 1997. Although the interception pre-dates RIPA, the case will be heard by the Investigatory Powers Tribunal whose terms of reference are to investigate complaints about the intelligence services or relating to the interception of communications and thus, this matter will be an important test case in the field.

3.6 Anti-Terrorism Crime and Security Act 2001

Most internet services providers claim to delete data once they are no longer needed for billing purposes, on average this is said to be three months. Any enforced retention period beyond the standard business practice is likely to have cost consequences for internet services providers in terms of (i) archive burdens in that a vast amounts of data might have to be stored; and (ii) retrieval, which is likely to be expensive and difficult to manage. Any costs consequences for an ISP are likely to be passed down to the operators of the web-sites it hosts or to other users of its services.

Data retention has become a major concern and rumours of the introduction of lengthy data retention periods (some sources have hinted at seven years) have been circulating for some time. With strong pressure exerted by law enforcement agencies following the attacks on the World Trade Center on 11 September 2001, many ISPs feared that the UK government would implement excessive retention requirements, ostensibly for the purposes of national security and the prevention and detection of criminal offences. The resulting Anti-Terrorism Crime and Security Act 2001 has not alleviated concerns. Although the Act gives the Secretary of State the power to make a contribution towards the costs of data retention, it need only be provided in such cases '*as he thinks fit*'. Hence payments are entirely at the government's discretion and may not cover the full costs incurred.

But costs aren't the only concern, for the Act merely provides a structure for compelling data retention without the detail. ISPs want clarity on precisely what type of data needs to be retained, how long must the data be retained for and how the data should be stored. Under the Act, the Secretary of State is due to issue a non-legally binding code of practice relating to data retention. Following the introduction of the code, the Secretary of State can still '*if it appears to [him] necessary to do so*' propose to parliament regulations having the force of law.

Businesses should thus be aware that ISPs will in all probability be compelled to disclose (under RIPA) and store (under the Anti-Terrorism Crime and Security Act) data transmitted by them over the internet or via e-mail. Where a business is a web-site operator, the obligations on an ISP will extend to data transmitted by users of that business's web-site. Businesses should also be aware that ISPs are likely to exclude in their terms of service with web-site operators any liability for the accuracy or consequences of such data stored and disclosed in this way.

3.7 Liability of a web-site operator to disclose a user's identity

RIPA and the Anti-Terrorism Crime and Security Act set out the statutory requirements on ISPs to reveal to *government bodies* traffic data or the content of communications of users. In addition, there is an obligation under UK civil law on web-site operators to disclose the identity of a user of its site to *private persons* where a person is contemplating bringing a claim against that user for content he or she has posted to a site (e.g. for defamation or for intellectual property infringement).

However, the Data Protection Act 1998 also imposes an obligation on ISPs processing personal data, to process it 'fairly and lawfully', which often means that an ISP should *not* disclose personal data to third parties such as private persons. (Fair and lawful processing is dealt with in detail in chapter 3.) A typical example of processing data is when a seller of goods over the internet requests a user to register on entering its web-site, or complete certain details when goods are purchased. So that the processing is fair and lawful, the terms and conditions on which that information is collected (i.e. the privacy statement) will usually inform the user what the seller will do with personal information collected and will either: (i) assure a user that his personal information will not be disclosed to anyone else, or (ii) request the user's consent to disclose his personal information to certain specified parties. The courts have stated that regardless of what that privacy statement might say, data protection legislation does not relieve the responsibility of an ISP to disclose the identity of a user to a person contemplating a civil claim (see *Totalise plc* v. *Motley Fool Ltd*). In fact, it seems that the identity must be disclosed in circumstances where there is evidence of wrongdoing and disclosure is necessary for legal proceedings.

Unfortunately, there are difficulties for ISPs arising from the court's approach. First, should an ISP give out personal information to anyone who threatens a claim? So far, where the court has ordered disclosure, the statements in question were clearly defamatory. Therefore, in obvious cases of wrongdoing, the identity of an anonymous user should be disclosed. However, where there is doubt, there should be scope for an ISP to argue before a court that it was entitled to be more cautious (*Totalise plc* v. *Motley Fool Ltd*; the second defendant, Interactive Investor, took a neutral stance to the application for disclosure, which the Court of Appeal held it was entitled to do, and should not have penalised bya costs award in favour of Totalise).

Second, how much information needs to be given? Earlier case law on disclosure of a wrongdoer's identity (dealing in circumstances unrelated to the internet) suggests that the information to be supplied is not limited to a name and address, but is '*all information necessary to enable a party to decide whether it is worth suing the wrongdoer*' (*Société Romanaise de la Chassure SA* v. *British Shoe Corp Ltd* [1991] FSR 1). Such interpretation could mean the disclosure of all information that the ISP holds for that user and, taken to the extreme, could extend to data relating to financial status such as assets or income, which almost always is a consideration when deciding whether or not to sue. Alternatively, data could be requested that relate to user habits such as traffic data, which could reveal user sympathies, as these may be relevant where, for example, it is additionally alleged that the user acted maliciously.(Maliciousness may give rise to a claim for malicious falsehood, or may assist in defeating a defence of fair comment.)

The implications of both the Anti-Terrorism Crime and Security Act and the Council of Europe's Cybercrime Convention (see section 4.3) should be borne in mind as both of which include data retention requirements. In theory, all information collected and stored in accordance with the Convention could become liable to be disclosed to a third party.

4. Forthcoming legislation affecting ISPs

4.1 The E-commerce Directive

The E-commerce Directive (2000/3P/EC) makes certain pronouncements on the treatment of an ISP. In order to encourage the setting up of e-businesses within the European Union, the Directive attempts to limit the liability of an ISP by ensuring that it is regarded across all member states as a carrier or mere conduit.

Important provisions of the Directive are set out below. Provisions relating to mere conduits and monitoring are likely to be relevant to both internet services providers and web-site operators, whereas the provisions relating to caching and hosting are likely to affect ISPs only.

No obligation to monitor
The Directive sets out that no general obligation should be imposed by member states on ISPs to screen or actively monitor third-party content, including obligations to filter content for evidence of illegal activity.

Mere conduit
The Directive provides an exemption from liability for ISPs where they play a *passive* role as a conduit of information for users by the transmission of information via a communications network.

Therefore, provided that an ISP does not:

- transmit its own information but only that of its users;
- initiate the transmission;
- select the receivers of the transmission; or
- select or modify the information during the course of transmission

then the ISP's role is considered to be passive or that of a 'mere conduit', and it should escape liability for third party content either as the primary wrongdoer as or as an accessory.

Storage/Caching
Caching is the process whereby a web browser stores a set of web page images temporarily either on the hard disk of the user or the server of the ISP, in order

to avoid having to download the same material repeatedly. Most browsers keep copies of the pages viewed by a user so they may be redisplayed quickly when the user returns to them, thus speeding up the time it takes to access information on the internet.

Liability will be avoided if the ISP:

- does not modify the information;
- complies with access conditions and any industry standards on updating the information;
- does not interfere with technology used to obtain traffic data; and
- acts expeditiously to remove or disable access to information once it is made aware that access has been removed or disabled at source, or that its removal or disablement has been ordered by a governing authority.

Hosting

In the case of hosting, protection is available providing the ISP does not:

- have 'actual knowledge' of the illegality of the information;
- delay in removing or disabling access to the information once it is made aware of any illegality by a 'qualified notice';
- initiate the transmission;
- choose the recipient; or
- modify the information.

What constitutes 'actual knowledge' or a 'qualified notice' has not been set out in the Directive, and this has led ISPs and commentators to express the view that the implementation of the Directive in any uniform or practical way will result in difficulty. Furthermore, it must be borne in mind that, whilst the Directive attempts to set out the sort of legislation one can expect in the UK and across the EU, implementation by member states can often reveal differing interpretations. In the UK, the DTI has published draft implementing regulations, which are currently under public consultation. The regulations provide no further clarification of 'actual knowledge' or 'qualified notice'.

4.2 The Tobacco Advertising and Promotion Bill 2000

This Bill is currently causing concern to ISPs because it provides that a person who publishes a tobacco advertisement in the course of their business, or who causes such an advertisement to be published, is guilty of an offence. The Bill also specifically states that it is an offence to 'distribute' any such advertisements. 'Distributing' includes transmitting an advertisement in an electronic form, or providing the means for such a transmission. Clearly, the activities of an ISP will be caught by one or both prohibited activities.

The Bill does contain a defence targeted at ISPs, in that an ISP charged with the offence of publishing advertisements by electronic means may escape conviction if it can show that it was unaware that the material was, or contained, a tobacco advertisement. However, despite the availability of a defence the Internet Services Providers Association is concerned that the Bill regards ISPs as potential 'publishers' (as opposed to neutral channels of communication). Such an approach, it is argued, renders the Bill in conflict with the neutral status given to ISPs as 'mere conduits' under the E-commerce Directive.

Due to slow progress and its controversial nature within the tobacco industry, enactment of this Bill looked dubious, but is currently awaiting Royal Assent.

4.3 Cybercrime Convention

Some of the crimes set out earlier are covered by the Council of Europe's Convention on Cybercrime, which was adopted by the Committee of Ministers on 8 November 2001 and has been open for signature by member states since 23 November 2001. Although, members of the Council are from Europe, non-members may also ratify the treaty. Examples of non-member countries that have participated in the preparation of the treaty are the US, Canada and Japan.

The Convention will be the first international treaty on crimes committed via the internet and aims to provide a common international policy for, in particular, computer-related fraud, copyright infringement, child pornography and hacking. It also sets out search and seizure procedures, measures for international cooperation between law enforcement agencies, interception of communications data and it is due to be supplemented by a protocol (currently in draft form) making any publication of racist and xenophobic propaganda via computer networks a criminal offence. The latter provision was omitted from the Convention itself on the basis of arguments from the US that such an offence would represent a violation of freedom of expression as guaranteed by the first amendment to the US Constitution.

Controversially, the Convention also contains provisions that compel the storage and processing of data about users for authorities investigating cybercrimes, which includes the collecting and storage of real-time traffic and content data related to specified internet communications or users. Information collected and stored by an ISP would then be liable to disclosure to a domestic or trans-border law enforcement agency. These proposals go a step further than RIPA, which deals with interception of data which is in the possession of an ISP only and does not impose any obligation upon an internet service providers to actively collect and store the data transmitted.

Initially, the data retention proposals of the Convention sparked much controversy, however to a large extent, the controversy has been overtaken by the Anti-Terrorism Crime and Security Act 2001 discussed above, which – depending on the code ultimately introduced under that Act – threatens to impose a similar obligation.

5. Minimising the risks associated with content

This chapter has discussed a number of ways in which an ISP might be liable for the content on a web-site. Where an ISP has itself placed content on a site, then it will be responsible for that content. However, sometimes an ISP (be it an internet service provider or web-site operator) might find itself liable for content placed by a third party, since in this latter respect, the law is not always clear where to lay the blame. Amidst the legal confusion however, some suggestions on how to minimise the risk of claims can still be made.

5.1 Monitoring

Where the offending material originates from a third party, the best way to reduce the chances of complaint and minimise risk of legal action is by exercising thorough control over postings to remove offending material. Yet the difficulty is that such editorial control needs to be rigorous and generally speaking, either an ISP will not have sufficient resources for foolproof editorial control to be workable or will not wish to incur the costs of providing it. Where editorial control is not foolproof, the courts have indicated that an ISP may be penalised and yet, had the ISP not carried out monitoring in the first place, it might have escaped liability, for example, in a defamation action (see above). With these factors in mind, and the fact that the forthcoming E-commerce Directive prohibits EU member states imposing an obligation on ISPs to monitor content, an ISP may feel it appropriate not to monitor third party material.

On the other hand, an ISP could consider exercising some monitoring by using automated systems (e.g. word triggering). There is support in US case law that unintelligent automated word exclusion does not equate with editorial control. (*Lunney* v. *Prodigy Services Co* 99–1430, order dated 1 May 2000. Although the Supreme Court did not discuss the type of instances where an electronic bulletin board operator might qualify as publisher, the courts below did. Key considerations were the exercise of responsibility for the publication and editorial control: 94 NY 2d 242 (2nd Cir. 1999) and [1998] WL 999836 (NYAD 2 Dept).)

The position has not yet been considered in the UK, however automated word triggering could be regarded as part of exercising reasonable care with respect to material posted, as required by, for example financial services legislation, or it could assist an ISP in fulfilling some of the defences against criminal liability, where it is a requirement that an ISP show that it had no reason to suspect the material being displayed by it was illegal (see above).

5.2 Notice and takedown

Even where an ISP chooses not to monitor third party content, an ISP can still be liable for illegal material if it is made aware of such material via another means. It is therefore important that an ISP should have procedures in place to remove such material once it becomes aware of any suspected illegality. This is usually referred to as a 'notice and takedown procedure'. A rapid takedown procedure should be put in place so that any material that an ISP suspects may be in some way illegal or offensive, or for which there is a complaint, can be quickly removed from a web-site. ISPs may reserve the right to shut down or block access to sites carrying such material. (In *Sir Elton John* v. *Countess Joulebine* the web-site's ISP had already shut down the site against the will of the Countess before the matter had reached the Court.)

How does an ISP assess whether the complaints it receives from a third party about content are genuine or not? Acting on a claim that has no reasonable basis can lead to undesirable publicity or even claims of a breach of human rights, particularly freedom of expression. This is a difficult area because, at present, the courts have declined to give legal guidance as to what would constitute an acceptable notice and takedown procedure.

Any notice and takedown procedure adopted should have a means of weeding out frivolous claims. For example, the complainant and person responsible for the material in question could be required to do one or more of the following:

- prove its identity;
- make a statutory declaration (if a company) or sworn statement setting out why a posting should or should not be removed within a defined period of time;
- agree to indemnify the ISP against any loss it incurs arising out of the takedown or reinstatement of material; and/or
- prove its solvency.

None of the above suggestions goes to the merits of a claim, but strict procedures may deter those who might otherwise be tempted to act vexatiously.

Next, the foundations for a good notice and takedown procedure are good internal procedures. These procedures must be sufficient to ensure that any complaints received from users regarding content are dealt with quickly adequately and that no complaint is accidentally overlooked. Practical suggestions that an ISP could implement to ensure the sufficiency of its internal procedures include:

- users should be provided with an obvious and accessible method to communicate complaints (e.g. a dedicated e-mail address for complaints regarding content, which may be accessed via a link on the ISP's web-site);
- clear channels for complaints and predetermined procedures for providing quick, reactive measures irrespective of the merits of the complaint;
- training to ensure staff are aware of complaints procedures and the importance of adherence to the complaints procedures;
- training to ensure that decision-makers are aware of matters affecting an ISP's liability; and
- since any decision *not* to remove the material could affect use of a defence by an ISP both under civil and criminal law, it is prudent to ensure that such decision is taken by a senior identified member of staff who makes the risk assessment of the decision.

An ISP should assess whether creating a separate 'walled garden' for certain content on the server is advisable, for example, in respect of pornographic material or content not suitable for children. Certainly, if the material alleged to make out an offence under the Obscene Publications Act remains accessible to children, it might be easier for the prosecution to prove that material has a tendency to deprave and corrupt those likely to view it.

5.3 Relationships with law enforcement agencies

At the same time, dialogue should be facilitated between an ISP and one or more law enforcement agencies. A cooperative relationship could:

- serve to persuade law enforcement agencies that the ISP is actively seeking to limit the presence of dangerous content on its site, which could result in an ISP receiving the benefit of the doubt in decisions to prosecute;
- enable law enforcement agencies to better understand the difficulties faced by an ISP attempting to control third party content;
- agencies could assist with the development of a cost-effective strategy for retaining/retrieving data by ISPs for law enforcement purposes; and
- assist in demonstrating that the ISP has taken all reasonable action to eliminate dangerous content in the event of a prosecution.

An ISP could also consider whether it will actively report and hand over any illicit material discovered on a site to a law enforcement agency or to simply delete it. It should be remembered that deleting material might amount to a destruction of evidence. ISPs should therefore consider handing over data or alternative actions to deletion, such as merely disabling access, providing appropriate care is taken to prevent committing an offence, such as in the case of the 'making' of indecent photographs of children merely by loading the images (see above).

5.4 Terms and conditions

Terms and conditions represent the contract between an ISP and a user for the provision of the ISP's service. Terms and conditions should be prepared and be clearly posted on the ISP's web-site so as to protect an ISP in it relationship with its user as far as possible. Where users are able to post content to a site, it is advisable that the terms and conditions include the following:

- a prohibition on a user posting any illegal material or material which infringes a third party's rights or is in any way defamatory or offensive;
- expressly permit the ISP to remove any data posted by a user at its sole discretion, without the need for complaint, or a need to establish whether any complaint is justified;
- a prohibition on replacing data that an ISP has removed;
- clearly state that any postings are not to be treated as statements of fact and are expressions of opinions only (certain defences against a defamation claim only apply to statements objectively classed as opinions);
- clearly state that all postings in no way represent the opinions of, or are endorsed by, the ISP;
- reserve the right for the ISP to monitor postings (without imposing an obligation on the ISP to monitor); and
- obtain a user's agreement to indemnify the ISP against all claims brought against the ISP for material which the user has posted (although the indemnity will be undermined by incorrect user information and user impecuniosity).

5.5 Disclosure of a user's identity

As an ISP may be obliged to disclose information that they hold on users to authorised third parties, that disclosure might put an ISP in conflict with its user terms and conditions or any separate privacy statement. To help minimise this risk, it is advisable that a ISP consider carrying the following:

- obtain assurances from a party requesting disclosure of a user's identity that it is genuinely investigating its legal remedies and that the information is not available from another source;
- obtain assurances from a party requesting disclosure of a user's identity that the degree of disclosure requested is necessary having regard to its relevance to the proceedings contemplated;

- obtain from a party requesting disclosure of a user's identity its agreement to indemnify the ISP against loss should any assurances prove false;
- reserve the right in any privacy statement for the ISP to disclose personal information to a third party where wrongdoing is alleged, without the necessity for any claim to be commenced or proved; and
- when there is any doubt about the legitimacy of disclosure of a user's identity to a third party, it is perhaps best to leave the decision to the courts.

5.6 Relationships with third party web-site operators or business partners

This chapter has shown how claims for intellectual property infringement could arise out by the use of third party content on a web-site, either by that content being posted by the ISP itself or posted by a third party.

An ISP should obtain a licence to display content which is not its own and should ensure that it obtains assurances, sometimes referred to a contractual warranties, from any person providing material that it too has obtained licences from third parties where necessary. It would be also prudent to obtain an indemnity against any loss sustained through an infringement claim. Similar warranties and indemnities should be obtained from users as part of the user terms and conditions, where users are able to post material to the web-site.

In addition to the use of third party content, linking and framing practices pose risks for an ISP. In these circumstances it is always advisable to obtain the consent of owner of the linked site to such practices. Where it is not practically feasible to obtain consent, an ISP should carry out the following:

- avoid using another's trade mark or logo as a link button, but rather use the web-site's domain name;
- avoid linking in a manner which reproduces the original text as this could give rise to claims for database or copyright infringement, instead an ISP should create a pathway to a page which has been put on the site by the site owner;
- avoid surrounding the text from another web-site with the ISP's own trade marks or distinctive content as this might confuse users about whose content they are viewing;
- set up frames so that there is a clear distinction between the ISP's content and the content of the linked site; and
- check the terms and conditions of the linked site to ensure that linking to that site or framing it is not prohibited or restricted by those terms and conditions.

5.7 Insurance

It is advisable for an ISP to seek and maintain sufficient insurance against the risk that it might incur damages and costs arising out of the potential areas of civil liability and fines or compensation arising out of the potential areas of criminal liability that have been discussed.

5.8 Regularly review the law and the business's internal procedures

As the laws relating to content liability are constantly evolving, an ISP's legal position and standard industry practices should change accordingly. Therefore, an ISP is advised to keep its position under regular review and ensure it is up-to-date with legal and industry developments.

Contracting for Services and Agreeing Service Levels

Introduction

E-businesses can be peculiarly reliant on third party service providers in order to function, so getting the relationship with such providers right is a critical task. The reliance arises because companies embarking on e-commerce rarely have the skills and services in-house to support their operations, either because they are new ventures themselves (without the wish or the finance to create a large infrastructure) or because they are traditional businesses which intend to create e-commerce operations but have no relevant experience.

The criticality is enhanced because the services contracted for are often fundamental to the business itself – for example, the provision of billing or customer relationship management (CRM) services and fulfilment (i.e. the delivery of their goods and services). And, for a new 'virtual' e-commerce company, there may be the additional complication that the contractor will be a much larger and more experienced organisation, giving limited scope for negotiation.

Thus the contractor often has two principal characteristics:

a) the provision of business-critical services which can directly affect the functioning and profitability of the e-business; and
b) involvement, often directly, in the relationship with the customers of the e-business.

This chapter considers the contracts which an e-business will enter into with such contractors, considering in particular:

- the types and structure of contracts, especially where there are multiple contractors;
- key issues in negotiating contracts; and
- the key issues in the contracts themselves.

1. Types of contracts and structuring the deal(s)

The typical e-business can find itself at the centre of a web of contracts:

A number of these contracts, and the issues of branding and intellectual property rights, are dealt with elsewhere in this book. However, the multiplicity of agreements, and their nature, can make negotiating and entering into them a daunting prospect. Some guidance on negotiation is set out below.

One answer to the complications of this scenario is to appoint a Systems Integrator (SI) whose role is to find and bring together the disparate service providers. This removes what may otherwise be an almost intolerable burden on the e-business, but can raise its own problems.

There are two main models, illustrated below with pros and cons.

Model 1: True SI

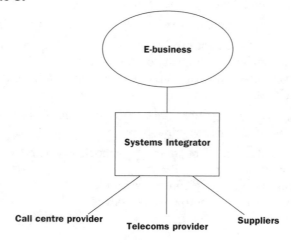

Characteristics: the SI enters into subcontracts directly with the various third parties; the e-business has one contract, with the SI.

Pros	Cons
A single point of management contact for the e-business	No direct contact with the various suppliers, so they are less aware of the e-business's business needs
Single point of billing	
SI takes legal responsibility for the performance of the suppliers	This assumes that that SI will actually enforce the subcontracts and that the SI is substantial enough to meet the legal obligations of all of the subcontractors
SI manages changes of suppliers	No direct control over the identity of what may be key subcontractors

Model 2: Systems manager

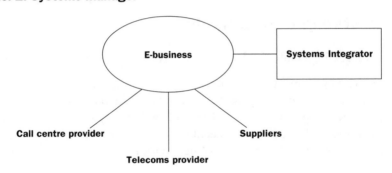

Characteristics: the SI does not directly contract with the various suppliers but manages them on the behalf of the e-business.

Pros	Cons
E-business ultimately controls all the relationships but does not have the burden of day-to-day management	There are opportunities for finger-pointing when there are service failures – was there a failure in management or not? Although the Manager can manage bill payment, there is no true single integrated invoice

The traditional objection to the true SI Model 1 is that there is no direct right of action by the e-commerce organisation against the subcontractors, which could leave it vulnerable if the SI is not good for the money or has commercial objections to enforcing the subcontracts. The problem is as set out below:

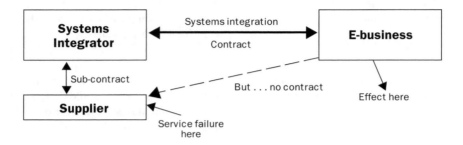

However, a new statute, the Contracts (Rights of Third Parties) Act 1999 does allow the e-business to enforce the subcontract directly, provided that the Systems Integration contract makes it clear that such a right is to be specified in the subcontract.

2. Structuring the contracts

The contracts which embody the services have two complementary roles:

- *passively*, they record the commercial agreement between the parties; and
- *actively*, the act of negotiating the contracts can help to highlight potential misunderstandings and to make it less likely that they will arise in practice. The contracts also act as a checklist of issues to be addressed in the negotiation process. The process of negotiation is looked at in more detail below.

Typically, the services agreement is likely to be in place for as long as five years and it has two main functions:

- to set out clearly the parties' obligations to each other at day one; and
- to allow the parties to evolve service provision over time and to end the relationship rationally.

These may appear to be competing ambitions: the aim must be to prepare a contract which balances them so as best to serve the commercial needs of both the parties. The contents of the agreement are examined at section 4 below.

Before considering the process of tendering for and negotiating the services contract, it is important to bear in mind the typical structure of the document. It is common to hear the term 'Service Level Agreement' (SLA) applied to these contracts; however this term is misleading. The SLA is typically a description of the services and the standard to which they are to be provided, but does not contain the basic terms and conditions, nor the charging provisions. In fact, the technical aspects of the SLA need to be seen in the context of the document as whole:

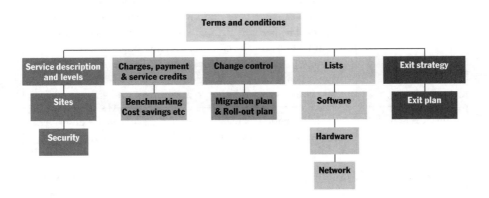

The elements are examined in more detail below, but to summarise:

Contractual element	Contents and purpose
Terms and conditions (T&Cs)	Typically, the 'legal' aspects of the agreement are set out at the start of the document, with the schedules, which deal with more technical or procedural issues being annexed to them. This should not conceal the fact that the T&Cs and the schedules form an integrated whole.
	The T&Cs typically begin with the defined terms which will be used throughout the document – these are really just shorthand to avoid setting out a complex description each time. For example, it is easier to refer to the 'Index' and only define it up front as 'the percentage change in the xyz index published by abc. . .'. Getting the definitions right is often the key to the rest of the contract as they force the draftsman to think clearly at the outset.
	The clauses then follow in as close to a logical order as possible. For example, you would expect the statement about the commencement date to be early on in the contract and the termination and exit clauses to be near the end.

Contractual element *continued*	Contents and purpose *continued*
	Conventionally, the last few clauses are 'boilerplate', i.e. clauses that always tend to be included. These include a clause on the service of notices and on other 'housekeeping' matters. The last clause usually sets out the legal system which will govern the contract and any litigation. It is tempting to skip through these clauses, but it is important to review them every time. One clause which will be of great importance is that relating to assignment and subcontracting.
Services schedule	The first schedule is usually where the services are described, together with the levels to which the services are provided and the consequences of failure.
Charges	Although the agreement will refer to the charges, usually the amount of the charges and the timing and means of payment are set out in a schedule.
Value for money	Linked to the charges is the question of how these are to vary over the period of the contract – assuming that there is not a fixed price.
Change control	Assuming that the services are to be provided for a number of years, the services will change over time and the contract should set out a procedure for managing and implementing the changes.
Exit	The contract will inevitably come to an end and, if the services are complex or critical, the e-business will want to ensure that there is an orderly transition to a new service provider.

The holistic nature of the service agreement can be illustrated by a pie chart:

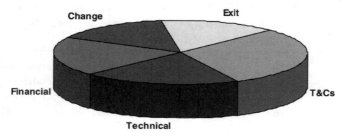

116

3. Procurement of services and negotiating the contract

Assuming that the e-business is intending to negotiate the service contracts itself, rather than via an SI, it will not only need to go through a disciplined procedure to ensure that it gets value for money, but also to manage the process of negotiating. As noted above, a new e-business may have limited leverage and experience of negotiating, so imposing the proper process is even more critical.

Some organisations, such as government bodies and utilities, are bound by public procurement rules which impose obligations to advertise the services and to follow prescribed procedures.

3.1 Requests for proposals and invitations to tender

Assuming the services are of sufficient value and criticality to warrant the effort, best practice is to go through a competitive tendering procedure. This enables the e-business to maximise its commercial strength at the initial stages so as to obtain the best deal. It is important to bear in mind some key principles in preparing the documents to be sent out.

Although there are no hard-and-fast definitions, there are two kinds of documents used for competitive tendering: a Request for Proposals and a subsequent Invitation to Tender. The characteristics of these are:

Request for Proposals (RFP)	Invitation to Tender (ITT)
A speculative document sent to a large number of potential tenderers, to elicit expressions of interest	A focused document sent to a manageable number (say, 5) potential tenderers, identified from the responses to the RFP
Contains a general statement of the e-business's business requirements	Contains specific requirements as to the services to be provided
	Contains a draft contract – see section 3.6 below

It is important for the e-business to bear four points in mind when creating these documents, and the ITT in particular:

- that it can be expensive for a tenderer to go through a formal tendering process, so the RFP and ITT should be seen as documents selling the services to potential service providers as well as seeking bids to provide those services;

- the e-business needs to make its requirements clear without specifying too prescriptively how the services are to be provided – it does not want to prevent innovative solutions being proposed;
- that any information sent out by the e-business should be marked as being confidential and the tenderers should be asked to sign up to a non-disclosure agreement (NDA) prior to disclosure. The NDA will generally need to be reciprocal: the tenderers will not wish to disclose sensitive information (such as pricing or technical solutions) without the e-business having agreed to keep it confidential; and
- the ITT should make it clear that it is not an offer and that the e-business is not obliged to accept the lowest or any proposal.

It is good practice for the e-business to include a form of services contract with the ITT and require potential suppliers to bid on these terms. The aim is not so much to wrong-foot the bidders as to create a level contractual playing field. The e-business can concentrate on reviewing the bids' relative technical and commercial merits without having to compare the small print of several sets of standard terms and conditions. Standard terms and conditions are unlikely to be helpful in any event. Again, from the e-business's perspective, they are likely to be unfavourable in a number of respects, including the remedies for failure to provide the services and the level of liability the suppliers are prepared to accept.

If the e-business does include draft terms and conditions with the ITT, it must bear in mind a number of points:

- there is no value in proposing unreasonable terms, which will not elicit sensible bids;
- certain terms will not be able to be tied down at this stage and only the principles to be adopted can be set out. As with describing the required services in the ITT, the e-business must tread a careful line between giving too little information for the suppliers to go on and being so precise that initiative and alternative views are stifled;
- the ITT must make it clear that the bidders must respond to the draft terms by either accepting them or raising all major issues in the response. The e-business should use the element of competition to its advantage.

It is usually recommended that an e-business should carry out parallel negotiations with at least two bidders, with a third in reserve. In practice, this is a counsel of perfection: rarely will an e-business have the time or the resources to do so. Experience suggests that the process works only if the same negotiation team carries out both sets of negotiation, which is both tiring and apt to lead to confusion. A more pragmatic solution is to rely on the process set out above to elicit all the major commercial, technical and legal issues while there is maximum competition and then to proceed with one favoured potential service provider while keeping another one 'warm'.

Clearly, this does not give the e-business the same commercial leverage as a true parallel negotiation, but it has the advantage of allowing resources to be concentrated; further, it may be possible to set some assumptions out at the outset. This raises the question of interim agreements, heads of agreement and the like.

3.2 Heads of Agreement, etc.

Various terms are used for documents signed prior to the formal contract – these include: Heads of Agreement, Memoranda of Understanding and Interim Agreements. None of these has any specific legal meaning and the key is to identify what the intention of the document is and whether the effort of negotiating one will be worth it.

It is usually not in the e-business's interest to sign a substantive contract before the commercial and technical details are fully worked out. However, there may be reasons why one or both of the parties want to sign an agreement prior to the completion of the formal contract:

Supplier's reasons

(i) **Lead times:** if, in order to fulfil its obligations under the final contract, the supplier has to place orders with third party suppliers, it could be left exposed if the contract is not completed. The supplier may want to agree with the e-business that if the contract is not signed, the e-business will still pay towards the third party order. Usually, this would depend on the reason for the failure to sign the substantive agreement.

(ii) **Exclusivity:** the supplier may offer price concessions on the basis that it is the 'preferred supplier' – i.e. that there is a period during which the e-business will negotiate exclusively with it. As noted above, this flies in the face of the use of competitive tendering so it is rarely in the e-business's interests to agree.

(iii) **Assumptions:** if the supplier has quoted prices on the basis of certain assumptions it may want these to be acknowledged in case it wishes to revisit the prices during negotiation.

(iv) **Confidentiality:** the supplier may want to require the e-business to refrain from disclosing to other potential suppliers in the bid process the financial and technical basis of its bid.

(v) **Internal management:** it may be important to the sales team that it has some acknowledgement from the e-business that it is serious about proceeding, so as to gain internal authorisation to commit resources to the negotiation process.

E-business's reasons

(i) **Assumptions**: the e-business may want to formalise certain assumptions, particularly over price, which it has made in deciding to proceed in the negotiations with a particular supplier. The aim would be to prevent the supplier reopening these points at a later date when it feels in a stronger bargaining position.

(ii) **Confidentiality**: the e-business may wish to establish that the contents of the ITT and other information gleaned by the potential suppliers in the course of negotiations should be treated as confidential.

(iii) **Wasted expenditure**: the e-business may want to recover its wasted fees and expenses if the negotiations abort for reasons connected with the supplier.

(iv) **Internal management**: the e-business may require some commitment from the supplier in order to gain board or other clearance to proceed with the negotiations.

In approaching the question of a pre-contract agreement, the e-business should consider two questions:

1. Will the effort of negotiating such an agreement detract from the resources available for settling the terms of the substantive contract?
2. Does it need the pre-contract agreement to be legally binding or simply to be a statement of its position so that it has some moral authority in the negotiations?

Experience shows that negotiating an interim agreement can often be an expensive distraction from the real business of getting the substantive transaction done.

3.3 Principles of negotiation

How the deal is negotiated is as much dictated by the circumstances and time available as principles, however there are some basic rules of thumb:

- there is a great temptation to plunge straight into meetings. The parties should be wary of this – meetings are enormously time-consuming and should only take place if there is an agenda and clear deliverables;
- generally, assuming that the potential service provider has made a formal response to the contract in the ITT, the e-business can issue a fresh draft, taking into account the points it accepts and noting the others;
- the potential service provider should then be asked to respond in writing to this draft and this can form the agenda for an initial meeting.

Set out below are some basic principles for negotiation, which could be tabled at the beginning of the process.

PRINCIPLES OF NEGOTIATION

Introduction

The aim of negotiation is, self-evidently, to reach agreement. However, experience shows that an unstructured approach to the process can lead to misunderstandings, delay and frustration. This note summarises some basic principles which the provider is required to adhere to. They are drawn from experience of many transactions and reflect also the Best Practice Guidelines drawn up for the National Outsourcing Association and a number of consultancies.

The principles are:

- *the negotiations will take place on the basis of the documents submitted by the e-business and not the provider's standard terms and conditions;*

- *the parties should agree who has authority on each side to make binding decisions in meetings and commit to having that person in each meeting;*

- *while complying with the principle above, the people attending each meeting should be kept to a minimum commensurate with having the right skills/decision makers present;*

- *generally, there should be as few lawyer-only meetings as possible;*

- *the parties should agree a timetable for meetings, for example two days of meetings per week with time in between for new drafts to be produced and considered;*

- *however, the parties should not have any particular meeting for the sake of it or if either party is not ready to comment on the most recent draft;*

- *the ebusiness's lawyers shall have control over the documents and shall exercise strict version control and control over electronic copies. Although the provider may, for convenience, submit electronic mark-ups of the documents, any agreed amendments will be made to the control documents held by the ebusiness's lawyers;*

- *amendments to documents should be clearly marked; and*

- *when points are conceded/agreed, a note should be taken and neither party should re-open a point unless there is a real and imperative commercial reason.*

---

4. Key issues in a services contract

4.1 Describing the services

Set out in schedules to the agreement there should be clear, detailed descriptions of the services and the levels to which such services are to be provided. These should be practical and workable, but it must be appreciated that the schedules are an integral part of the contract and that therefore they should be treated as legal as well as technical documents. The following box sets out some basic principles for agreeing the service levels:

PRINCIPLES FOR DRAFTING THE SERVICE LEVELS

There shall be a clear list of the services to be provided to the e-business by the provider with associated obligations to provide the services to an agreed quality and standard.

Services will be clearly defined, i.e.:

- *stating what services are to be provided and how quality is to be measured (e.g. quality control);*

- *what time scales are allowed for service delivery and availability of service (in terms of quality and quantity of services – i.e. usability);*

- *stating the period over which the services are to be available (taking account of agreed unavailability);*

- *stating actual quality and permitted deviation from a standard as a percentage of the total (and provide a means to quantify this);*

- *stating responsibility for monitoring and reporting;*

- *stating a maximum permitted tolerance of service level quality and targets for re-performing inadequate services and time to re-perform the affected service; and*

- *stating service boundaries and responsibilities for all network services and including detail as to network responsibility.*

For each element of each of the services there shall be a specific and/or a general response time or other measure of quality, reflecting the speed of each service and the throughput of that service.

Where appropriate, for each element of each of the services there shall be a specific and/or a general response time or other measure of quality, reflecting the speed of each service and the performance of that service.

For all services, there will be a procedure for reporting, logging and escalating problems. Problems will be categorised (e.g. into critical, major, minor or cosmetic) and there will be obligations to respond within appropriate time scales.

4.2 Controlling quality

Failure to provide the services to the standards set out in the descriptions will be a breach of contract entitling the e-business to sue for damages. However, unless the e-business is also prepared to terminate the agreement, it will not wish to damage the relationship by resorting to the courts. The contract should therefore set out less contentious alternatives to make sure that there is recourse for the e-business should service provision be inadequate. The usual method is to link service levels to predetermined credits against charges. The aim is for service credits to be an automatic remedy which apply without dispute. The contract therefore has to set out clearly how services levels will be measured and credits calculated. Beyond service credits there may be other levels of remedies, including the payment of more substantial damages, ending with total or partial termination (see below). The issue of risk allocation is considered in more depth at section 5 below.

4.3 Controlling change

It is inconceivable that the e-business's requirements will remain static and therefore the agreement must incorporate a mechanism for managing change. The aim of the process must be to ensure that the e-business has confidence that it is receiving the right services at the right price. This breaks down into a number of steps:

1. *Identifying the changes*. It is important that an organisation contracting out business critical service realises that it is not abdicating responsibility for its CRM, billing or other strategy. It is never wise to leave a supplier in the roles of both specifying a requirement and then fulfilling it. Instead, the contract should allow for a review process that enables both parties to agree the e-business's future requirements but with ultimate control residing in the e-business.
2. *Providing changed services*. These generally are of three kinds:
   a) Volume changes to existing services – including taking more mainframe resources or taking additional bandwidth. In such cases the agreement would normally specify a formula for varying the existing unit charges to reflect increases, or potentially decreases, in volumes. Whether the unit price is increased to reflect decreases in usage depends on whether the parties have agreed volume discounts for the initial services and whether the supplier is permitted to protect its revenue stream under the contract irrespective of actual volumes.
   b) Other changes to existing services. The contract should contain a more formal process for the supplier to quote to provide such changes and for the e-business to be provided with information justifying such charges.

This should reflect the fact that the supplier has a built-in advantage when it comes to tendering for such work over alternative suppliers.

c) New services. Here, there should be a formal market testing procedure where the e-business can require the supplier to quote against other potential suppliers.

4.4 Intellectual property rights (IPR)

Where the supplier is creating IPR – whether in graphics, documents or software – the e-business needs to work out whether these rights are significant enough to be identified and, if so, whether it needs to own those rights. It is easy for an e-business to get hung up over ownership of copyright and other IPR. Often, a better question is to consider who should be able to use such rights and on what basis. For example, if the supplier owns the rights, does the e-business need a licence to use them, and, if so, should this be on an exclusive basis or should the supplier be able to use the rights for other customers? Should the licence only be in relation to the receipt of the services or should it extend in time beyond the contract – for example, so that a future service provider can use the IPR to provide the services.

4.5 Controlling prices

The e-business will also expect to see a mechanism for controlling price increases over the life of the agreement. Given that the costs of certain components of the prices – such as bandwidth in a telecoms contract – are likely to come down over time, this should be reflected in the charges. The parties may agree an indexation mechanism, akin to that in telecommunications licences, such as the application of an 'RPI-x' formula. A more sophisticated approach is benchmarking (or 'comparative analysis'), where the supplier's charges are compared against those of comparable alternative suppliers providing comparable services and adjusted to reflect market trends. The problem with this kind of approach is drafting a mechanism which allows for the identification of comparable suppliers and services so as to produce a meaningful benchmarking process.

4.6 Dispute management

This breaks down into two areas:

1. *Preventing disputes*: In addition to the strategic reviews mentioned above, the agreement should provide for regular liaison meetings and exchange of information. It should also set out which office holders at the e-business and

supplier are authorised to agree changes to the services or to make other decisions relating to the supply of the services; and

2. *Resolving disputes*: the contract should set out the basic mechanisms for internal escalation of disputes and their reference to an independent expert, alternative dispute resolution or the courts. As a breakdown in the user/supplier relationship is likely to be very damaging to both parties, serious thought should be given to the merits of alternative dispute resolution.

4.7 Termination

Both parties, but particularly the e-business, should give some thought to the circumstances in which the contract can be brought to an end. The most obvious time is at the expiry of a fixed-term arrangement. However it is usually difficult for a complex services arrangement to 'drop dead' on a particular date so fixed-term contracts are rare. More usually, the parties can bring the contract to an end on the service of notice after the initial term, otherwise the contact rolls on. Where there is a long-term contract (e.g. ten years), the e-business may wish to have the option to terminate earlier, albeit on payment of a termination fee.

The typical triggers for termination are considered later in this chapter.

5. Risk allocation

As noted above, the e-business is unlikely to wish to terminate the contract for poor service provision unless it has no option. Instead, it will look to other remedies, such as service credits. However, typically a service provider will look to set these at a very low level (often a few per cent of the relevant charges, measured over a month) which leaves the e-business with difficulties should its actual losses exceed this but should it not wish to terminate and sue for damages.

In fact, some service providers use service credits as a kind of limit of liability and try to specify that the e-business may not recover any other kind of financial remedy without terminating the agreement. The e-business should resist this kind of provision, which benefits only the service provider, and should also consider what other remedies it may want to recover during the term of the agreement.

This involves the e-business making an appraisal of the business impact of a failure to provide the services and a judgement as to what level of loss it is reasonable to expect the service provider to accept. The service provider will not accept unlimited liability, and will take the view that it is not there to underwrite the e-business. It will look at its potential exposure in the light of the value of the contract (often in terms of profit rather than revenue).

While being mindful of this approach by the service provider, the e-business should not accept a level of liability that does not provide some protection for its business. The contact generally has to address two scenarios when it comes to the liability of the service provider: liability prior to termination and liability on termination for breach by the service provider. Set out below are the basic principles governing remedies and liability.

5.1 Remedies

Any failure by a service provider to provide the services in accordance with the contract is a breach of contract, which would entitle the e-business to sue for damages or to terminate the contract. A court order either compelling performance of an obligation or restraining a breach could also be sought, but would generally be more appropriate in the context of, say, an exit strategy.

In practice, of course, no e-business would wish to sue an incumbent supplier and therefore the recovery of damages by way of court action is generally unpalatable as an option unless the contract is terminated. It is therefore necessary to have other remedies within the contract. Otherwise, the e-business risks having no effective control over the performance of the supplier (the supplier, of course, being aware that termination would be a risky and extreme option).

This section on remedies therefore concentrates on those that should appear in a prudently drafted services agreement to come into effect prior to termination.

Assuming that there are clear service levels and a mechanism for discerning and measuring compliance or failure, the contract must address the consequences of any failure. A number of mechanisms are used, and their advantages and disadvantages are set out below.

Remedy	Pros	Cons
Escalation (referral of issue up the management chain) – could include generating a service review or a formal correction plan.	Simple – focuses the attention of the correct levels of management on a particular issue. Less contentious and more 'positive' than money-based remedies.	Unless linked to another remedy, such as service credits, has no teeth and can be used as a stalling tactic by the service provider.
Service credits, liquidated damages and rebates of charges.	Simple (can be linked mechanically to service failures).	If set too low, can allow the service provider to avoid rectifying a problem

Remedy	Pros	Cons
	Avoids the need to sue for damages. Scalable: can increase to reflect severity and/or persistence of problem. Hit the service provider in the pocket.	if it is cheaper to pay service credits. Often are more of a management tool than a true representation of loss.
Re-performance of failed services.	May be more attractive to the service provider than paying out money. Focus on fixing the problem rather than getting money back.	Only relevant where it makes sense to re-perform: more applicable to discrete jobs or batch work (e.g. printing).
Services in kind (e.g. free consultancy).	May be more attractive to the service provider than paying out money.	E-business has to be sure that there will be real benefit in the services.
Specific costs or losses – must link to the facts of the deal, but examples could be: ■ recovering the costs of wasted advertising; ■ recovering the costs of obtaining fill-in services from a third party; or ■ lost cost of money.	Can be a very useful bridge between service credits and termination – avoiding some of the cons of service credits. A way of getting damages, linked to service failure, without suing or terminating.	Service providers do not like them!
Partial termination.	Allows the failing service to be cut out of the agreement without having to terminate the entire agreement.	Service providers resist. There must be a mechanism for exit and for reducing the remaining charges. May not be technically or commercially feasible.
Loss of some other benefit, e.g. exclusivity or inclusion in a re-tender or cancellation of a related contract (e.g. maintenance or support).	More palatable than a money-based remedy, but does focus the mind of the service provider.	May have little direct meaning if there is only one service provider in the market.

Remedy	Pros	Cons
Intellectual property rights: ■ where the e-business has the IPR, this could involve terminating a licence to the supplier or removing exclusivity; or ■ where the supplier has the IPR, this could involve a licence coming into effect or material which is in escrow being released.	May enhance the ability of the e-business to go elsewhere without actually having to terminate.	Only relevant where there is specific IPR which is not generally available. May involve a process of going to a third party (e.g. source code escrow agent) or be expensive to set up.
Others specific to the circumstances?		

In practice, a number of these types of remedies may be used in an agreement, but it is almost invariable practice to have escalation and service credits.

5.2 Liability and damages

The overriding principles governing what the e-business can recover in damages for service failure are complex but can be summed up in two deceptively simple statements:

a) the aim of contractual damages is to put the innocent party in the same position as if the contract had been performed. The obvious example of this would be the incremental costs incurred in receiving the relevant services from an alternative service provider; and

b) damages must flow directly from the breach.

In practice, it is the second statement which causes most debate – what are 'direct' (as opposed to 'indirect' or 'consequential') losses? Are lost profits recoverable as direct losses?

There are also some basic rules, which govern the way that the courts will award damages. Essentially, the innocent party has the onus to prove:

a) that there was a breach of contract;
b) that losses were suffered and how much these losses were; and
c) that those losses were of a kind which can be recovered – i.e. are direct.

There is also a duty on the innocent party to 'mitigate' its loss – in other words, to be reasonable in its conduct so as to minimise its exposure.

In theory, the contract could be silent as to these issues and allow the courts to make the decisions. In practice, no supplier will accept this position and will seek to limit its liability in two parameters: the kinds of loss it will accept as being recoverable and the absolute financial amount of exposure it will bear.

There are rules governing the enforceability of limitation of liability clauses, however, where the parties have negotiated the clause fully, it is wise to assume that it will be enforceable. It is therefore important that the e-business is happy with the clause and is not intending to rely on legal technicalities.

It is for the parties to agree the parameters as regards types of loss and the financial cap. There are some rules of thumb, however:

- most suppliers will accept as a matter of course that the reasonable incremental costs of going to another supplier are recoverable;
- at the other extreme, it is no longer tenable for suppliers of services to have a blanket exclusion of liability for business losses such as loss of profit – whether these losses are accepted are a matter for negotiation, rather than principle. Where a service is business-critical and particularly where it is intrinsic to the e-business's ability to generate money, it would be perfectly appropriate to seek to recover lost profit where a service failure impedes that money generation. Clearly, the ability to prove and quantify the loss needs to be considered;
- one option would be to be silent in the contract as to whether business losses are recoverable and leave it to the courts to determine whether loss of profit (for example) is a direct loss. It is preferable to set out expressly in the contract a list of losses which are pre-agreed to be direct;
- sometimes liquidated damages may be more palatable to the supplier than referring to loss of profit expressly;
- other losses which could be listed include those set out in the note on remedies above;
- the financial cap generally bears some relationship to the contract value – for a services contract, for example, a multiple of the annual value would be a good starting point; a cap of less than one year's charges would be on the low side;
- a distinction is often made between a per event cap and an aggregate cap. A pragmatic view might be to regard these as being the same, given that the e-business is unlikely to sue unless the contract is terminated and that termination is likely to stem from one event.

Where services are intrinsic to the success of an e-business's business, it would be perfectly reasonable for the e-business to insist both on recovering business losses and that such losses could be considerable in amount.

6. Re-tendering, termination and exit

No one likes to enter into a service relationship thinking about what would happen if the deal collapsed or the e-business simply wanted to change to a cheaper or better supplier. However, the consequences of not addressing at the outset how the parties are to manage these situations can be dire. From the e-business's point of view, it can find itself trapped with an unsatisfactory supplier with no real ability to do anything except renew the contract. From the supplier's perspective, a messy 'divorce' could mean bad publicity so handling the end of a contract smoothly and professionally should be a high priority.

There are three main scenarios that the parties to an existing services relationship can find themselves in:

1. The contract is approaching its end and the e-business wants to re-tender to decide whether to renew the contract or change suppliers.
2. The contract is being terminated at its end with a change of suppliers or the taking of services in-house.
3. The contract is being terminated for breach, with a consequent change of suppliers or the taking of services in-house.

In each case, either the contract will set out adequately what the parties' rights and obligations are or it will not. This section considers how to assess what the true situation is and suggests how to deal with the all too usual situation where the contract is inadequate.

6.1 Re-tendering

Assuming that neither party is in breach, and even if the e-business is satisfied with the services, it is likely that the e-business will want to go through a re-tendering process even if the aim is only to renegotiate the existing contract. If the e-business allows an existing contract to roll on, it is unlikely to benefit from the competitive edge offered by other potential suppliers, in terms of quality and range of service and price.

To do this, the e-business first has to make sure that it allows itself sufficient time. Given that from start to finish the original contracting out is likely to have taken a number of months, the e-business should ideally start thinking about the re-tendering 12 months before the contract expires or can be brought to an end by notice.

If there is to be a meaningful re-tendering exercise, the e-business will want to issue an invitation to tender to a number of potential suppliers. In order to elicit sensible bids, this ITT will need to contain basic information about the assets and services which the potential new suppliers will inherit.

6.2 What does the e-business need to know?

The e-business will need to be able to give any potential new supplier information about:

- Physical assets: as these are needed for service provision, potential new suppliers may need to know what equipment is being used in the provision of services, what state it is in and what can be transferred at what cost;
- Contracts with third party suppliers, especially of software, maintenance or other critical services. Again, the new supplier will want to know what these are and whether they can be transferred to it, and, if so, at what cost in terms of consent fees;
- Staff: the Transfer of Undertakings (Protection of Employment) Regulations 1981 (TUPE) can apply on the change of suppliers and the effect can be to transfer the relevant employees of the sitting supplier to the new one. Potential new suppliers need to know whether TUPE will apply and, if so, exactly who will transfer and on what terms. The issues here include:
  - the existing supplier faces the possible loss of skilled employees to a competitor. On the other hand, if those employees would have been made redundant on the ending of the contract, the existing supplier avoids having to pay any redundancy costs and can end up with a windfall situation. Subject to its overriding obligation to provide the services in accordance with the contract up to the point of termination, it could also judiciously redeploy the best employees and move less valuable staff to the undertaking which will transfer to the new supplier; and
  - the new supplier faces taking on a group of employees whom it does not know and who have been trained by another supplier. This may or may not suit the new supplier, particularly if it inherits outstanding liabilities, the old supplier's less valuable staff and the possibility of a redundancy bill.
- Services: in order to set out in the ITT what the e-business wants, it needs to know what it currently receives. This means that the e-business must have information to hand both as to the nature of the current services and also the levels to which they have been provided and any problems with that service provision; and
- Access to information and general cooperation: potential new suppliers will also want to know what general level of access to information, key personnel, premises and other material it will have and what obligations the sitting supplier will have to cooperate in the handover of services.

If the contract sets out rights for the e-business to obtain and disclose this kind of information and deals with the process of hand-over of service provision, then the existing parties merely need to comply with their obligations.

6.3 Termination and transfer of suppliers

There are two scenarios here: the contract is being terminated for breach or one party has exercised a right to terminate at the end of the agreed term. The latter is relatively straightforward; it is termination for other reasons which requires further consideration.

6.4 Termination for breach, etc.

The first issue is to assess what rights of termination the contract contains. From the e-business's point of view, the triggers for termination could include:

- breach of a material obligation of the supplier. What is 'material' may not always be clear and the contract may include a non-exhaustive list of breaches which would be treated as being material. Where a breach is capable of being put right, it is normal to specify a reasonable period during which the supplier must remedy the breach;
- if the supplier is in financial difficulties;
- convenience: if the contract is for a long fixed duration, then the contract may allow the e-business the right to break it at certain points, on the payment of a fee;
- change of control: if the ownership of the supplier is of importance to the e-business, the contract may specify that the e-business has a right to terminate the contract if the ownership changes;
- change of nature: similarly, if the supplier disposes of business interests or assets such that the e-business loses confidence in its long-term commitment to servicing clients in the area of the contract, the e-business may have a right to terminate; and
- loss of external accreditation/licensing: if the supplier loses, for example, ISO accreditation or a telecommunications licence, the e-business may also be able to terminate.

In respect of the last three options, it may be that the e-business would not exercise the right to terminate but would use the possibility as a lever to ensure that the supplier provided suitable reassurance about its long-term ability to provide the services.

The supplier will also want the right terminate for the e-business's breach or insolvency. Given that the only serious breach an e-business can commit is to fail to pay, it is unlikely that the e-business would concede an immediate right to terminate and the contract would usually instead provide for the payment of interest on outstanding amounts.

6.5 Rights on termination

Irrespective of the cause of termination, whether by expiry or on breach by either party, both the e-business and the supplier will want to see an orderly transfer of service provision. The species of rights which should be considered are:

- information: as noted in connection with re-tendering, the e-business will need information about how the current services are being provided, who is providing them and using what assets and contracts;
- contracts: the e-business will want to be able to compel the supplier to assign relevant third party contracts either to the e-business or to a new supplier, including any important software licences;
- hardware and other physical assets: the e-business may need the option to purchase necessary equipment being used by the supplier and will want to set out also the basis of valuing that equipment; and
- intellectual property: where the supplier uses its own software in the provision of the services and this cannot be obtained in the market place, the e-business may require a licence for it or the new supplier to use the software, at least on a temporary basis. Where this is the existing supplier's proprietary software, this may be a sensitive point.

The e-business may also want the right to solicit key staff members, irrespective of the TUPE situation, and, in extreme circumstances, a right to enter the supplier's premises to take back relevant equipment and information.

Although the exit strategy which the parties agree will be similar whatever the circumstances of termination, it must of course take account of who, if anyone, is at fault. If the e-business is at fault, it can expect to have less stringent rights and to pay for all cooperation provided. If the supplier is at fault, some assistance should be provided free of charge as a kind of self-help remedy for the e-business.

6 The Legal Risks of Webvertising

Who was it that said existing, analogue advertising law controls were well able to cope with digital media marketing? Whoever it was, and it may have been me, has been proved very wrong.

Stephen Groom
Head of Br@ndlegal Osborne Clarke

Introduction

At the height of the internet boom, webvertising was seen as a golden opportunity to bring marketing messages to customers via this far-reaching media.

The recent growth of the internet means that more advertising and marketing messages are read worldwide and that compliance with (worldwide) advertising laws has become more complex.

This chapter deals with the principal legal issues that arise under UK law when advertising online.

1. Netiquette for advertisers

Before launching into the legal and regulatory issues of webvertising in the UK, advertisers should always bear in mind the unofficial code of practice for online users, otherwise known as 'netiquette'. Sending unsolicited advertisements or marketing materials will be considered unacceptable by many recipients and may lead to complaints or direct action (e.g. so-called 'flaming') from users or the ISP carrying the ad.

The internet is a great way of reaching a large audience for your products, but it is also a place in which it is very easy to cause great inconvenience and annoyance to a very large number of people.

An advertiser can minimise the risk of problems by following a few simple rules of netiquette which mainly come down to understanding the internet before using it as a marketing medium.

A few rules of netiquette to bear in mind are:

a) Targeted advertisements for products which actually meet a need of the recipient will generally be more acceptable than generic material sent out on a blanket basis.
b) Do not unnecessarily upset, offend or anger people by the content of an advertisement.
c) Do not send out unsolicited emails or marketing messages.
d) Include a prominent 'unsubscribe' mechanism.

2. Regulation of webvertising in the UK

2.1 The Codes

In the UK a self-regulatory system has been developed by the advertising industry, which is represented by the British Codes of Advertising and Sales Promotion (the Codes). The Codes contain a comprehensive set of rules for advertisements and sales promotions.

The basic principles of the Codes are that advertisements should be:

a) legal, decent, honest and truthful;
b) prepared with a sense of responsibility to consumers and to society;
c) in line with the principles of fair competition generally accepted in business.

The Codes complement statute and common law, but do not have effect as law themselves.

2.2 The Committee of Advertising Practice

The Codes are written by the advertising industry through the Committee of Advertising Practice (the CAP). All the main trade and professional bodies representing advertisers, agencies, service suppliers and media owners are members of CAP. In addition to writing the Codes, CAP also has some powers of enforcement. It can for instance recommend to its media owner members that they refuse to accept particular ads. Even if an advertiser is not a member of CAP (or one of the other trade bodies), it will be required to observe the Codes.

2.3 Online advertising

All advertisements and promotions in non-broadcast media are covered by the Codes. This includes certain internet advertisements and promotions.

3. ASA

3.1 Regulated webvertising

The Codes are regulated by the Advertising Standards Authority (ASA). The ASA regulates the following types of internet advertising and promotion:

- online advertisements in paid for space including banners, pop-up and other advertisements, but excluding any generic product information on an advertiser's home pages; and
- sales promotions anywhere online.

The ambit of ASA regulation is restricted as the ASA does not have the resources to regulate all types of advertising that appear on the internet.

3.2 Complaints

If a consumer feels (s)he has been misled or offended by an internet advertisement regulated by the ASA, (s)he can complain to the ASA, who will investigate the complaint. A company or organisation can also complain to the ASA against another company or competitor. It is also possible for the ASA to investigate advertisements even in the absence of any complaint.

The ASA will only deal with complaints under the Codes. The ASA council (consisting of twelve independent and advertising members) will adjudicate in respect of the complaint. Both the complainant and the advertiser are notified of the ASA adjudication. If the complaint is not upheld, no further action is taken. Upheld complaints may result in the advertisement being required to be withdrawn or amended (see section 3.3 below).

3.3 What sanctions can the ASA impose?

The ASA has a number of sanctions it can use to ensure that advertisements that breach the Codes are amended or withdrawn. Media owners play an important part in ensuring compliance with an ASA adjudication (see section 3.5 below).

If an online advertisement has been held to be in breach of the Codes, the advertisers can change or withdraw the advertisement. In the vast majority of cases, advertisers act quickly to make any changes necessary to bring their ads in line with the Codes. If the ad is not changed or withdrawn, the CAP can ask publishers and media owners to refuse more space online for an advertisement until it has been changed.

Furthermore any incentives available through membership of some of the advertising trade bodies may be withdrawn from advertisers who do not comply with ASA decisions.

In the case of persistent or deliberate offenders, the ASA can refer an advertiser, its agency or publisher to the Office of Fair Trading which in turn can seek an injunction to prevent the same or similar claims being made in future ads.

3.4 Adverse publicity

In addition to the sanctions available to the ASA, the ASA's adjudications are published online (http://www.asa.org.uk), with a hard copy summary of all the decisions being made available to interested parties on a regular basis. The adjudications of the ASA are read by the media, government departments, the advertising industry and consumer bodies. They are often the subject of intense media interest especially if complaints are withheld arising from well-known organisations or their brands. Most advertisers would want to avoid any such adverse publicity.

3.5 Traditional vs. internet adjudications

The self-regulation system relies on the participation of media owners to enforce the adjudications of the ASA. Trade associations of traditional media owners require that their members must refuse bookings for advertisements that have been the subject of upheld complaints by the ASA. This requirement has been agreed between the Trade Associations and CAP. As a result, virtually all media owners comply with ASA adjudications in the traditional media.

The Interactive Advertising Bureau UK (http://www.iabuk.net), the trade association for interactive advertising, electronic commerce and online marketing, is a member of CAP and may require its members to comply with the Codes. The IAB supports e-commerce, interactive advertising and online marketing by establishing standards for the industry, developing innovative research projects and keeping members informed of developments in the sector.

However, the IAB (or any other existing trade body for online advertisers) cannot enforce the adjudications of the ASA. Webvertisers may therefore choose to ignore adverse adjudications by the ASA.

As a result, ASA adjudications in respect of online advertisement may have less bite in practice than adjudications in respect of advertising on traditional media. Nevertheless, the online advertisers will still suffer the bad publicity from an adverse ASA ruling.

3.6 Is self-regulation effective for online advertising?

As generic product information of a company on its home page falls outside the regulatory ambit of the ASA, advertisements which may breach the Codes if advertised in traditional media, may be accessible on the internet via the advertiser's home page. This gap in the regulatory system is illustrated by a controversial campaign of the retail chain French Connection in the summer of 2001.

French Connection's advertising campaign 'Kinky Bugger' was deemed to contain an unacceptable level of sexual innuendo for broadcast on UK television. A subsequent poster campaign with the caption 'Sorry' directed the public to French Connection's web-site to see the 'Kinky Bugger' advertisement (http://www.fcukinkybugger.com). The public complained that the poster was offensive and the ASA held that the poster should be withdrawn.

Meanwhile, the 'Kinky Bugger' advertisement could be viewed online without regulatory consequences.

3.7 Admark

To increase consumer confidence in online advertising, CAP launched the 'Admark' scheme for internet advertising on 17 May 2001. Admark is an opt-in scheme that allows member advertisers and publishers to indicate that their online advertisements are 'legal, decent, honest and truthful', by displaying the Admark icon on their 'paid for' adverts and providing information about the scheme on their web-sites.

The benefit for consumers is that they can recognise that the advertiser has agreed to comply with the Codes and ASA adjudications by the Admark icon displayed on the advertiser's web-site. Consumers can also search for members on the Admark web-site (http://www.admark.org.uk) and see which of the online brands have opted in to the admark scheme.

Admark does not cover advertisers' own claims on their web-sites (apart from sales promotions) as these are not regulated by the Codes or the ASA. Advertisers will benefit from consumer reassurance by joining the scheme for an annual fee. In addition to payment of a fee, membership will impose additional obligations on the advertiser under Admark's terms and conditions.

4. Statutory provisions

Companies that advertise online should consider a number of statutory provisions applicable to webvertising. This chapter deals with the most relevant statutes.

4.1 Trade Descriptions Act 1968

The Trade Descriptions Act 1968 makes it an offence to apply a false trade description to any goods or services. A trade description includes an indication of quantity or size, method of manufacture, descriptions for purpose or place or date of manufacture, or any other history of the goods and/or services.

As all goods sold online are sold by description, particular care is required. A trade description can only be false if it is false to a material degree. Therefore some minor inconsequential mis-description of goods may not necessarily be unlawful.

When considering whether an ad includes a false trade description the whole advertisement must be considered as well as the reaction of a reasonable customer to it. For example, a poster advertisement showing 'Ribena Tooth Kind' bottles as bristles on a toothbrush were held to be a misleading description of the 'Ribena Tooth Kind' drink as it implied that the product actively benefited oral health. A claim made by the advertisers in a trade press advertisement that 'Ribena Tooth Kind does not encourage tooth decay' was also found to be misleading as being an absolute rather than a comparative claim. The ASA adjudication was upheld in the High Court.

The offence is one of strict liability and the advertiser may not rely on a disclaimer. However there is a special defence for publishers of advertisements which is referred to as the 'advertiser's defence'. Where a person is in the business of publishing advertisements and receives an advertisement in the ordinary course of business and did not know, or had no reason to suspect, that the publication would amount to an offence, they will be able to claim advertiser's defence.

The regulatory Codes discussed earlier on in this chapter also contain a prohibition on making misleading claims in advertisements.

4.2 Trade Marks Act 1994

The Trade Marks Act is another relevant statute to keep in mind when advertising online.

What is a trade mark?
A trade mark is a sign that distinguishes goods or services of one business from those of another. Marks that may be registered as a trade mark include names, shapes, letters, numerals, signatures and designs.

Trade mark owners will often draw attention to their registered trade mark rights by use of the ® symbol following the mark. Alternatively, a search on the Patent Office's web-site (http://www.patent.gov.uk) can help reveal whether a mark is registered (or has been applied for).

Use of a registered trade mark
Marketing or advertising goods can require the consent of the trade mark

owner if for example the logo, name or shape of the product is registered as a trade mark.

Some recent court cases have looked particularly at a situation where a vendor, without the consent of a trade mark proprietor, is marketing goods within the European Economic Area (EEA) which were placed on the market outside the EEA.

Tesco and Levi's case

The court case brought (*inter alia*) by Levi Strauss against Tesco and Costco for selling Levi's jeans (amongst other designer goods) in their shops at a much lower price than the official Levi's distributors in the UK, illustrates the issue of obtaining a trade mark owner's consent before marketing their imported goods.

Consent of a trade mark proprietor to the marketing within the EEA of products bearing their mark which have previously been placed on the market outside the EEA by that proprietor, is required before such goods may be marketed in the EEA.

A judgment from the European Court of Justice followed a referral from the High Court in proceedings pending between the same parties. The European Court of Justice held that a person who markets the products of a trade mark proprietor has to demonstrate that the proprietor has renounced his right to oppose the placing of his goods on the market within the EEA.

Use of competitor's trade mark

Furthermore, using a competitor's trade mark online – for example, as a comparison between products or services available on the advertiser's web-site and those of the competitor – will be allowed under the Trade Marks Act 1994 only as long as use of the competitor's trade mark does not take unfair advantage of the mark and is in accordance with honest practices in commercial matters. Comparative advertising is more fully addressed in section 5 below.

Use of unregistered marks

If dealing with unregistered trade marks, the advertiser may still risk a claim for passing off (see chapter 1).

Exceptions

Subject to certain provisions, the Trade Marks Act 1994 allows use of a registered trade mark by any person for the purpose of identifying goods or services as those of the owner or licensee of the mark.

For example, an online car dealer may refer to the fact that it sells a particular type of car and use that car's trade mark to denote that it sells that particular type of car.

Use of someone's registered trade mark is also allowed to indicate the kind, quality, intended purpose or other characteristics of the goods or services. For example, it is not an infringement under the Trade Marks Act 1994 to state that the goods and services sold on the web-site are suitable for use with a particular type of product.

Remedies

Where trade mark infringement takes place, the trade mark owner has various remedies. These include an injunction to stop the infringer from using his trade mark, delivery up of all infringing goods or erasure of the mark or destruction of all infringing goods. The trade mark owner may also sue for damages or for an account of profits resulting from the infringement. In addition to any claim for damages, it may be costly for an advertiser if it has to change or withdraw an advertisement as a result of infringing someone's trade mark.

4.3 Passing off

In addition to any statutory liability, online advertising may also risk liability under common law, most notably for defamation or passing off claims.

The law of passing off aims to prevent people being misled as to the nature, quality or origin of advertised goods and services.

Advertisers need to be aware of the law of passing off as it places restrictions on the content of descriptions for goods and services so that they do not take unfair advantage of other traders' reputations and goodwill.

Examples of how a misrepresentation may lead to a claim in passing off include claiming a connection with another well-established business, imputing the authority or consent of the holder of the goodwill, and using the name or mark of another trader.

Advertisers accused of passing off may have certain defences available to them. Depending on the details of the claim, the advertiser may be able to use as a defence the fact that a mark is not distinctive, that consent was obtained, or that the traders have concurrent rights.

4.4 Defamation

Advertising that makes statements which are derogatory about other companies or individuals may give rise to liability for defamation.

Every person who is responsible for a defamatory publication is a potential defendant. Therefore the advertiser and the owner and/or operator of a web-site may be potentially liable for a defamatory advertisement.

Defences to claims for defamation are available. These include justification – where it can be shown that the statement and its defamatory meaning are true and fair comment – broadly speaking, where the statement complained of is an honest expression of a reasonably held opinion.

The principal remedies for defamation claims are the payment of damages and obtaining an injunction to prevent publication of the advertisement. In certain cases, corrective advertising can also be ordered.

To minimise potential liability for defamation an advertiser should:

- check that all statements of fact contained in the advertisement are true and can be proved to be true;
- if a statement is a comment rather than a statement of fact, make it clear that it is an opinion;
- ensure opinions expressed are fair; and
- ensure that indemnity insurance is in place.

5. Comparative Advertising Regulations

The Control of Misleading Advertising (Amendment) Regulations 2000 allow product owners to compare their products with those of competitors either directly or indirectly, subject to certain requirements being fulfilled which are set out in the Regulations.

5.1 Requirements for comparative advertisements

Comparative advertising is defined as any ad which *'in any way, either explicitly or by implication, identifies a competitor or goods or services offered by a competitor'*. If an advertisement comes within this definition it will automatically be illegal unless it satisfies the seven requirements set out in the Regulations.

The most important of these seven requirements are:

a) advertisers must compare like with like, which means that an advertisement must compare goods or services meeting the same needs or intended for the same purpose;
b) the advertisement must objectively compare one or more material, relevant, verifiable and representative features of the goods and services (which may include price); and
c) the advertisement must not discredit or denigrate the trade marks of the competitor.

A comparative advertisement will only be lawful if all seven requirements are met.

5.2 Special offers

The Regulations include an eighth rule for special offers. In respect of an advertisement for a special offer, any comparison must indicate the date on which the offer ends, whether it is subject to availability, or whether specific conditions apply, and must state a date when the special offer starts.

5.3 Enforcement of the Regulations

Product owners can complain to the Office of Fair Trading or the ASA if they have been subject to comparative advertising which they think breaches these rules.

Under the Stop Now Orders (EC Directive) Regulations 2001 (which implement the Injunctions for the Protection of Consumer Interests Directive), certain other organisations representing consumers may now also apply to the court directly to enforce the Regulations.

6. Copyright and other intellectual property rights

All materials used in webvertising must be cleared for copyright and other intellectual property rights to ensure that they do not infringe the rights of a third party.

6.1 Obtaining a licence

The advertiser and/or the web-site owner must ensure that it obtains a licence from all third parties who may own intellectual property rights in the advertisement. The licence must cover use on the internet and must be for the whole period that the advertisement is available online.

7. Distance Selling Regulations 2000

The Distance Selling Regulations give the consumer various rights where the supplier and consumer do not meet face to face. Online sales are an obvious example of distance sales.

7.1 When do the Regulations apply?

The Regulations apply only in a business-to-consumer relationship, whereby the consumer is defined as any person not acting in the course of business. If a company acts outside its business (for example, the purchase of computers by a flower shop), then the Regulations will apply.

7.2 Exclusions

Various goods and services are excluded from the Regulations such as contracts for a regular delivery of newspapers, financial services and contracts for the provision of accommodation, transport, catering or leisure services.

7.3 Rights of information

The online supplier of goods and services must give the consumer various pieces of information set out in the Regulations.

In respect of online advertising, the most relevant information includes:

a) informing the consumer of the full costs of the goods and services including all taxes and charges; and
b) the period for which an offer or the price remains valid.

7.4 Right to cancel

The consumer has a right to cancel a contract concluded online within seven working days following either delivery of the goods or conclusion of the contract if it is for services.

If the consumer exercises his right of cancellation, he has a right to return the goods at the supplier's expense and has the right to be reimbursed for the purchase price within thirty days of rejecting the goods.

7.5 Non-cancellable contracts

In respect of some distance contracts the consumer is not given the right to cancel.

Non-cancellable contracts include: contracts for the supply of audio or computer software if they are unsealed by the customer, magazines, personalised goods and gaming, betting or lottery services.

8. Foreign laws of webvertising

8.1 US advertising laws

The Federal Trade Commission's guidelines for internet advertising give an overview of how US consumer protection laws apply to commercial activities online.

The guidelines state the basic principles of US advertising law that apply to online advertising:

- advertising must be truthful and not misleading;
- advertisers must have evidence to back up their claims;
- advertisements cannot be unfair.

The Guidelines further provide that disclosures which are required to prevent deception or to provide consumers with material information about a transaction must be presented clearly and conspicuously.

8.2 European advertising rules

Even though legislation of the member states of the European Union will be similar to a great extent on issues governed by European legislation, local legal advice should always be taken. In some countries alcohol advertising is banned. In others, advertising directed at children is heavily regulated. It is also worth noting that non-sensitive issues in one country, e.g. lingerie advertisements, may lead to massive public outcry in others.

Different views that may exist on nudity in advertisements throughout Europe are illustrated by claims brought in Brussels and France in respect of advertisements containing an element of nudity.

An Adecco television spot featuring an unattractive and overweight employer in his fifties doing a striptease in front of a young woman, and ending up wearing nothing but an employment contract, was withdrawn by commercial broadcaster RTBF after various complaints. Adecco wanted a court order requiring the broadcaster to carry the spot. RTBF argued that the advertisement was immoral and encouraged sexual harassment in the work place. The court rejected RTBF's arguments and upheld Adecco's 'right to be humorous'.

In France the self-regulatory ad watchdog BVP ordered that a poster advertising French clothing which featured a near naked woman squatting doggy style opposite a sheep (but not revealing too much) with the ad captions 'I need a sweater' was ordered to be taken down.

Cultural differences in areas such as sex and gender in advertising may differ substantially, even between neighbouring European countries, and care should be taken when putting such advertisements online.

9. Pricing

Misleading consumers as to the price of goods or services is unlawful. The Consumer Protection Act 1987 provides a prohibition on misleading price indications of goods or services. It is also an offence, if the price indication contained in advertisements becomes misleading, for the advertiser not to take reasonable steps to prevent consumers from relying on the price indication.

9.1 Online pricing

Case law in the UK generally suggests that prices identified on a web-site are an invitation to treat and that the consumer offers to buy the particular product for that price. The offer may or may not be accepted by the advertiser.

Companies selling products online outside the UK should ensure that the method of pricing and currency conversion is not misleading to consumers, for example by stating the equivalent of the price in pounds sterling.

Areas of particular caution are where prices of goods fluctuate or when prices vary depending on when the product is ordered.

9.2 What amounts to misleading pricing?

Customers may be misled as to the price if:

- the price indicated is less than the actual price;
- the applicability of the price does not depend on the fact or circumstances on which its applicability does in fact depend; or
- the price includes any hidden charges (such as taxes, delivery costs etc).
  The method of determining a price may also be misleading.

9.3 Specific rules

In some circumstances specific rules apply to price indications, for example when a price does not apply to all methods of payment.

9.4 Pricing

The checklist below may help to ensure the provisions on price indications are met:

 CHECKLIST

→ is the price the consumer will have to pay for the product clearly stated?
→ is the price indication accurate and does it cover the total charge payable?
→ if a price only applies to a limited number of goods or services or not to the goods or services as advertised, is this made clear?
→ are there any hidden charges such as postage, packaging and delivery?

→ if VAT is payable, is VAT included in the price?

→ is any price comparison accurate and valid?

→ if prices are liable to change is this stated?

→ if the goods and or services available outside the UK, are the prices for each country where the goods and services are available stated?

→ do any specific pricing rules apply?

10. Particular products and their rules

The advertising and marketing of particular products may attract specific legislation which should be particularly considered. The following sub-paragraphs deal with some particular products although this is not an exhaustive list.

10.1 Tobacco

Advertising laws for tobacco products are being more restrictive across Europe and in some countries are banned altogether.

The position in the UK is that tobacco advertising on television and radio is banned, whilst non-broadcast tobacco advertising is allowed, subject to stringent restrictions on the distribution and the content of such advertisements.

The contents of non-broadcast cigarette and tobacco advertising are regulated by the Cigarette Code which runs in parallel with, and its rules are applied in addition to, the Codes (which are discussed in section 3 of this chapter).

All cigarette advertisements must be vetted by CAP before they may be displayed or published. The pre-clearance procedure operated by CAP is supervised by the ASA. A CAP clearance certificate does not automatically protect advertisements against complaints to the ASA, which deals with complaints about advertising content and is the final arbiter of the meaning of the Code rules.

The Cigarette Code applies to a variety of tobacco-related products except, amongst other products, cigars and herbal cigarettes.

The general principles and procedures of the Cigarette Code may be found on the ASA web-site. The Code mainly aims to prevent people from starting smoking or to prevent encouraging existing smokers.

10.2 Alcoholic products

The Code and other non-legal regulatory codes impose important restrictions on the advertisement of alcoholic products. The Food Labelling Regulations

1996 for example restrict the use of various terms indicating a specific product as a 'wine', 'non-alcoholic wine' etc in the advertising of alcoholic products.

For the purposes of the Code, alcoholic drinks are those that exceed 1.2% alcohol by volume.

The main aim of the Codes is that advertising should not encourage excessive drinking and should not be aimed at people under 18 (or likely to appeal to people under 18).

The Code also restricts the medium on which alcoholic products may be advertised. No medium should be used to advertise alcoholic drinks if more than 25 per cent of its audience is under 18 years of age.

Low alcohol drinks (those that contain between 0.5 per cent and 1.2 per cent alcohol by volume) are also covered in the Code. Advertisers should ensure that low alcohol drinks are not promoted in a way that encourages their inappropriate consumption and should not depict activities that require complete sobriety.

10.3 Children

The restrictions relating to advertising and children fall into three main categories:

a) restricting advertisements with children as the subject matter;
b) prohibitions on material which puts children's welfare at risk (for example, selling indecent photographs of children online); and
c) restrictions on advertisements aimed at children.

Various statutory and regulatory restrictions apply to advertisements with children as its subject matter. The Adoption Act 1976 for example forbids any advertisement for any person (not being an adoption agency) to indicate its willingness to arrange the adoption of a child.

The Protection of Children Act 1978 places restrictions under the second category set out above and provides a prohibition on advertising the sale or display of indecent photographs of children.

The Codes also set out specific rules concerning advertising aimed at children, for example it states that advertisements and promotions addressed to or featuring children should not exploit their loyalty, vulnerability or lack of experience.

10.4 Other particular products

Special restrictions apply to a variety of other particular products which are outside the scope of this chapter, for example medicinal products, weapons, organic products and fireworks.

11. Gaming, betting and lotteries advertisements

There are various legal and regulatory provisions relating to betting, lotteries and gaming advertisements. Generally speaking advertisements that invite people to make bets are heavily restricted and advertisements which encourage youngsters to bet are unlawful.

11.1 Statutory provisions

Under the Gaming Act 1968 advertising that publicises gaming is prohibited, subject to certain exceptions, for example advertising of bingo, which is allowed.

The advertising of lotteries is also unlawful, subject to certain exceptions (most importantly in respect of the National Lottery).

11.2 The Codes

The Codes also incorporate specific rules for betting and gaming ads, aimed primarily at discouraging excessive gambling. Care should also be taken so as not to exploit the young or socially vulnerable. An advertisement should not be directed to people under 18 and people shown gambling should not look under 25.

11.3 The *Victor Chandler* case

In 2000, the Court of Appeal held that Victor Chandler, a bookmaker, whose business was located abroad was entitled to solicit custom within the United Kingdom by broadcasting advertisements on Teletext.

Victor Chandler's argument was that advertisements under the Betting and Gaming Duties Act 1981 were limited to advertisements in document form and that the means by which the advertisements broadcast on Teletext were made available for viewing did not involve the issue, circulation or distribution of any document.

As the Betting and Gaming Duties Act was enacted in 1952, Parliament would not have contemplated the means by which advertisements can now be created circulated and distributed electronically. However this case shows that even Acts enacted in the 'brick age' may cause problems for Internet advertisers.

12. Advertising holidays on the internet

Advertising holidays online may attract specific problems and complaints. The most common types of problems are:

- the advertised flight price is not inclusive of all airport or other taxes; or
- the flight price advertised is subject to limited availability or other restrictions.

Misleading advertisements for holidays and other travel can cause great irritation and upset to travellers.

Advertisers should ensure that their ads for holidays and travel do not mislead consumers about anything likely to influence their decision to purchase the holiday or travel.

12.1 What do the Codes say?

The Codes contain a number of requirements for holiday and travel advertisements. As a general rule, no advertisement should mislead consumers in any way and the Codes require the following:

- all prices should be stated inclusive of all taxes and charges and any extras should be specifically mentioned;
- any terms and conditions or limitations on the holiday or travel must be clearly stated, for example, if the price is calculated on two people sharing a room;
- all amenities advertised should be available and any restrictions (for example non-availability during off-peak season) should be clearly stated;
- illustrations and photographs used in the advertisements must be up to date and accurate;
- sales promotions which offer free holidays must not incorporate any hidden costs for the winner (for example compulsory insurance, airport taxes and other fees).

12.2 Other rules

Advertisers are also bound by the codes of practice of other regulatory bodies such as ABTA and IATA. The general statutory laws relating to misleading advertisements also apply.

12.3 Complaints

The ASA receives hundreds of complaints each year regarding advertisements for holidays and travel which mainly relate to omissions of price and other offer restrictions and misleading descriptions of holidays.

easyJet
An example of such complaints relates to an internet advertisement for flights

that could be booked through easyJet's web-site. The complainant was quoted £68 for flights to and from Aberdeen but was unable to book them because of a problem with the easyJet site. The claimant was told in a telephone call with easyJet that the flights were not available at the prices quoted on the web-site. The complainant challenged the availability of flights at the advertised prices.

easyJet argued that the complaint referred to their online booking engine and that it did not constitute advertising. The ASA held that, because the complaint concerned web pages that were accessed before the customer entered into a transaction, those pages constituted an advertisement. However in this case, easyJet provided the ASA with documentation showing that it had sold seats at the advertised prices on the flights the complainant had tried to book. Therefore in this case, the complaint was not upheld.

13. Spamming

The sending of unsolicited emails is an intrusive way of advertising and marketing and has various data protection implications. The main restrictions on spamming are set out below.

13.1 Data Protection Act 1998

E-mail marketers are required to comply with the Data Protection Act 1998 ('the DPA'). (Please refer to chapter 3 for a comprehensive discussion of the provisions of the DPA.) The DPA provides that individuals must be able to give written notice stating that they do not want their details to be used for the purpose of marketing.

As a result, when collecting data for the purposes of e-mail marketing advertisers should give individuals the opportunity to opt out of receiving unsolicited e-mails. For advertisers that purchase or use publicly available lists of personal data instead of collecting their own data, individuals should additionally be given the opportunity to opt out of receiving further unsolicited e-mails at the first point of contact.

It is however best practice in either situation to have the list 'cleaned' before any unsolicited e-mails are sent. This is the process of sending the list to the e-mail Preference Service (http://www.e-mailpreferenceservice.co.uk) which removes the details of all individuals who have registered with them that they do not want to receive spam mail from the list.

If an individual has registered with an e-mail preference service or has notified a company that it does not wish to receive (further) unsolicited marketing e-mails, for these to continue will be unfair processing of personal data.

Codes

The ASA regulates the use of personal data for direct marketing purposes as well as the content of mailings. The Codes cover three principal areas related to personal information:

- Obtaining personal information: The advertiser's name and general purpose for which a person's details are being collected should be made obvious at the time the information is requested from that individual. If there is an intention to make the individual's details available to third parties or if the data may be used for a significantly different purpose, this should be clearly stated.
- Corrections: Advertisers are required, where requested, to correct any inaccuracies to an individual's personal information.
- Accuracy and deletion: Advertisers are required, on request, to delete a name from their mailing list and to stop future mailings to that individual. Mailing lists should be kept accurate and up to date.

The Codes have specific rules to ensure that the above principles are adhered to by advertisers. For example e-mail advertisements must state the full name and address of the advertiser so that it can be retained by the addressee.

13.2 E-commerce Directive

The E-commerce Directive requires that the following provisions are met in respect of e-mail marketing:

- all e-mails must give the name, geographic address, e-mail address of sender and the details of any 'supervisory authority' to which it belongs, so that recipients can readily take action to avoid receiving such communications in the future;
- all unsolicited marketing e-mails must be identifiable as such and must identify the person on whose behalf it was sent;
- all unsolicited marketing e-mails must be clearly identifiable as such as soon as they are received so that they can be deleted without having to read them;
- senders of unsolicited marketing e-mail must consult regularly and respect any opt-out registers.

13.3 Direct Marketing Association

The Direct Marketing Association (DMA – the direct marketing industry watchdog) has a code of practice for electronic commerce, which sets out the standards of ethical conduct and best practice for ecommerce which their members must adhere to ('the DMA Code of Practice').

The DMA Code of Practice for electronic commerce has the following specific provisions in respect of unsolicited e-mail:

- unsolicited e-mails must be clearly identifiable as such;
- random untargeted commercial e-mails must not be sent;
- appropriate e-mail preference services must be used and e-mail communications must not be sent to individuals who have registered an objection to receiving such communications;
- unsolicited e-mails must include a mechanism for the addressee to register an objection to receiving further unsolicited communications;
- unsolicited e-mails sent as a result of a scheme must make clear to the recipient that their personal information has been obtained through such a scheme.

14. Advertising financial promotions

14.1 Financial promotions

Issuing a financial promotion in the UK that has not been approved by a person authorised under the Financial Services and Markets Act 2000 (FSMA), may be a criminal offence punishable by imprisonment, a fine or both.

The FSMA contains a wide definition of what constitutes a 'financial promotion'. Material on the internet could be defined as a 'financial promotion' if it invites people to enter into investment activity or if it is likely to lead people directly or indirectly to enter into or offer to enter into investment activity .

Promotions of financial products over the internet from other countries may also be caught by the UK financial promotion restrictions under the FSMA if the promotion is directed at persons in the UK.

Factors taken into account in determining whether or not a promotion has been directed towards UK persons include explicit statements that the promotion is not directed at, nor should be relied upon by UK persons or the prevention of UK persons entering into the investment activity.

There are various exemptions and exclusions which apply and the circumstances of each case will be taken into consideration when determining whether the advertisement is considered 'a financial promotion' and whether any exclusions or exceptions apply. Apart from committing an offence under the FSMA, breach of the Act can also lead to civil proceedings by the FSA for an injunction and for recovery of any money paid by investors.

14.2 Disclaimer

Although a disclaimer posted on the site in respect of a financial promotion may make clear that the promotion is not directed at, nor should be relied upon by the UK, such a disclaimer may not alleviate the risk of committing an offence under the FSMA as it is only one factor which is taken into account when considering whether the advertisement is unlawful.

Trident case

In November 2001, the Financial Services Authority successfully took legal action against an offshore firm trading as Trident Market Advisors, which targeted UK investors. Trident used mailshots to attract UK customers' interest and offered customers share dealing and investment advice services, although it was not authorised to undertake such business by the FSA.

The FSA stopped Trident's unauthorised business at the end of 2000 and in November 2001 successfully won a High Court case against the company whereby the court declared that Trident had issued an investment advertisement in the UK without the required approval from the FSA.

This case illustrates the importance of recognising that special rules may apply in respect of the service advertised and the importance of taking legal advice on the legality of the advertising in each target country.

15. Consumer Guarantee Directive

The Directive on the Sale of Consumer Goods and Associated Guarantees will be implemented in the UK by regulations which will run alongside the Sale of Goods Act 1979. The Directive aims to harmonise consumer protection laws in the European Union for those customers who purchase defective goods.

15.1 Consumer rights period

The Directive will provide a two-year period in which a consumer who purchases goods with defects present at the date of delivery from the supplier, may be entitled to a repair, replacement or price reduction or a refund within that two-year period.

The Directive also places a burden on the supplier to prove that, if a defect which appeared within the first six months after purchase, the product was sold without that defect.

15.2 Sellers' obligations

Sellers must deliver goods to consumers which conform with the contract of sale under the Directive. Goods must therefore:

- comply with the description given by the seller and have the qualities ascribed to the goods by way of sample or model;
- be fit for the purpose for which the consumer requires the goods (and which he told the seller about when the contract was made);
- be fit for the purpose for which the particular goods are normally used;
- be of the quality and performance which are normal in goods of that type and which the consumer can reasonably expect given the nature of the goods and taking into account any public statements on the specific characteristics of the goods made about them by the seller, the producer or his representatives, particularly in advertising or on labelling.

The Directive will not change the current law in the UK in respect of misleading descriptions in advertising, but will serve as additional ammunition for consumers and consumer representative bodies, such as Trading Standards.

Therefore online advertisers should be particularly careful in describing goods and/or services advertised.

16. Some cases highlighting risks

In this section a few recent cases are summarised to indicate how things can go wrong for online advertisers.

16.1 Keeping competition web-sites updated

In March 2001, Free Money Limited's rules of entry of its competition web-site stated that a daily prize of £1,000 could be won and that winners were drawn every day. A complaint was received by the ASA on the basis that daily prizes had not been given for a long time and that Free Money had not updated their 'previous winners' page.

The ASA noted that the daily £1,000 draw had been unavailable for a long period of time. This was referred to on Free Money's home page. However the rules of entry to win a daily prize of £1,000 were still accessible on the site and the frequently asked questions section also referred to the daily prize of £1,000.

The ASA concluded that the claims referring to the daily £1,000 prize were invalid and in breach of the Codes as they were misleading and not true.

The lesson to be learned from this adjudication is to keep web-site material current and updated to make sure that any claims which are no longer valid are immediately removed.

16.2 Specific products and their rules

In June 2000, the ASA received a complaint in respect of a web-site advertising magnetic products. One of the products advertised was a magnetic wristband which the advertisement claimed could give relief for various medical conditions, including eczema, blood pressure and asthma.

In respect of the magnetic wristband, the complainant challenged whether it could give relief for the advertised medical conditions.

The advertisers said that they had intended to list the benefits of the products and encourage sufferers from the advertised medical conditions to try their products. The advertisers had not provided the ASA with any written evidence to substantiate their claims. The ASA concluded that the advertisers' claims were not substantiated and upheld the complaint. It asked the advertisers to remove the advertisement from their web-site and to seek advice from CAP's Copy Advice Team before advertising again.

The Codes provide specific rules for the advertising of health and beauty products. Broadly speaking, these state that any medical and scientific claims made about such products must be backed by evidence. They also state that advertisers should not offer medical advice or a diagnosis or treatment unless this is conducted under the supervision of a qualified health professional. An advertiser should always check whether there are any specific rules, either under the Codes or any statutory rules, which may apply to the products advertised.

16.3 Industry complaints

The ASA ruling in respect of Design Holidays' claim to be the largest and longest established tour operator for a particular resort in Spain illustrates how claims made on an advertiser's web-site may lead to an industry complaint from a competitor.

In June 2000, a competitor of Design Holidays challenged the claim because they believed that they were in fact the largest tour operator for the resort and that they had been selling holidays to the resort for longer than the advertisers. The complaint was upheld and the advertisers amended their claim to being 'one of the largest and longest established operators'. Advertisers should not use a claim in respect of their products or services unless they can supply documentary evidence to prove the claim, as this may lead to complaints not only from consumers but also from within the industry.

16.4 Text messages

In November 2001, the ASA received a complaint about a mobile phone text message sent by a computer games company. The message stated 'please report to your local army recruitment centre for your second tour of duty. Commandos 2 on PC, it's more Real than Real Life – out today from Eidos'. The recipient's mobile phone identified the sender as 'SNBS'. The complainant, who was a man and an ex-member of the British Army, objected to the message on the grounds that it could cause undue fear and distress.

The advertisers had not intended to insult their customers and apologised for any distress caused by the insensitivity of the text message. The ASA upheld the complaint and considered that at first glance the text messages could distress recipients.

Direct marketers should consider the appropriateness of their messages to unprepared recipients, as not only could it cause anxiety and distress to customers, but they could be made to discontinue their marketing campaign.

17. Limiting liability for unlawful adverts

Depending on the type of liability, both the advertiser and the ISP may be liable for unlawful adverts. (An ISP may be able to limit its liability to the advertiser through its terms and conditions, see chapter 2.)

The online advertiser may, by contract with its ISP, be obliged to ensure compliance with relevant legislative and regulatory provisions and may have to indemnify the ISP for any unlawful adverts it carries on the advertiser's behalf. An advertiser's first step in minimising liability is to include a disclaimer on the site.

Of course, if an advertiser's banner ad is placed on a third party web-site, it may not be possible to include such a disclaimer.

17.1 Disclaimer

A disclaimer may help to reduce the risk of legal action but in cases of strict liability (for example in defamation) it may not alleviate liability.

A disclaimer could include wording to the effect that:

- the goods and services advertised are supplied on standard terms and conditions to which English law and jurisdiction apply;
- the goods advertised on the site are primarily marketed to a particular country (or countries) and orders from other consumers will not be accepted;
- all liability is excluded to the fullest extent allowed by English law.

Legal advice should be taken before including any disclaimers in respect of the validity and ambit of such disclaimer.

17.2 Checklist

Secondly, a legal compliance checklist will assist the advertiser to identify and check relevant areas where legal or regulatory liability may arise.

The checklist below sets out some key areas to consider and may help to minimise the legal risks of webvertising.

 CHECKLIST

→ obtain legal advice in respect of the advertising.

→ ensure that any statements made in relation to the products or services advertised are accurate and not misleading.

→ ensure that any prices quoted are clearly stated, accurate, complete (no hidden charges), and that any terms and conditions which may apply to the price are clearly stated.

→ ensure that the information relating to the advertisement is kept up to date.

→ ensure that any promotion is removed after it has run its course.

→ ensure that any sales promotion is well planned and can be fulfilled for all customers who have responded to it.

→ ensure that consent is obtained for any direct email marketing.

→ ensure that all statutory requirements such as Distance Selling Regulations have been complied with.

→ ensure that any special rules for the goods or services advertised have been checked and are complied with.

→ ensure that the advert will not be offensive or controversial in the countries where the marketing or advertising is aimed at.

→ ensure that any designs, logos, pictures and other creative materials used in the advert have been cleared.

→ if a disclaimer is used, ensure that it has been checked by legal counsel.

→ obtain indemnity insurance for when things go wrong.

---

18. Overview

Advertising online may be a cost-effective way to communicate your marketing message to a large audience but there are additional legal risks inherent in using the internet as a marketing medium.

This chapter has aimed to set out the main legal risk areas of webvertising. It is advisable to take legal advice in respect of online adverts and marketing, especially when the target group extends over various countries.

7

Domain Names and Dispute Resolutions

Introduction

In this chapter we discuss domain names and seek to explain the dispute resolution procedures that have been put in place where a dispute concerning domain names arises. This chapter also provides practical tips in resolving disputes, and makes use of a case study to provide examples of how issues in dispute can be resolved.

 CASE STUDY I

Company A has recently decided to take part of its business online. The Director has sought legal advice and realises he must carry out various tasks in order to achieve his goal. The first thing he must do is obtain an appropriate domain name.

1. The name

1.1 Terminology

Every web-site on the internet is identified by a unique number comprising of four groups of digits, these are known as Internet Protocol Numbers. In essence this is a domain name in its original form. However, strings of digits are difficult to remember, and so domain names are used and domain name servers translate the domain names back into Internet Protocol Numbers.

1.2 Technical information

Domain names are categorised into three levels: the top level, the second level and the third level.

The top level domain (TLD) is the part of the domain name that was originally intended to denote the type of user/site. Most commonly this is the .com or .co.uk part of the domain name. When looking at a domain name one can make certain assumptions about the type of web-site. For example, a web-site with a co.uk TLD should in theory be the site of a commercial organisation situated in the UK.

The second level domain can be found to the left of the TLD. Using the example of the author's domain name, this would be the 'osborneclarke' section. It is this second level that enables businesses to carry over their branding to the web and it is the combination of this and the TLD that most people normally refer to as being 'the domain name'. Consequently, this is the part of the domain name that gives it its true value. There can be only one osborneclarke.com, though by comparison there could hypothetically be a number of businesses or individuals trading under the name Osborne Clarke. Those businesses could even have registered 'Osborne Clarke' as a trade mark in different classes of goods and services and in any number of territories.

Finally, particular pages of a web-site may be identified through the third level domain, which appears to the right-hand side of the TLD. For example, the '/home' in http://www.osborneclarke.com/home. This part of the domain name is not registered.

1.3 Value

Normally the owner of a web-site will be seeking to attract as many visitors as possible. There are a number of ways in which this can be done, and choosing the appropriate domain name is often high on the list of priorities.

In attempting to find a web-site, a user will often resort to using a search engine such as Google or Yahoo. The problem often associated with using a search engine is that they will often list a number of web-sites that match the search criteria. This can be frustrating for a user and result in potential visitors giving up the search at this stage. In recognition of this, web-site owners often strive to obtain a domain name that their visitors/potential visitors can easily recall.

Businesses have been particularly keen to obtain domain names that will make e-commerce as easy as possible. In choosing a domain name, a business will often seek to obtain a domain name that corresponds with their brand positioning, for example, by using a domain name that includes their corporate identity and trade marks. By doing so, businesses increase the chances of their customers/potential customers being able to find their web-sites.

The differences between domain names and trade marks is important here. A number of different businesses may register the same trade mark in different classes of goods or services and in different territories. In contrast, each domain name is unique and registration of a particular name gives the domain name owner the ability to establish a presence on the web that can be viewed by anyone having access to the internet irrespective of their location. Additionally, registration of a domain name is not contingent on classes of goods or services. Unlike the position with trade marks, once a domain name has been registered, that particular domain name cannot be registered by anyone else until the contract for registration has lapsed.

⚖ CASE STUDY II

Company A has decided to purchase the domain names 'companya.co.uk' and 'companya.com'. They are of the opinion that the domain names will be of value to them and correspond with their market branding. They have decided to obtain both the .co.uk and the .com prefixes because they are a commercial enterprise in the UK, and although they don't have a US branch, it is quite possible that they will have in the near future.

The first thing they must do is find out whether the names are available.

---

1. The domain name system

1.1 Internet Assigned Numbers Authority

The Internet Assigned Numbers Authority (IANA) is responsible for allocating top level domain names, Such as .com and .co.uk.

1.2 The Internet Corporation for Assigned Names and Numbers

The Internet Corporation for Assigned Names and Numbers (ICANN) oversees the management and registration of SLDs.

1.3 VeriSign

VeriSign remain an authorised domain name registrar, but no longer monopolises the market. A list of accredited competitors is available at http://www.icann.org/registrars//accredited-list.html. VeriSign will continue to manage the .com, .net and .org TLDs until 2003; after which ICANN will select a successor.

1.4 Nominet

Since August 1996, Nominet has been responsible for allocating UK domain names. Nominet categorises the UK TLDs as:

- co.uk – for commercial enterprises;
- org.uk – for non-commercial organisations;
- net.uk – for the host machines of ISPs;
- ltd.uk and plc.uk – for use by registered companies only.

 CASE STUDY III

Company A approaches ICANN for the purchase of companya.com and Nominet for the purchase of companya.co.uk. ICANN confirms the availability of the domain name and registers Company A as the new owners of companya.com. Unfortunately, the domain name companya.co.uk has already been purchased and registered by a third party. Company A are prepared to purchase the domain names from the current owners at an appropriate price, and enter into negotiations.

Negotiations are successful and the domain name companya.co.uk is re-registered as being owned by Company A. Unfortunately, things do not always go as smoothly as this.

1. Disputes and dispute resolution

1.1 Why dispute?

In recent times domain names have become the centre of an increasing number of disputes in the UK and internationally. The main reason for this pheno-menon is the value that can be attached to this new form of property. At the height of the internet boom the value of certain domain names spiralled into astronomical sums.

Although the amounts of money now attached to domain names can generally be said to have decreased, the value of domain names is still sufficient to justify action against infringement.

In contrast to actions such as trade mark infringement, there is no cause of action for domain name infringement. By registering a domain name, one does not acquire the monopolistic rights that attach to a trade mark. As a result, a business will often attempt to register all the possible variants of TLDs to prevent registration by third parties. By registering companya.com and companya.co.uk , Company A has made an attempt at doing this in the case study above.

ICANN oversees the management of the Domain Name System (DNS). Its powers have evolved through the consensus of the internet community rather than through some form of enabling legislation.

At present there are four ICANN approved dispute resolution providers, namely:

- the World Intellectual Property Organisation (WIPO);
- the National Arbitration Forum;
- CPR;
- disputes.org/eResolution Consortium.

According to WIPO, around 65 per cent of all ICANN cases are referred to them (the vast majority of which result in a transfer of the domain name to the Complainant).

The four 'providers' follow ICANN's Uniform Dispute Resolution Policy (the Policy) for domain name disputes and it is worth noting that the Policy has been adopted by all competitive registrars in the .com, .org and .net TLDs. This means that when someone now registers a gTLD, they are agreeing to be bound by the Policy. It may also apply to nTLDs where the registrar for the country in question has signed up to the Policy.

As with all forms of ADR, there are both benefits and drawbacks. While the procedure is quicker and cheaper than traditional litigation, the remedies available are less extensive. For example, the most that a successful party can hope to achieve will be a cancellation or transfer of the domain name in question. The arbitrators will not award damages to the party, whose rights may well have been infringed.

One also needs to consider the applicability of the procedure; the Policy only applies to so-called 'abusive registrations', i.e. registrations that meet the following criteria:

- the domain name must be identical or confusingly similar to a trade mark or service mark in which the Complainant has rights; and
- the domain name holder must have no rights or legitimate interest in the name; and
- the domain name must have been registered and used in bad faith.

1.2 The procedure

For full details on the procedure one should refer to ICANN's web-site at http://www.icann.org. It should also be noted that the four dispute resolution providers also have their own Supplemental Rules (governing such things as fees) which can be found on their individual web-sites. A model complaint and model response can be obtained from WIPO (see their web-site at http://www.arbiter.wipo.int/domains).

The ICANN procedure will proceed through the following major stages:

- a written complaint is filed with one of the providers;

- the Registrant responds in writing;
- an Administrative Panel of one or three persons is selected (the 'Panel');
- the Panel makes its decision and notifies the parties, the Registrar (e.g. Network Solutions) and ICANN;
- the Registrar implements the decision.

1.3 Practical tips for a Complainant

The first issue to consider is, has the domain name been registered in bad faith, i.e. has there been an abusive registration? If not, then the procedure will not be appropriate and traditional litigation should be considered as an alternative.

According to the Policy the following may amount to 'bad faith':

- the registration was made for the purpose of selling, renting or otherwise transferring the domain name registration to the Complainant who is the owner of the trade mark or service mark or to a competitor of that Complainant, for valuable consideration in excess of the registering party's documented out-of-pocket costs directly related to the domain name; or
- the domain name was registered in order to prevent the owner of the trade mark or service mark from reflecting the mark in a corresponding domain name (provided that the registering party has engaged in a pattern of such conduct); or
- the domain name has been registered primarily for the purpose of disrupting the business of a competitor; or by using the domain name, the registering party has intentionally attempted to attract, for commercial gain, internet users to its web-site or other on-line location, by creating a likelihood of confusion with the Complainant's mark as to the source, sponsorship, affiliation or endorsement of the registered party's web-site or location, or of a product or service on its web-site or location.

The list is not exclusive. There may, of course, be additional matters that support an allegation that a registration has been abusive. For example, any evidence that the Registrant has registered other domain names of other brand owners in similar circumstances may serve to influence the Panel against them.

It may also be worth checking variants of the domain name; for example, if the domain name in dispute is *brandx.com* a 'whois?' search should be made under *brandx.co.uk*, *brandx.net* etc. A registrant who has warehoused names in such a manner may find it hard to convince the Panel that the registrations were not made in bad faith.

It should be noted that the procedure does not prevent either party from issuing proceedings. The Panel does not implement its decisions until ten days have elapsed following the decision. During this time either party may send a copy of any Court proceedings to the Panel whereupon no further action will be taken until either the case settles or there is a decision of the Court. This will be of particular interest to complainants who feel that they do not wish to accept the decision of the Panel and wish to have a 'second bite of the cherry' in the Court.

1.4 Practical tips for a Registrant

When challenging a complaint, the starting point is obviously to produce as much evidence as possible to either counteract or explain the evidence contained in the document sent to the Panel by the Complainant.

In addition the following will support a claim of 'legitimacy':

- before receiving notice of the complaint, has the registering party used, or made preparations to use, the domain name or a name corresponding to the domain name in connection with a bona fide offering of goods or services; or
- has the registering party been commonly known by the domain name, even if it has acquired no trade mark or service mark rights; or
- is the registering party making a legitimate non-commercial or fair use of the domain name, without intent for commercial gain, to misleadingly divert customers or to tarnish the trade mark or service mark at issue.

One particular area of difficulty that may arise for a respondent is whether or not to offer to sell the domain name to the Complainant. Often this may be the most practical solution to disputes of this nature; particularly when the Registrant is prepared to establish a web presence under a different domain name. One needs, however, to be very careful when making offers to sell, particularly when the asking price is likely to be a great deal more than the costs of registration and transfer. If possible, the party making the complaint should be manoeuvred into a position whereby they make the first offer.

Enquiries should also be made of the client as to what, if any, trade mark searches were made and in what territories, before registering the name in question. The WIPO Panel decision in allocation.com showed that the Panel will not expect a Registrant to have made exhaustive searches, but negative searches within the territories targeted by any proposed web-site may amount to powerful evidence on behalf of a respondent to the UDRP process.

Registrants may be tempted to consider avoiding the complaint by looking to sell the domain name on to a third party as quickly as possible. It should be noted however that there are restrictions on transferring domain names whilst the procedure is ongoing (or within fifteen days after the Panel's decision). Those restrictions also apply for as long as Court proceedings are pending (unless the party to whom the domain name is being transferred agrees to be bound by the Court's decision).

1.5 Why opt for the ICANN procedure when traditional litigation is available?

Points in favour of using the procedure under the Policy instead of rushing off to court with a claim form in hand, include:

- the speed of the process (usually concluded in as little as two months);
- cost (£1,000–£2,000 depending on the number of panellists);
- lack of formality;
- the experience of the Panel;
- convenience; there is no need to attend any hearings (which may be particularly advantageous when you or your client are in a different country to the Panel).

1.6 What are the downsides?

One may 'succeed' in the ICANN process only to find your opponent then issues proceedings:

- it is limited to abusive registrations;
- the procedure cannot be used to resolve disputes between anyone other than the Registrant and the Complainant;
- the Panel will not award damages or legal costs.

1.7 What approach have the Panels been taking?

A visit to the WIPO web-site at http://arbiter.wipo.int/domains/decisions may be time well spent if one is contemplating either filing a complaint or is required to respond to one. It would be a Herculean task to read them all in any detail but a consideration of a number may pay dividends insofar as they show the approach that the Panel takes to issues, many of which are similar from case to case.

As we will see, in the *One in a Million* case, the mere registration of the domain names, without anything further, was enough for the Court of Appeal to deprive the Registrants of the domain names. The WIPO Panel now seems to take a similar approach. Initially, it held that even where a domain name is registered in bad faith, it could not take any action because the domain name was not being used (see *BuyVuarnetSunglasses.com*). In the more recent case of *clericalmedical.com* however, the Panel found that mere registration could amount to bad faith (see also *telstra.org* where passive holding of a domain name was found to amount to 'being used in bad faith'). This approach by WIPO in many ways mirrors the attitude of the Court of Appeal to cyber squatters.

However, the decision in *microinfospace.com* provides an illustration of situations where the complainant may be best advised to issue proceedings. In this case the Complainant was the owner of the trade mark 'Infospace' and operated a web-site at *infospace.com*. The Respondent was using the domain name *microinfospace.com* in China. Though it was found that the registration had not been made in bad faith, the Panel was not in a position to consider evidence vis-à-vis confusion. That evidence may well have resulted in a more successful outcome for the Complainant had Court proceedings been commenced for passing off and trade mark infringement.

Where the domain name is considered to be generic, the 'first come, first served' maxim will apply (see *concierge.com*). Contrast this however with the decision in *easyjet.net* where the Panel found that the name was not generic. That decision also provides a further example of the consequences of bad tactics on the part of the Registrant (which included offering to sell for a six figure sum and linking his site to the site of a competitor of the Complainant).

Respondents may also do well to produce evidence showing that the Complainant has previously acquiesced in the use of their mark (see the *militec.com* and *drawtite.com* decisions concerning distributors), though if such use is in breach of an agreement with the Complainant this may amount to bad faith (see *heelquick.com*).

1.8 Nominet

For UK country code domain names (e.g. co.uk), Nominet provides a dispute resolution service. Unlike some national registries, Nominet has not adopted the UDRP. Details of the Nominet procedure can be found at their web-site at http://www.nic.uk/ref/drs.html. The current Nominet procedure was introduced in 2001 and is already being hailed as a significant improvement on the previous procedure. Of particular importance is that, under the new procedure, a complainant can now obtain a transfer of the domain name. Though given that Nominet does not have the power to make awards of damages or give orders for legal costs to be paid, there will be times when the Court remains the most appropriate forum in which to commence proceedings.

One feature of the Nominet dispute resolution procedure is the early attempt at mediation, not found in the Policy. This would appear to be in keeping with the introduction of the Civil Procedure Rules in the English Courts, which encourage mediation.

The Nominet procedure applies only to what it calls 'abusive' registrations, i.e. the domain name has been registered, acquired or used in a manner which has taken/is taking unfair advantage of or is unfairly detrimental to the complainant's rights.

Once a complaint has been submitted to Nominet, the following procedure will apply:

- The complaint is sent to the respondent within three days of receipt by Nominet (assuming that it complies with Nominet's rules).
- Once the respondent is deemed to have received the complaint he will have fifteen days to submit a response.
- Within three days following receipt of the response, Nominet send the response to the complainant.
- Within five days of receiving the response from Nominet, the complainant may submit a reply.
- The matter is then referred to informal mediation (in a manner which Nominet in its sole discretion considers appropriate).
- If the dispute has not settled through mediation within 10 days then Nominet will send a notice to the parties saying that they will appoint an expert once the complainant has paid the necessary fee (currently £750 plus VAT for disputes concerning up to five domain names).
- Within five days of receipt of the fee, Nominet will appoint an expert (Nominet holds a list of approved experts).
- In the absence of any exceptional circumstances, the expert should forward his decision to Nominet within 10 days of his appointment (note the decision will be in writing and should give reasons).
- Within three days of receipt of the expert's decision, Nominet will send a full text of the decision to each of the parties, the decision will also be published on Nominet's web-site.
- If the expert decides that the domain name registration should be cancelled, suspended, transferred or amended then the decision will be implemented within ten days (unless within that ten-day period either party appeals or the respondent issues Court proceedings).

Nominet has included a sanction against the practice of 'reverse hijacking' of domain names. If the expert finds that a complaint has been brought in bad faith, and the complainant has been found on three separate occasions within a two-year period to have brought a complaint in bad faith, then Nominet will not accept any further complaints from that complainant for a period of two years.

In the event that one of the parties issues Court proceedings concerning a domain name which is the subject of an ongoing Nominet dispute resolution procedure, then Nominet will suspend its proceedings pending the outcome of the Court case.

1.9 Cyber squatting

Imagine that a director at Company A receives a letter from a third party. The letter informs the director that the third party has registered the domain names company-a.com and company-a.co.uk in his own name. The letter contains an offer for Company A to purchase the domain names from the third party at an inflated price.

Cyber squatting describes the situation where a third party has registered a domain name that is identical or similar to the corporate identity or brand of a business. This practice continues and is carried out by so-called 'cyber squatters' in the hope that a domain name purchased at market rates can be sold on to a business at an inflated price for a profit.

This type of practice is nothing new. Similar activities have come before the Courts previously in respect of company name 'squatting'. The case of *Glaxo plc and another* v. *Glaxo Wellcome and others* [1996] FSR 388 gave the Court an opportunity to set the tone.

Following a press release announcing a takeover bid by Glaxo Plc for Wellcome Plc, the Defendants registered a company under the name GlaxoWellcome Limited. The Claimants discovered what had happened and offered to buy the company for £1,000. The Defendants however demanded £100,000. Finding that the Defendants' scheme was dishonest and aimed at appropriating the Claimants' goodwill, Mr Justice Lightman remarked:

> 'The court will not countenance any such pre-emptive strike of registering companies with names where others have the goodwill in those names, and the registering party then demanding a price for changing the names. It is an abuse of the system of registration of companies' names. The right to choose the name with which a company is registered is not given for that purpose.'

Accordingly, Mr Justice Lightman granted the Claimants a mandatory injunction requiring the company and subscribers to change or facilitate the change of name.

The Court took a similar approach in *Direct Line Group Ltd and others* v. *Direct Line Estate Agency Ltd and others* [1997] FSR 374. The Defendants, who had engaged in similar practices previously, formed a number of companies with names that incorporated the trade mark 'Direct Line'. Mr Justice Laddie granted the Claimants an interim injunction, commenting that the court would view with extreme displeasure any attempt by traders '*to embark upon a scam designed to make illegitimate use of other companies' trade marks*'.

These cases set the tone for the leading authority on domain name disputes, the Court of Appeal case of *British Telecommunications Plc* v. *One In A Million Ltd and others* [1999] FSR 1.

By way of background, the Defendants had registered a significant number of domain names comprising well-known names and trade marks (including those of Marks & Spencer Plc, J.Sainsbury Plc Ltd and Ladbrokes Plc). The Defendants argued that there were a number of ways in which they could make their intended profit, including selling the domain names to third parties who may have legitimate rights in the names or even to the owners of the goodwill.

The question before the Court was twofold. First, did the Defendants' conduct amount to passing off? Second, had there been trade mark infringements under section10 (3) of the Trade Marks Act 1994?

A first instance injunction restrained the Defendants from passing off and from infringing the Claimants' trade marks. They were also ordered to transfer the domain names to the owners of the goodwill, the Court having found that the Defendants had clearly threatened to infringe the Claimants' rights in the future. The Judge also observed:

> '*Any person who deliberately registers a domain name on account of its similarity to the name, brand name or trade mark of an unconnected commercial organisation must expect to find himself on the receiving end of an injunction to restrain the threat of passing off, and the injunction will be in terms which will make the name commercially useless to the dealer.*'

The Judge did not, however, find that the mere registration of the domain names, without something more, amounted to passing off.

Taking the matter to the Court of Appeal, the Defendants argued that the domain names that they had registered could be used for purposes that were legitimate.

Surprisingly perhaps, whilst upholding the first instance decision vis-à-vis trade mark infringement, the Court of Appeal went even further with regard to the issue of passing off.

In summary it found that:

- there was a jurisdiction to grant injunctive relief where a Defendant was equipped with or was intending to equip another with an instrument of fraud;
- a name which would, by reason of its similarity to the name of another inherently lead to passing off, was such an instrument;
- the Court would intervene by way of an injunction in passing off in three types of case: firstly, where passing off was established or threatened; secondly, where the defendant was a joint wrongdoer with another in passing off, actual or threatened; thirdly, where the defendant equipped himself with or intended to equip another with an instrument of fraud;
- the registration of a distinctive name (such as 'marksandspencer') made a

representation to persons who consulted the register that the registrant was connected or associated with the name registered and thus the owner of the goodwill in the name. This amounted to passing off;

- that the registration of such a distinctive name as a domain name was an erosion of the exclusive goodwill in the name which damaged or which was likely to damage the owner of the goodwill;
- domain names comprising distinctive names were also instruments of fraud. Any realistic use of them as a domain name would result in passing off;
- it was the value of the goodwill in the 'household names' (and not the fact that they could be used in some way by a third party without deception) which had caused the Appellants to register the names. The registrations were made with the purpose of appropriating the Respondents' property.

Lord Justice Aldous explained when a domain name will be considered to be an instrument of fraud:

> 'The Court should consider the similarity of the names, the intention of the defendant, the type of trade and all the surrounding circumstances. If it be the intention of the defendant to appropriate the goodwill of another or enable others to do so, I can see no reason why the court should not infer that it will happen, even if there is a possibility that such an appropriation would not take place. If, taking all the circumstances into account the court should conclude that the name was produced to enable passing off, is adapted to be used for passing off and, if used, is likely to be fraudulently used, an injunction will be appropriate.'

One in a Million is viewed by some as taking the law of passing off too far (particularly in that the court was prepared to draw an inference that passing off would take place simply because of the Defendants' alleged intentions). It is, however, worth noting that the case was relied upon, largely unsuccessfully, by the Claimants in a subsequent interim injunction application in MBNA America Bank NA & anr v. Freeman.

In this particular case, the Defendant Mr Freeman had registered the domain name mbna.co.uk. Mr Freeman explained to the judge that the letters stood for 'marketing banners for net advertising' and were part of an idea of his to sell banner advertising on web-sites. Mr Freeman's web-site was not actually operational.

MBNA were conducting business from their site at mbna.com and began proceedings against Mr Freeman for trade mark infringement (on the grounds of taking unfair advantage of the mark) and passing off. The Claimants relied on One in a Million in support of their proposition that if Mr Freeman's intention had been to use the domain name to take advantage of MBNA's goodwill, with a view to increasing the number of visitors to his web-site, then there was no reason why the court should not infer that an appropriation of their goodwill would take place.

While the court granted an interim injunction preventing Mr Freeman from disposing of the domain name pending trial, it did not restrain the operation of the site. Though the outcome may have been different had the Claimants shown that there was a risk that they would suffer financial loss or damage before the trial, the fact that Mr Freeman had a proposed legitimate use for the name would appear to have saved him.

It is worthy of note that in *One in a Million*, the Defendants did not appear to have any such 'legitimate proposals'. Moreover, they had threatened to sell some of the domain names to third parties and also to involve the media; such tactics surely worked against them.

Use of a domain name can still amount to an instrument of fraud, even though its use does not inherently lead to passing off. In *easyJet Airline Co Ltd & ors* v. *Tim Dainty (t/a easyRealestate)* (Ch.D.28/2/2001) the Defendant had registered the domain name easyRealestate.co.uk and created a site using a get-up in plain white lettering against a bright orange background. easyJet applied on summary judgment for an injunction to restrain the Defendant from passing off and for an order that the domain name be transferred to easyJet. The Defendant argued that easyJet should not be entitled to exclusive use of the word 'easy', that easyJet did not as far as he knew have any estate agency business and finally that he had no intention of taking advantage of easyJet's goodwill.

easyJet succeeded in obtaining summary judgment on the basis that though they were not entitled to appropriate the word 'easy' there was a likelihood of deception because of the get-up of the web-site. In other words, it was not the registration of the name itself but rather the get-up of the site that would probably lead to passing off.

Even if a domain name is descriptive of the type of goods or services being offered, it is not necessarily the case that the Courts will tolerate its use. If another party has established goodwill in a similar domain name, and the Defendant's use of its own domain name is likely to cause confusion, then the Court may intervene. By way of example, in *Lawyers Online Ltd* v. *Lawyeronline Ltd* (Ch.D Birmingham District Registry 29/9/00) the Claimant, who operated a web-site at lawyersonline.co.uk, succeeded in obtaining an interim injunction to restrain the Defendant's use of lawyeronline.co.uk despite the fact that the domain name was descriptive. The Court was satisfied that there was an arguable case that goodwill attached to the domain name and that there had already been confusion.

To summarise, in the wake of *One in a Million* the days of the successful cyber squatter may be over. Domain name disputes are now much more likely to occur where more than one party believes that it has some legitimate right to use the name.

1.10 Conclusion

The growth of the internet as a business medium has led to a whole new type of dispute centring on the registration and use of domain names. Many businesses appreciated too late the value of registering as domain names their corporate or brand identities. This led to opportunists, who initially seemed to be 'ahead of the game', warehousing domain names and effectively blocking the registrations of legitimate users. Although the days of the successful cyber squatter would appear to be over, at least in the United Kingdom (litigators are now far more likely to be advising on less clear-cut disputes) the recent introduction of the .biz and .info TLDs has created another outbreak of cyber squatting, and the development of multilingual domain names may cause confusion.

When disputes do arise, consideration should be given as to whether or not the matter is suitable for some form of alternative dispute resolution, such as the ICANN or Nominet procedures. Resolving matters in this way may prove to be the most cost effective way of achieving your objectives or those of your client. However, there will be situations where such methods are unsuitable and proceedings should be issued.

With regard to the future, changes are in store for the domain name system. In November 2000 the ICANN Board selected seven new TLDs, namely: .aero, .biz, .coop, .info, .museum, .name, and .pro. Registrations of the .biz and .info domains are already underway and Nominet may shortly be introducing a new *.me.uk* suffix.

These changes may well serve to ease some of the pressure on the domain name system. They may also, however, serve to increase the number of disputes, at least initially, as individuals and businesses race to be the first to register the most sought-after names.

 CHECKLIST OF PRACTICAL TIPS

→ Select a domain name that corresponds with the nature of your/your client's business.
→ Having selected a domain name conduct (and record) trade mark searches in the territories to which the web-site will be targeted.
→ If other businesses have trade mark rights in a particular territory, consider including a notice on the web-site making it clear that the target audience is restricted geographically (see *Euromarket Designs Inc.* v. *Peters and another*).
→ Make sure that the domain name is used.

→ If a certain type of goods or services is suggested by the domain name, try to ensure that this corresponds with the actual goods or services being sold.

→ Be cautious about making offers to sell the domain name, particularly to parties who may arguably already have rights in the name and particularly for extortionate sums.

→ Register variants of your/your client's domain name to prevent confusion amongst clients and customers (links could even be established from those sites to the main web-site, thereby maximising the number of 'hits').

→ Do not stockpile domain names that have no connection with your/your client's business.

→ If you discover that another party is infringing your/your client's trade mark, be wary of the consequences of 'threats actions' when writing letters before action (see *Brain* v. *Ingledew, Brown, Bennison & Garrett* [1996] FSR 341 and *Prince Plc* v. *Prince Sports Group Inc.* [1998] FSR 21).

8 Employment and Human Rights

Introduction

This chapter considers the employment issues which arise when a company such as Traditional Company Limited (chapter 2), decides to provide e-mail and internet access to its employees. In addition to the obvious problem of reduced productivity amongst employees who engage in lengthy e-mail conversations or surf the web to find the best holiday deal, an employee's abuse of the e-mail and internet systems may lead to claims against the company as diverse as libel, sex or race discrimination or breach of copyright.

To stand a chance of defending such claims, the company will have to show that it has taken all reasonably practicable steps to prevent the abuse perpetrated by its employees. This will only be possible if the company has provided clear guidance to all employees on the appropriate use of the systems through a comprehensive IT policy. In addition, the company needs to manage the situation actively on an ongoing basis, checking that employees are complying with the policy by monitoring their use of the systems and taking the requisite disciplinary action against those who breach the policy.

Having said that, the company needs to ensure that the monitoring of employees' e-mail and internet use is done lawfully, within the applicable Regulations and without infringing an individual's right to privacy under Article 8 of the Human Rights Act 1998.

1. E-mail abuse

The issues which the company may face as a result of the misuse of e-mail by its employees are many and varied. At one end of the scale this could entail dealing with a practical joker who has sent a compromising e-mail from a colleague's PC and at the other end of the scale, the company could find itself on the losing end of a high-value claim for defamation or it could be vicariously liable for discrimination.

In this section we look at issues which could have a significant financial impact on the company.

1.1 Defamation

What is defamation?

Defamation is a generic term for libel and slander. If a defamatory statement is made in print, for example in a newspaper, or in some other permanent form (which is likely to include e-mail), the individual who is the subject of the statement will have a claim for libel. If the defamation is verbal only, the claim will be for slander.

A defamatory statement is one that lowers the standing or reputation of a person in the estimation of right-thinking members of society generally or which would cause that person to be avoided, ridiculed or to be disparaged, whether personally or professionally.

In order to bring a claim, the defamatory statement must have been 'published' which means that it must have been communicated to someone other than the person who is the subject of the statement.

There are a number of defences that a defendant to a defamation claim could raise. These include:

a) *Justification* – on the basis that the statement is true or substantially true.

b) *Fair comment* on a matter of public interest – on the basis that the statement consists of comment or opinion, the opinion is honestly held and the defendant is not motivated by malice.

c) *Qualified privilege* – on the basis that there is a common interest between the maker and recipient of the statement or an obligation on the maker to communicate the particulars of the statement. For example, if a manager with supervisory responsibility for an under-performing employee sends a report in the context of a performance management procedure to the Human Resources manager, explaining the employee's particular deficiencies.

d) *Innocent dissemination* – on the basis that the defendant does not have primary responsibility for the offending statement. For example, the publisher of a book which contains a defamatory statement.

e) *Innocence* (referred to as Offer of Amends) – on the basis that the defendant, who published the offending statement innocently and in good faith, offered to make amends, for example to publish a correction and apology and to pay damages. If this is not accepted by the defamed party, it provides a defence for the defendant at trial.

A company or other corporate body may also sue for libel or slander when a defamatory statement is published which is damaging to its business.

How it applies to e-mail

The law of defamation applies to e-mail and information posted on the internet, in the same way that it applies to more traditional forms of publishing. Businesses have always been subject to the risk of their employees committing libel, for example by defamatory statements contained in internal memoranda or employee newsletters, but the risk appears to be much greater with e-mail. This increased risk is partly due to the ease and speed with which e-mail messages can be transmitted to large numbers of recipients, both internally and externally. Also, people adopt a more casual approach in e-mail communications than they do in written correspondence, treating it more like the spoken than written word.

Examples

Take a disaffected employee who has sent an e-mail to a few of his colleagues which contains vociferous criticism of his manager and casts aspersions on the manager's private life or his ability to do his job. Before e-mail, the employee may have had the same conversation with his colleagues, but it would not have been committed to print. The offending e-mail may be transmitted onwards to the whole workforce by the touch of a few keys, either in error or purposely to cause mischief. The manager who is the subject of the e-mail may well have a claim for libel for the damage caused to his reputation.

In 1997 Norwich Union paid out £450,000 and made a public apology in the High Court to Western Provident Union after some of its employees circulated an e-mail internally which said that Western Provident was in financial difficulties and that it was being investigated by the Department of Trade and Industry. Such a statement could clearly be very damaging to its business.

The company's liability

As the provider of the e-mail facility through which an employee's defamatory statement is circulated, the company may be liable for publishing the statement. The employee who made the statement will be jointly liable, but as the company has more funds, the defamed individual or business is more likely to pursue the company.

The company may have a defence on the basis that it unwittingly provided a conduit through which the defamatory statement was published but it will have to show, among other things, that it took reasonable care in relation to the publication of the defamatory statement. If the company has not provided clear guidance to its employees on the correct use of e-mail, including an express prohibition on making defamatory statements, and does not undertake at least some degree of e-mail monitoring, this will be a difficult requirement for it to satisfy.

The company may also be liable by way of vicarious liability for the defamatory statement if the employee who sends the e-mail containing the offending statement is deemed to be doing an authorised act in an unauthorised manner. It is easy to see how an employee who uses e-mail in their work will be considered to be carrying out an authorised act, albeit in an unauthorised way.

1.2 Harassment

What is harassment?

A claim of harassment may be brought by an individual in the context of the Sex Discrimination Act 1975 (SDA), the Race Relations Acts 1976 (RRA) or the Disability Discrimination Act 1995 (DDA). There is no statutory definition of harassment in these Acts but it is well established that harassment on grounds of sex, race or disability amounts to unlawful discrimination.

The European Commission Recommendation on the protection of the dignity of men and women at work provides a definition of sexual harassment as:

> '*conduct of a sexual nature or other conduct based on sex affecting the dignity of women and men at work...*'

It makes clear that such conduct is unacceptable if:

- it is unwanted, unreasonable and offensive to the recipient;
- decisions regarding the employment, promotion or salary of the recipient are dependent on the acceptance or rejection of the conduct; and/or
- it creates an intimidating, hostile or humiliating working environment for the recipient.

The harassment may consist of physical, verbal or non-verbal conduct. Sexual attention becomes sexual harassment if it continues after the recipient has made clear that he or she regards the conduct as offensive. However, a one-off incident may constitute sexual harassment if it is sufficiently serious.

It is important to note that an essential characteristic of sexual harassment is that it is unwanted by the recipient and that it is for each individual to determine what behaviour is acceptable and what is considered to be offensive. The motive or intention of the individual carrying out the unwanted conduct is irrelevant. What may appear to be a harmless joke and amusing to one person may constitute harassment to another.

Although the above definition and explanation relates to sexual harassment, it can be applied by analogy to race and disability claims.

There is, in fact, a new definition of racial harassment which has been formulated for the purpose of the European Race Equality Directive (2000/43) which must be implemented in the UK by July 2003. It provides that racial harassment is:

> '*unwanted conduct related to racial or ethnic origin . . .with the purpose or effect of violating the dignity of a person and of creating an intimidating, hostile, degrading, humiliating and offensive environment.*'

The problem with e-mail

E-mail has become a means by which harassment can be perpetrated in the workplace. It may be used by an employee as part of a concerted and calculated campaign of harassment against another employee, with large numbers of unwanted and offensive e-mails hitting the victim's inbox over a prolonged period. Alternatively, it may be a one-off incident, perhaps with one e-mail only, containing a thoughtless joke or remark, causing the problem.

As with defamatory statements, the risks are increased by the fact that the offending e-mails may be forwarded to a much wider audience than originally intended and in a very short space of time.

Example

In 2001, a black secretary working at a City law firm handed in her resignation, saying that she had accepted the offer of a job elsewhere. Shortly afterwards, two of the male lawyers for whom she worked engaged in an e-mail exchange about her departure and a possible replacement. One of the lawyers wrote something to the effect of:

> '*Can we go for a real fit busty blonde this time? She cannot be any more trouble and at least it would provide some entertainment!*'

The secretary saw the e-mail and brought a claim against the two lawyers and the law firm for sex and race discrimination.

Liability of the company

The company has a legal obligation to protect its employees from harassment and to provide a safe working environment. As with defamation, if the employee who sends the offending e-mails is deemed to be doing an authorised act in an unauthorised manner, the company will be vicariously liable for the harassment. Again, it is easy to see how an employee who uses e-mail in their work will be considered to be carrying out an authorised act, albeit in an unauthorised way. The company will be liable whether or not the acts were done with its knowledge or approval and it can defend itself only if it can show that it took all reasonably practicable steps to prevent the harassment. Dissemination of an e-mail and internet policy to all employees, followed by training in that policy will assist the company in establishing this statutory defence.

1.3 Disclosure of confidential information

During their employment, all employees are under a duty to protect the confidential information of their employers. This is part of the duty of fidelity which employees owe to their employers and which is implied into all contracts of employment. In addition, the company's employees may be subject to an express clause in their contracts of employment or employee handbook which prohibits the use and/or disclosure of the company's confidential information. The clause may give examples of the sort of information which the company considers to be confidential, for example customer lists, pricing information and databases.

The introduction of e-mail and the fact that employees tend to have access from their desktops to the company's databases and computer files, increases the risk of commercially sensitive information being disclosed to its competitors or used by its employees for their own purposes.

Example
An employee is considering resigning and establishing himself in competition with the company. He has access from his desktop to all the company's databases and sensitive files, including documents containing client contact details and tenders for new work. The employee sends a whole range of documents as attachments to otherwise innocuous looking e-mails to his wife at home. If the employee does set up on his own, the information will be invaluable to him.

In 2000, the Conservative Party's head of marketing and membership leaked a speech by a senior member of the shadow cabinet to journalists by e-mail. The e-mail was found on his system and he was asked to leave Conservative Central Office shortly afterwards.

1.4 Inadvertent contracts

An agreement by e-mail is capable of forming or varying a contract in the same way as a paper document. The case of *Hall* v. *Cognos Limited* (17 February 1998, Case No. 1803325/97) in 1998 illustrates the dangers of employees inadvertently forming contracts on behalf of the company, or alternatively varying existing contractual terms to which the employer is then bound.

In this case, Mr Hall's right to claim for reimbursement of expenses was subject to detailed rules, which formed part of his contract of employment. Having missed the deadline for submitting a particular expenses claim, he emailed his line manager to ask whether he could enter it late. The manager replied by e-mail, saying 'yes, that is OK', following which Mr Hall submitted his claim. Cognos Limited refused to pay these expenses. It relied on a clause in Mr Hall's contract which said that any amendment or modification to his contract had to be in writing and signed by both parties if it was to have effect. Mr Hall claimed breach of contract in the Employment Tribunal.

The tribunal considered two issues:

1. Whether e-mail correspondence was capable of constituting a document which was in writing and signed by both parties; and
2. Whether Mr Hall's line manager had ostensible authority to agree to a variation of the terms of the contract relating to expenses.

In answer to the first issue, the Tribunal held that once an e-mail had been printed out, it was in written form and as each e-mail contained the Christian name of its author, it was also signed.

On the second issue, the Tribunal held that as it was Mr Hall's line manager who had agreed to him submitting the late claim, Mr Hall was entitled to rely on the manager's apparent authority to vary the terms of his contract. Cognos Limited was, therefore, bound by the variation agreed by the line manager.

2. Internet abuse

In this section we consider some of the problems which the company may face in connection with its employees' abuse of the internet.

2.1 Personal surfing during work time

Providing internet access to employees from their desktop may have an unwelcome impact on productivity levels. With access to a large array of entertainment, the ability to shop for holidays and to download pirate software, it is easy to see how a few hours can be lost in a day. For example, in 2000 the Xerox Corporation in the US sacked forty employees for 'inappropriate visits to web-sites'. Some of these employees were recorded as spending up to eight hours a day on the internet visiting non-work-related web-sites. In the UK such conduct is likely to constitute misconduct and could lead to an employee's dismissal.

In the case of *Mrs L. J. Franxhi* v. *Focus Management Consultants Ltd* (29 July 1999, Case No. 2102862/98), Mrs Franxhi claimed unfair dismissal and sex discrimination after she was dismissed by Focus for extensive use of the internet during working hours for the purposes of booking her holiday. When challenged about this by her boss, Mrs Franxhi initially lied, saying that she had used the internet once only during her lunch hour. At the time of her dismissal, Mrs Franxhi was already subject to a written warning for using the company's stamps for personal postage. Mrs Franxhi alleged that her dismissal was due to her being pregnant.

The Employment Tribunal rejected this allegation and held that Mrs Franxhi's conduct constituted misconduct justifying her dismissal. The Tribunal said that Mrs Franxhi's use of the internet was more than the occasional fleeting one that might conceivably have been regarded as open to all employees and that, even though there was no express prohibition on using the internet for personal purposes, as a senior employee she must have known that her prolonged use was unacceptable, just as extensive use of any other company asset for private purposes would be unacceptable.

2.2 Pornography

A number of surveys have been carried out by web-monitoring companies which reveal that a significant proportion of internet activity in the UK relates to pornography.

The number of cases and news reports relating to employees who have been dismissed for accessing pornography on the internet during working hours suggests that this is a widespread problem for employers. For example, in 2000 the mobile phone company Orange sacked between thirty and forty employees after an internal investigation revealed that they had been downloading pornography from the internet and circulating it in the office. Orange had a policy covering use of the internet which prohibited access to offensive and inappropriate material.

In a 1997 case brought by an employee who had been dismissed for downloading obscene material, the Employment Tribunal observed that in the absence of an express provision or policy which stated that unauthorised use of the internet constituted gross misconduct, the mere use of the internet by an employee for unauthorised purposes (including pornography), would not generally justify summary dismissal. This decision illustrates the importance of having comprehensive rules on what is acceptable in terms of internet use.

Having said that, downloading pornography is clearly an inappropriate activity during working hours and a waste of company resources. In these circumstances, an employer could deal with the employee through its normal disciplinary or poor performance procedures, which could ultimately lead to dismissal if the employee does not heed warnings.

Harassment claims may also arise as a result of employees accessing pornographic sites in the office, as the case of *Mrs M. Morse* v. *Future Reality Ltd* (22 October 1996, Case No. 54571) illustrates. Mrs Morse shared an office with several men who spent a considerable amount of time viewing sexually explicit and obscene images, which they had downloaded from the internet. Mrs Morse accepted that the men's activities were not directed at her personally and that the circulation and discussion of the images generally went on in the background. However, it made her feel uncomfortable and she resigned, claiming sex discrimination. She cited the offensive pictures, bad language and general atmosphere of obscenity in the office as the basis of her complaint.

The Employment Tribunal held that the activities of the men had a detrimental effect on Mrs Morse and as such their conduct constituted sexual harassment. Future Reality Ltd was held liable because it had not taken any action to prevent the harassment. The award for injury to feelings in this case was only £750 and Mrs Morse received an additional three months' compensation for loss of earnings. If the conduct of the male employees had been directed personally at Mrs Morse, the awards would have been significantly higher.

Criminal liability

There is also potential criminal liability for an employee who downloads and/or circulates pornographic material. Under the Obscene Publications Act 1959 it is an offence to send material that could deprave or corrupt the recipient and under the Protection of Children Act 1999 it is an offence to possess or download child pornography.

An employer could also be found liable under these provisions if the employee's activities are found to have been carried out with the consent or connivance of the employer, or the activities are found to be attributable to the neglect of the employer. If the company knowingly allows employees to download pornographic material and circulate it around the office by e-mail, it will clearly be guilty of an offence. However, if it merely fails to provide any guidelines on the appropriate and inappropriate use of the internet and fails to monitor employees' use of the internet, it could be found liable due to neglect.

2.3 Breach of copyright laws

If employees download copyrighted materials from the internet, the employer may be vicariously liable for the breaches of copyright committed by its employees.

3. Monitoring employees

So far, this chapter has identified the most common risks associated with the inappropriate use of e-mail and the internet by employees. To defend itself against the various claims which may arise, the company will need to show that it has taken all reasonably practicable steps to prevent the offending behaviour of its employees. In order to satisfy this requirement, the company needs to be aware of what is being sent by way of e-mail and internet traffic by its employees. This will involve it in monitoring. This section considers what the company can do lawfully in terms of monitoring its employees' e-mail communications and internet use.

The company must strike a balance between protecting its business interests and respecting the rights of its employees to privacy, as conferred by the Human Rights Act 1998, the Data Protection Act 1998 and the Regulation of Investigatory Powers Act 2000.

3.1 Human Rights Act

The Human Rights Act 1998, which effectively incorporates into UK law the European Convention on Human Rights (the Convention), came into force in October 2000. Article 8 of the Convention confers the right to privacy of individuals both at home and at work. It is relevant in this context as it has an impact on the company's ability to monitor its employees' e-mail and internet use.

Article 8 (1) provides that:

> 'Everyone has the right to respect for his private and family life, his home and his correspondence.'

The European Court of Human Rights (ECHR) has made clear that the notion of 'private life' includes an individual's working life. The right to respect for correspondence clearly encompasses e-mail, telephone calls and other forms of communication.

The ECHR case of *Alison Halford* v. *United Kingdom* [1997] IRLR 471 ECHR concerns the interception of an employee's telephone calls at work by her employer.

Ms Halford was an Assistant Chief Constable with Merseyside Police. In 1997 she brought a claim, alleging that her employers had tapped her telephone calls at work in order to obtain information about a sex discrimination claim she had brought against them in the Employment Tribunal. Ms Halford argued that the interception of her calls constituted a violation of Article 8.

The ECHR found that because Ms Halford had not been given any prior warning by her employer that her telephone calls from work were liable to be intercepted, she would have had a reasonable expectation of privacy for such calls. Consequently, the interception was an unlawful breach of Article 8. Ms Halford was awarded £10,000 as compensation for invasion of privacy.

Because Ms Halford was employed by a public authority, she was able to lodge a claim based directly on a breach of Article 8 of the Convention. Employees of a company such as Traditional Company Limited (which is a private employer) do not have direct, free-standing rights under the Convention. An employee would need to bring a claim against the company under domestic legislation and rely indirectly on Article 8, reminding the court or tribunal of its duty to act in a manner compatible with Convention rights. For example, if an employee was dismissed for gross misconduct after monitoring by the company revealed that he was sending offensive messages by e-mail, the employee could bring a claim for unfair dismissal in the Employment Tribunal, arguing that in breaching his right to privacy, the company had acted unreasonably and his dismissal was consequently unfair. To succeed in his claim, the employee would have to show that he had a reasonable expectation of privacy in relation to his e-mail communications.

The corollary of the Halford decision would appear to be that an employer is free to monitor communications if it makes clear to its employees that they should have no expectation of privacy in the workplace. On this basis, if the company has a clear policy, which states that the e-mail system is not private and will be subject to regular monitoring, it should avoid liability. However, because of the potential for infringement of human rights associated with workplace monitoring, the legislature has introduced the Regulation of Investigatory Powers Act 2000 and, more importantly for the company as an employer, the Lawful Business Practice Regulations 2000, both of which came into force in October 2000.

3.2 The Regulation of Investigatory Powers Act 2000 and the Telecommunications (Lawful Business Practice) (Interception of Communications) Regulations 2000

The Regulation of Investigatory Powers Act 2000 (RIPA) creates a statutory tort of unlawful interception of communications on a private network. Broadly speaking, a person who has the right to control the operation or use of a private telecommunication system must not intercept any communication in the course of its transmission, unless he has lawful authority to do so. In this context, a private telecommunication system will include the company's e-mail system (unless it is wholly internal and has no capacity for sending or receiving e-mails via an outside telephone line). An employer will have lawful authority to intercept if it has the consent of both parties to the communication. An unlawful interception could give rise to a claim by the sender or recipient of the e-mail intercepted, with the injured party being entitled to make a claim for damages. It may also give rise to criminal liability.

RIPA contains provisions which enable the Secretary of State to introduce statutory regulations dealing specifically with work-place monitoring. Pursuant to these provisions, the Secretary of State has introduced the Telecommunications (Lawful Business Practice) (Interception of Communications) Regulations 2000 (the Regulations).

As explained above, in order to comply with RIPA, the company needs the consent of both the sender and the recipient of an e-mail before it can legitimately intercept it. This causes obvious practical difficulties. How does the company go about obtaining consent from a potential recipient of an e-mail from one of its employees?

The Regulations assist the company in overcoming this problem by permitting monitoring and recording of communications by employers in a variety of circumstances *without* the need for the consent of their employees.

Regulation 3(1) provides that employers may monitor or record their employees' communications for the following purposes:

- to protect national security;
- to prevent or detect crime – for example, to detect fraud or offences under the Obscene Publications Act 1959, which would include downloading and circulating pornography;
- to investigate or detect the unauthorised use of the telecommunications system – for example, to check that employees are not sending abusive, defamatory or discriminatory e-mails;
- to ascertain or demonstrate standards which are achieved or ought to be achieved by employees using the system in the course of their duties – that is, for quality control and staff training;
- to establish the existence of facts – for example, to verify that a contract has been entered into by telephone or e-mail;
- to ascertain that employees are complying with external or internal regulatory rules or guidelines – for example, the rules of the Financial Services Authority; or
- to ensure the effective operation of the system – for example, to detect viruses.

Employers may monitor *but not record* employees' communications for the following purposes:

- to determine whether communications are relevant to the business – for example, checking e-mails and voice-mails of employees who are absent on holiday or due to sickness;
- to monitor communications to a confidential counselling or support service.

The circumstances in which an employer may intercept communications, as set out above, are wide-ranging and cater for most circumstances in which an employer would want to monitor its employees. However, the Regulations stipulate that any interception must be carried out solely for the purpose of monitoring or recording communications which are relevant to the employer's business. At first sight, this would appear to exclude the interception of an employee's private communications. However, if an employee's private e-mail breaches an express company policy on the use of e-mail or internet because, for example, it contains pornographic images or discloses confidential information to a third party, then it is certainly arguable that the communication is relevant to the business.

The Regulations also place an obligation on the employer to make all reasonable efforts to inform every person who may use the telecommunication system that their communications may be intercepted. In relation to employees, this can be effected by including a provision in the company's e-mail and internet policy, which states that monitoring of e-mail will occur on a regular basis. It is a more difficult prospect to inform all third parties who send e-mails to the company that their communications may be monitored. The company should consider including an automatic statement at the foot of all out-going e-mails, advising recipients that their communications may be monitored. This will not solve the problem if the e-mail communication is initiated by the third party. Having said that, the employer is only required to make 'all reasonable efforts' in this regard and it would have a strong argument that it was impracticable, if not impossible, to inform all third parties that their incoming communications may be monitored.

3.3 Data protection

The Data Protection Act 1998 will apply to any e-mail that is monitored, recorded or stored if that e-mail contains information about an identifiable living individual. Data protection is considered in detail in chapter 3.

In 2000, the Information Commissioner issued a draft Code of Practice entitled 'The Use of Personal Data in Employer/Employee Relationships', which deals specifically with employee surveillance, including monitoring e-mail and internet use. At the time of writing, the Code of Practice is still in draft form, following a lengthy consultation period.

There has been a good deal of disquiet about the lack of accord between the Regulations and the Code of Practice, which in its current form is comparatively restrictive in its approach to monitoring. However, the Government has insisted that there is no clash between the two, explaining that the Regulations offer a broad framework, whereas the Code of Practice proposes more precise details.

The Code makes clear that employers should monitor only where there is a genuine business need and where the methods used to carry it out are proportionate to the legitimate aims of the employer and are not unduly intrusive of an individual's privacy. What does this actually mean?

E-mail monitoring

In relation to e-mail monitoring the Code of Practice provides that employers should always take account of the privacy of those sending and receiving e-mails. More specifically, the Code provides that:

- An employer should not monitor the content of e-mail messages unless the business purpose for which the monitoring is undertaken cannot be achieved by simply looking at the record of e-mail traffic on the system. For example, if the business reason for monitoring is to address time-wasting, then reviewing data traffic should be sufficient to achieve this objective. On the other hand, if the aim of the monitoring is to detect harassment, bullying or other discriminatory behaviour, then reviewing data traffic will not help and the employer should be justified in scanning the content of e-mails.
- If an employer intends to check its employees' e-mails in their absence due to sickness or annual leave, it should notify them in advance that this will occur and should restrict such monitoring to identifying work-related e-mails and ensuring that the business responds properly to its customers and other contacts. The employer should not open messages that are clearly personal.

Internet monitoring

In relation to monitoring employees' internet activities, the Code of Practice provides that:

- Employers should explain clearly and precisely to employees any limits or prohibitions on their use of the Internet for non work-related reasons and should not monitor the sites visited or content viewed by employees unless it is clear that the purpose for which the monitoring is undertaken cannot be achieved by simply recording the amount of time spent by the employee on the internet.
- As far as possible, a company policy on internet use should be enforced by the use of technology designed to restrict access, rather than by monitoring employees' use of the internet. For example, there are software products available that can detect excessive amounts of skin tone in an image and thereby prevent the display of pornographic material.

There are further specific provisions relating to monitoring and pornography. For example:

- the information obtained by the employer from the monitoring process should be disregarded unless it reveals that the downloading of pornography poses a significant risk to the employer; and

■ in using the results of monitoring to take disciplinary action against employees, the employer should bear in mind the ease with which web-sites can be inadvertently accessed by employees through unintended responses of search engines, unclear hypertext links, misleading banner advertising or mis-keying.

These provisions appear rather lenient to employees who access pornographic material at work. Despite the Code's comment that '*it is hard to see that monitoring of Internet access is justified unless there is evidence that activity is taking place or likely to take place which is likely to lead to real distress or offence*', it is important to remember that an employee who is subjected directly or even indirectly in the workplace to a pornographic image that is not legally obscene may nevertheless have grounds for claiming sex discrimination (see *Morse* v. *Future Reality Limited* above).

The Code suggests that as far as possible, employers should target those employees who it reasonably suspects of being guilty of certain types of misconduct, rather than monitoring all employees.

Many employers carry out occasional spot checks as a way of monitoring employees and the Code makes it clear that if more general monitoring is necessary, then spot checks or audits are preferable to continuous monitoring. Without spot checks, an employee who has not otherwise come under suspicion (and who will not therefore be subject to targeted monitoring) could make defamatory remarks or disclose confidential information without detection. These are unlikely to be picked up simply by examining traffic data or by software applications.

It is arguable that an employer who does not carry out spot checks is not fulfilling its duty to do everything reasonably practicable to prevent harassment, defamation, breach of copyright and so on by its employees. In that case, the employer is unlikely to succeed in defending itself against such claims. Also, provided employees are warned that they will occur, spot checks support one of the key aims of monitoring which is prevention of misuse rather than detection.

A final few words of caution: the company must identify the specific business purpose for which any monitoring is introduced. All forms of monitoring should be carried out sparingly and in proportion to the harm which employees could cause to the business.

4. Drafting and implementing an e-mail and internet policy

It is clear, in relation to all the issues we have discussed in this chapter, that a well-drafted and comprehensive policy on e-mail and internet use is essential to minimise the significant legal risks faced by the company as a result of providing access to e-mail and the internet to its employees.

On the one hand, the company faces liability as a consequence of its employees' misuse of the systems, for example if they send defamatory e-mails or ones which are offensive and deemed to constitute harassment of the recipient. On the other hand, the company faces claims from those same errant employees, if the monitoring it carries out is unlawful or if it dismisses employees in circumstances which are deemed to be unfair.

Provided the policy is effectively implemented (which essentially means disseminated and communicated), it should assist the company in its defence to a claim that it is vicariously liable for its employees' actions by demonstrating that it has taken all reasonably practicable steps to prevent the harassment, defamation or other misconduct.

In drafting the policy, the company needs to make sure that the right balance is struck between protecting its legitimate business interests, restricting employees' activities and invading their privacy.

4.1 The scope and content of the policy

There should be a general policy statement which explains the rationale for the policy and raises awareness of the potential consequences for the company of misuse by employees. One of the objectives of the policy should be to promote a culture of caution in relation to e-mail and internet use.

The policy should set out the extent to which employees are permitted to use e-mail and the internet for private purposes and warn employees that their e-mail communications and internet activities may be monitored, thereby removing their expectations of privacy and satisfying the requirement of RIPA in relation to the company making all reasonable efforts to inform those who may use the system that their communications may be intercepted.

The policy must set out clearly the consequences for employees who misuse the systems. It should warn employees specifically of those offences that will be regarded as constituting gross misconduct. For example, if the company wanted summarily to dismiss an employee who was found to be accessing and downloading pornography in the office, it must make clear that such conduct will be considered as gross misconduct and that the employee will be dealt with in accordance with the company's disciplinary policy.

If the company engages independent contractors or agency workers who have access to its e-mail and the internet, it should ensure that the policy applies to them also or that the agency who provides the workers applies equivalent rules and guidance relating to e-mail and internet activities.

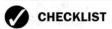 **CHECKLIST**

Provisions to include in the policy
The e-mail and internet policy should contain clear rules on the following issues:

In relation to e-mail:

→ Personal use – whether personal e-mail messages are prohibited or allowed on a limited basis. If personal use is permitted, guidance on what the company considers is reasonable use should be provided, for example only during lunchtime or after working hours.
→ E-mail style – for example, employees should draft e-mails with the same formality as hard copy letters or memos, they should not use capital letters (which is considered to be the equivalent of shouting) and for external e-mails they should include appropriate signature files with relevant contact details and appropriate disclaimers.
→ Inappropriate messages – for example, a prohibition on messages which may be offensive to the recipient(s) on the grounds of sex, race, disability, religion and gender, and a prohibition on responding to or forwarding chain letters, humorous stories and jokes.
→ Defamatory e-mails – for example, a prohibition on e-mails containing criticisms or disparaging remarks of colleagues, other individuals or organisations.
→ Confidential information – for example, rules on using encryption when sending confidential information by e-mail and a ban on e-mailing confidential information to home computers.
→ Contractual commitments – for example, rules relating to the negotiation of contracts by e-mail and a warning about inadvertently entering into contractual commitments.

In relation to the internet:

→ Personal use – specifying whether accessing the internet for personal use is prohibited or allowed on a limited basis, for example only during lunchtime or after working hours and for a maximum of 30 minutes in a day.
→ Downloading inappropriate material such as pornography, pirate software or computer games. In relation to pornography, there should be a warning that this may constitute a criminal offence as well as gross misconduct.
→ Breach of copyright – for example a statement that employees must take care not to breach copyright laws when downloading material and/or forwarding it to others.
→ Posting information on the company's web-site, for example, any information must be accurate and up to date. It may be advisable to restrict the ability to amend or add to the web-site to a small group of individuals.

The policy should also contain a warning that the e-mail system is not private. It should explain the extent to which e-mails and internet access will be monitored, for example, whether the content of e-mails and sites visited will be monitored in addition to recording e-mail traffic and time spent on the internet. It should also contain details of the practice relating to back-up and retention of e-mails on the system.

There should be a clear statement to the effect that breaches of the policy will be treated as disciplinary offences under the company's disciplinary procedures. It should also give an indication of the penalties to be applied for such breaches, specifying in particular which breaches will constitute gross misconduct and warning that the appropriate penalty for gross misconduct is summary dismissal.

The company may also wish to include information on how employees should report inappropriate use of e-mail or the internet (including provisions for anonymous reporting) and rules designed to safeguard the security of the system, for example, rules relating to the use of passwords, security of work stations and the use of floppy disks and CD-ROMs.

4.2 The implementation of the policy

The effective communication of the policy is vital if it is to be effective in educating employees of the risks, creating a culture of caution and assisting the company in its defence of any claims.

The principal means of promoting the policy are likely to include:

- induction training for new employees and regular training for existing employees, perhaps with a presentation by an IT professional which explains the contents of the policy and the consequences of breaching the policy. It would also be advisable for the company to ask employees to sign and return a copy of the policy, confirming that they have read and understood its contents;
- training for managers who will have responsibility for implementing the policy;
- occasional features in the company's in-house publications and/or global e-mails reminding employees of the policy;
- discussions in team meetings of particular problem areas which have arisen.

4.3 Managing employees who breach the policy

In order to avoid unfair dismissal claims, the company must ensure that it deals with those employees who breach the policy consistently and in accordance with the company's normal disciplinary procedures. If the company turns a blind eye to inappropriate use of e-mail for the first six months after its introduction and then decides to dismiss an employee for similar misuse of the system, the dismissal may be deemed unfair. Not all breaches of the policy will justify dismissal. In many situations it will be appropriate for the company to impose informal and formal written warnings before considering dismissal.

In cases of gross misconduct where dismissal may be appropriate, the company must have investigated all relevant facts adequately with the result that it has a reasonable and genuine belief in the employee's culpability. It must also be able to satisfy the employment tribunal that it acted reasonably in treating the reason for dismissal as a sufficient reason for dismissing the employee. For example, if an employee is found to have accessed and downloaded pornography from the internet, the tribunal will consider whether the company's decision to dismiss him falls within the band of reasonable responses to the employee's conduct which a reasonable employer could adopt.

If the company's policy specifically states that accessing and downloading pornography constitutes gross misconduct for which the appropriate sanction is dismissal, then the tribunal will almost certainly conclude that the company acted reasonably in dismissing the employee. This may not be the case if the policy does not contain such a provision. In *Dunn* v. *IBM UK Ltd* (I July 1998, Case No. 2305087/97), Mr Dunn admitted accessing pornographic sites at work but had not been warned that this could result in disciplinary action. There was no company policy which prohibited this conduct and the tribunal found that his summary dismissal was unfair. It did, however, reduce his compensation by 50 per cent on the grounds that he had significantly contributed to his dismissal.

The tribunal will take into account not only whether the company had reasonable grounds for dismissing the employee, but also whether it adopted a fair procedure. The company must inform the employee in detail of the case against him and hold a disciplinary hearing at which the employee has an opportunity to explain his side of the story and/or make representations in mitigation. In addition, the company must provide the employee in advance of the disciplinary hearing with copies of any documents on which it relies, for example, copies of relevant e-mails. The employee should also be given the opportunity to appeal to a higher level of management against any finding and/or sanction imposed. He is entitled to be accompanied at the disciplinary and appeal hearings by a union/employee representative or colleague of his choice.

If, when carrying out the investigation into the employee's misconduct, the company breached the Regulations and/or infringed the employee's right to privacy under Article 8 of the Human Rights Act, a tribunal may consider that the company has acted unreasonably and find that the dismissal is unfair.

The danger of jumping to conclusions and not allowing the employee an opportunity to put forward his or her side of the story is well illustrated by a US case in which a police officer was dismissed after his employers had carried out a review of his computer records and discovered that he had visited whitehouse.com, a pornographic site. The officer claimed that he had typed the address in error and that he had actually intended to visit the official site for the White House at whitehouse.gov.com. He successfully sued his employer and was awarded $100,000 in damages.

Group dismissals

Many of the news reports about dismissals for misuse of e-mail and the internet relate to groups of employees rather than individuals, no doubt because the dismissal of forty employees by a company for accessing and downloading pornography is far more newsworthy than a story about a single employee engaging in such conduct, unless that employee is a high-profile individual.

If the company reasonably believes that a number of employees in a particular area of the business are guilty of serious breaches of the policy, but despite carrying out a thorough investigation it cannot identify which employees are to blame, it may be reasonable to dismiss all of those who could have been responsible. This situation could arise if, for example, each of the employees identified by the company as having breached the policy, claims that one of his or her colleagues must have accessed their computer when they were out of the room and sent the defamatory e-mail or visited the inappropriate web-site.

The case of *Monie* v. *Coral Racing Ltd* [1998] IRLR 464 established the principle that where an employer believes that one or more of a number of employees is guilty of an offence and, despite proper investigation, cannot identify which of them is culpable, it may be reasonable for the employer to dismiss all those who could have been responsible.

In the case of *Parr* v. *Whitbread Plc t/a Thresher Wine Merchants* [1990] IRLR 39 the Employment Appeal Tribunal set out guidelines for tribunals faced with such group dismissals. It said that a tribunal should consider whether the acts of misconduct would justify dismissal if they were committed by an individual, whether the employer has carried out a reasonable investigation and whether as a result of that investigation, the employer has reasonable grounds to believe that more than one person could have committed the acts of misconduct. In addition, the employer has to show that it acted reasonably in identifying the employees who could have committed the acts and that it has established that each employee was individually capable of doing so. The employer also has to show that it could not identify the individual perpetrator.

5. In summary

Introduce a comprehensive e-mail and internet policy at the outset which stresses:

- prohibited uses;
- rules of etiquette in relation to e-mail;
- disciplinary penalties for breaching the policy;
- the fact that e-mails and internet access are not private;
- the company's policy on monitoring.

Ensure that the policy is communicated to all employees and that they receive training and regular updates on its provisions and implications.

Consider the extent to which monitoring is required in order to protect the company's interests. Take a cautious approach and, in particular:

- establish the specific business purpose for which the monitoring is to be introduced;
- target monitoring on those areas where it is necessary and proportionate to achieving the business purpose;
- carry out spot checks (rather than continuous monitoring of all employees) to assist the company in arguing the statutory defence to discrimination claims and in defending defamation claims;
- make reasonable efforts to inform third parties who use the system that their communications may be monitored.

Take a consistent approach to the management of employees who breach the policy. In response to a suspected breach:

- investigate thoroughly;
- do not jump to conclusions, allow the employee to put his side of the story;
- follow a fair disciplinary procedure and make provision for an appeal by the employee against any disciplinary sanction imposed.

9 From Bricks to Clicks: Taxation

Introduction

E-commerce taxation is not a term of science, and there are few UK tax provisions which specifically relate to it alone. Rather, general principles of tax law need to be taken and examined in the light of the particular business moving from bricks to clicks. In the future, this may change, as the advent of e-commerce poses one of the largest challenges facing fiscal authorities in recent years. The increasing popularity of B2B (business-to-business) and B2C (business-to-consumer) transactions highlights not only how wide the Inland Revenue and Customs and Excise tax nets are, but also how seemingly paperless transactions can fall within the gaps.

1. Tax challenges for the fiscal authorities

Fiscal authorities around the world are bracing themselves to face various challenges; and they must move quickly. What are the challenges? They include stemming the loss of revenue occurring as a result of paperless transactions, ensuring that the legislation is flexible enough to adapt to the changing behaviour of taxpayers, and meeting the demands of the public requiring an internet-based interface with the relevant tax authorities.

A recently stated, and perhaps ambitious, UK government plan is to have every UK resident online by 2005. The B2B and B2C opportunities (and resulting potential loss of revenue) are high on the priority list for the tax authorities.

2. Tax challenges for a business moving from bricks to clicks

The challenge for a business going from bricks to clicks is to stay ahead of competitors and meet customer demand for online services and products.

To help meet this challenge, a business must concern itself with both tax compliance and tax planning issues. These issues include:

- Choice of business vehicle, e.g. company, trust, sole trader, partnership, joint venture (consider also the need for asset and liability protection, applicable tax rates, the need for employees and particular compliance regimes).

   For the purposes of this chapter, we have assumed that the business is trading through a company, incorporated and resident in the UK for tax purposes. However, this chapter also discusses, at times, the position for a non-UK resident entity doing business in the UK.

- Determination of 'home jurisdiction'. Tax authorities view some instances of treaty shopping as being tax avoidance (there are commercial considerations that need to be applied to the location of the clicks enterprise). A business's home jurisdiction is the country that has primary taxing power over that business. Businesses cannot 'shop around' for the country that has the most favourable tax regime unless they can show that there are sound and commercial reasons for choosing that jurisdiction.

- Consider whether a 'presence' should be established in jurisdictions where a large amount of trade is expected (e.g. establishing a taxable presence in another country in the form of a company may entitle that company access to government concessions and certain tax reliefs in that country).

- If a presence is established, how will any profits / losses be repatriated back to the UK?

- For transactions remaining within the UK, consideration should also be given to the manner in which the income and losses flowing from the internet operations will be accounted for, and how the tax compliance regime will be satisfied.

- How will the start up costs and capital be treated?

- Can the UK company access any UK government concessions or incentive programmes and, if so, what needs to be done?

- What are the future intentions for the e-business if it is successful? And what if the e-business is not successful? Is the structure flexible enough to deal with either scenario? What will happen to the 'physical' business going forward?

- Will management agreements (or other instruments) be used to link the 'physical' business with the 'virtual' business as regards staff, intellectual property, goods and the like?

- How will the e-business trade? Will it need assets currently used or owned by the physical business? Will assets need to be transferred? Will the transfer of any business (or part of a business) satisfy the 'transfer of a business as a going concern' value added tax (VAT) rules?

- The business should consider whether it wishes to set up employee incentive plans to retain the best employees and to encourage others to join the team.

- What reliefs (if any) are available for registration of domain names and other intellectual property? What reliefs (if any) are available for any disposals of such assets and the related goodwill?
- How will the venture be financed?
- Will the company eventually be listed? What if the company is registered offshore and then seeks listing in the UK? (There may be a need to transfer some assets of the business back into the UK, which may trigger tax liabilities).

To enable a brief discussion of some of these issues, this chapter is divided as follows:

- General introduction to the UK tax regime, including VAT and stamp duty.
- Tax compliance issues.
- Government concessions and initiatives.
- Expanding the business in the UK.
- Expanding the business internationally.
- The future for e-business and e-commerce.

The Appendix to this book provides some web-site addresses that may prove useful when making the decision to move from bricks to clicks.

Just before moving on to introduce the UK tax regime, it is worth pausing briefly to consider how an e-business might be structured to engage in transactions over the internet. The two structures that are most common are:

1. Using the internet merely as an interface or virtual shop window whilst maintaining factories, store houses, employees and the like behind the scenes (perhaps in the UK). Under this scenario, the more traditional 'physical' shop is maintained.
2. Using the internet as a shop window, but selling a virtual form of the product (where applicable). For example, selling virtual books, which are downloaded by the paying consumer. This structure has particular tax implications, as we shall see, in relation to VAT.

Businesses making the decision to go from bricks to clicks are unlikely to be engaging in the latter kind of business at the initial stage of investment in e-business. Accordingly, this chapter will not focus on e-businesses selling 'virtual' products in significant detail.

3. General introduction to the UK tax regime for corporate business moving from bricks to clicks

To assist a review of e-commerce tax aspects for a business, it may be helpful to have a quick look at some of the UK concepts of direct tax, together with some basic concepts of VAT. Many of these concepts will be referred to later in this chapter.

3.1 Business asset taper relief

A significant measure contained in the 2002 Budget was the improvements to the business asset taper relief regime.

What is the business asset taper relief regime? Broadly, taper relief is available to reduce the chargeable gain on disposals made after 5 April 1998. Different rates of taper relief apply to business assets and non-business assets. The longer the asset is held, the greater the relief available.

Broadly, business assets include assets used in a business; shareholdings in unlisted trading companies; employee holdings of up to 10 per cent in non-trading companies; shareholding of 5 per cent or more in a quoted trading company; any shareholding in such a company held by any employee or director; and assets held by a shareholder, whose shares are business assets and are used in the company's trade.

Pursuant to the 2002 Budget, maximum taper relief is available after the asset has been held for two years (previously, taxpayers had to hold the asset for four years to obtain maximum relief). A higher rate taxpayer will achieve an effective tax rate of 10 per cent for disposals of business assets held for two years.

The new regime applies to all disposals on or after 6 April 2002 and not just to disposals of assets held for more than two years after 6 April 2002.

Taper relief for non-business assets remains unchanged as at the date of writing. A chargeable gain is eligible for taper relief for a non-business asset with a qualifying holding period of at least three years.

The rules outlined above are complex. The obtaining of maximum taper relief is notoriously capricious and specific advice should be sought on whether you meet the conditions to obtain taper relief.

Where taper relief falls to be applied to the whole or any part of a gain on the disposal of a business or non-business asset, that relief is applied by multiplying the amount of that gain or part of a gain by a specified percentage.

3.2 UK direct tax

If a bricks to clicks business is being run through the medium of a UK resident company, then perhaps the first tax to consider is corporation tax. A company resident in the UK pays corporation tax on the whole of its world-wide profits (subject to double tax relief for foreign taxes).

A company not resident in the UK, but which has UK source profits, is charged corporation tax on its UK source profits only if it trades through a branch or agency in the UK, and if the UK source profits are derived through that branch or agency. Where the non-UK resident company is resident in a country with which the UK has a Double Tax Agreement (DTA), the branch or agency in the UK must be a 'permanent establishment'. (The concept of permanent establishment is discussed later in this chapter under the heading 'Expanding the Business Internationally'.)

It is also worth noting that a non-UK resident company which does not have a branch or agency in the UK, although not liable to corporation tax, will be liable to income tax on its UK source profits (e.g. rents from UK property) at the basic rate of tax.

A UK resident company is potentially liable to pay corporation tax on any chargeable gains arising from the disposal of an asset. If an asset has been the subject of capital allowances, these are deducted from the acquisition value as part of the calculation of any chargeable gain.

Capital gains may be set off against capital losses only in the same or in future accounting periods, and they may not be surrendered to reduce the capital gains of another company in the same tax group (although new rules introduced in the Finance Act 2001 have helped in this regard).

What about trading losses? Broadly these may be set off against income or capital profits for the accounting period in which the loss is made or surrendered to reduce the profits of a company within the same group (subject to suitable elections). Trading losses may also be carried back to be set off against profits of the preceding accounting period, or carried forward indefinitely against profits from the same trade.

What about income tax for directors and employees of the company? Directors' and employees' liability to income tax is usually recovered by the deduction of tax at source, under the PAYE (Pay As You Earn) system. Under the PAYE system, the company will deduct from the directors' or employees' salary the appropriate amount of income tax and national insurance contributions, and account for those deductions to the UK Revenue. The company will also have to account for the employer's national insurance contributions on most payments made or benefits provided to employees or associates of employees.

Direct tax implications for the business

So, what can be made of these direct tax aspects when considering a clicks business? Any e-commerce transactions that remain wholly within the boundaries of the UK do not pose any greater risk to the UK tax base than any transactions which are undertaken by the bricks business within the UK. The transactions will need to be recorded, the corporation tax computed, and the amounts to be paid included in the company's self-assessment return. The tax (and VAT) implications of expanding the business in the UK are dealt with in greater detail below. However, it is when the cross-border and international tax (and VAT) issues arise that the threats to the tax base occur.

3.3 Value added tax

Value added tax (VAT) is a tax on business supplies of goods and services, and on imported goods. It is levied by Customs and Excise on supplies made by a 'taxable person' in the UK in the course or furtherance of a business. VAT is also an EU-legislated tax, stemming from a series of European Community (EC) Directives. The primary UK source of legislation on VAT is the Value Added Tax Act 1994, with much of the detail contained in Regulations and Orders. Where UK legislation is clearly in conflict with EC law, EC law prevails.

The principle behind VAT is that it should be borne ultimately by the consumer of the goods and services supplied. If a company is registered for VAT, then generally it will be able to deduct an amount equal to VAT on supplies made to it from the VAT charged by it on its supplies, and it will only account to Customs and Excise for the difference. VAT is, therefore, paid on the 'value added' at each stage of the supply to the ultimate consumer.

Supplies are divided into three main categories – standard rated (in the UK, this is 17½ per cent), zero rated (0 per cent) and exempt. If a supplier makes exempt supplies, then it is treated as the ultimate consumer: it is neither required to account for VAT on supplies it makes, nor is it able to recover VAT on supplies it receives which are attributable to those exempt supplies.

It was announced in the 2002 Budget that there will be a new flat rate of VAT for small businesses in a government effort to reduce the VAT administrative burden. The flat rate will be made available to taxpayers with:

- no more than £100,000 taxable supplies; and
- no more than £125,000 total business income.

The flat rate will be available from 25 April 2002.

The government hopes that the flat rate scheme will save business time by removing the need to calculate and record output tax and input tax to calculate the net VAT due to Customs. Taxpayers simply record the VAT-inclusive value of all their business supplies in a period – including exempt supplies. Taxpayers then apply the flat rate percentage for their trade sector to your total income and that is the VAT you pay. Advice should be sought on the applicable flat rate.

In relation to goods, exports (outside of the EU) are within the scope of VAT (but generally zero rated), whereas generally imports are supplies which are outside the scope of VAT albeit subject to 'import VAT' (see further on imports and exports below). The position with supplies of services is a little different. The basic rule is that services are treated as supplied where the supplier 'belongs' for VAT. Generally, the location of the supply mirrors the location of the supplier. A supplier will belong in a country if he or she has a business establishment in that country, or if there is no business establishment, the relevant location will be where the supplier resides. If the supplier has both a usual place of residence and a business establishment in different countries, then Customs and Excise will determine which country has the closest link for connection to the supply. There are a number of important exemptions to this rule, including:

- where a supply of services is made in relation to land, that service is treated as supplied in the country where the land is situated;
- where a person supplies, say, certain intellectual property, consultancy services and staff (in VAT jargon, 'Schedule 5 Services'), to a person who belongs outside the UK and in a country (other than the Isle of Man) that is not within the EU, the supply is treated as made in the country where the recipient belongs. The supply of such services is, therefore, outside the scope of the VAT;
- where a person belonging in the UK makes a Schedule 5 service to a person who belongs outside the UK but in a country that is within the EU, the supply is treated as made in the member state where the recipient belongs. The supply of such services is, therefore, outside the scope of UK VAT if the recipient receives the supply for the purpose of a business carried on by him.

The VAT rules relating to the import and export of goods and services within and outside the EU are complex and fraught with numerous exemptions and exceptions, which are beyond the scope of this chapter. Please seek specialist advice if your Clicks business will be providing services or supplying goods outside the UK.

Further on, this chapter refers to the 'VAT group'. Two or more companies may be registered as a group for VAT purposes if one 'controls' the other(s) (control is taken from the Companies Act 1985 definition, e.g. if a company held a majority of voting rights in another company it would exercise 'control').

A group has to be registered as a group, and its members must be registered as part of that group. Within a VAT group, one member, called the 'representative member', is responsible for completing the VAT returns of the whole group and is liable for the payment of the whole group's VAT (although this liability is joint and several between VAT group members). The additional consequences are:

- transactions between members of the VAT group are outside the scope of VAT; and
- the representative member is treated as making and receiving all supplies on behalf of the group.

There are many anti-avoidance provisions in this area, and Customs and Excise have the power to refuse group VAT status to groups of companies to 'protect the revenue'.

In the 2002 Budget, the Chancellor announced changes to VAT law in a stated effort to ease the VAT burden on businesses. The following are the broad VAT changes:

- easing the impact of VAT on small and medium-sized enterprises by:
  - increasing the VAT registration threshold from £54,000 to £55,000,
  - introducing an optional flat rate scheme designed to cut compliance costs (see above), and
  - reforming the VAT annual accounting scheme;
- the arrangements for VAT bad debt relief will be simplified, removing the requirement for supplier business to send letters to their debtors notifying them that they are claiming relief.

Indirect tax

What will the impact of indirect tax be upon the clicks business? In many cases, where the transactions are wholly within the UK, the VAT rules will apply as usual; use of the internet should have no effect on VAT liability. Once again, the threat to the VAT base occurs when cross-border and international transactions are considered, and this will be explored in the section dealing with expanding the business internationally.

Stamp duty

Stamp duty is a 'tax' on certain documents or instruments (usually those evidencing transactions). From a practical perspective, the e-commerce business medium hails a new era of paperless transactions, and individuals (as taxpayers and as business people) should be aware of the steps that the Inland Revenue may take to avoid any potential loss of revenue.

Most bricks to clicks businesses will maintain a physical presence here in the UK, which means that they should not incur any additional stamp duty obligations (other than the ones with which they should already be familiar and comply with). Accordingly, the Inland Revenue will still be able to access its normal revenue base. For example, real property sales will remain identifiable, ascertainable and dutiable and the requirement that share transfers be lodged with the appropriate government bodies such as Companies House is intended to stop any taxpayer avoiding paying stamp duty on share transfers. The two-level 'supervision' system should help to ensure that individuals meet all their stamp duty responsibilities whether or not they trade over the internet.

One relevant issue is ascertaining the jurisdiction of execution for e-commerce transactions. Broadly, documents executed offshore are not dutiable in the UK until they are brought back into the UK (albeit that interest or penalties might be payable from the date of execution). Note, however, the

2002 Budget amendments will extend the current penalty regime for documents executed in the UK to documents executed outside the UK where they relate to UK land or buildings. In this regard, the business might wish to consider setting up its infrastructure abroad (whilst taking into account the other aspects – such as the inability to obtain government concessions and reliefs discussed elsewhere in this chapter) if it does not or is unlikely to require the executed documents in the UK. However, it is worth noting that documents cannot be presented in English courts unless they are properly stamped, that stamp duty is payable on certain assets regardless of where the document is executed and that a non-UK 'home jurisdiction' may have stamp duty charges of its own (which, in turn, may be at higher rates than those in the UK).

At present it is difficult to ascertain when execution occurs in virtual transactions, and as a consequence of that execution, at what stage stamp duty becomes payable, if at all. Businesses should keep a close eye on Inland Revenue press releases to keep up to date with government announcements (if and when they are made) regarding the stamp duty and e-commerce relationship.

Significant anti-avoidance and simplification measures were introduced for stamp duty as part of the 2002 Budget. One important measure is that there will be no stamp duty on transfers of and agreements to transfer goodwill. Further changes are heralded as part of a stamp duty rewrite expected next year (paving the way for 'e-conveyancing'). It is stated that the reform will build on recent measures to tackle avoidance, and will:

- Support the government's e-business agenda, in particular the introduction of paperless electronic conveyancing, and
- Update the framework of the tax, bringing it into line with more modern taxes.

4. Compliance

To date, neither the Inland Revenue nor Customs and Excise has specifically addressed the e-commerce compliance hurdle. However, as discussed below, they are encouraging taxpayers to submit tax returns and lodge forms over the internet to assist them with administration. This may lead to some form of e-commerce compliance regime, which will attempt to catch e-commerce transactions. Given that any move in this regard would have significant impact, there is likely to be considerable press coverage, which will instruct taxpayers new to the clicks business on what to do.

4.1 Electronic submission of tax returns

Both the Inland Revenue and Customs and Excise are considering, or have already commenced, programmes to facilitate the lodging of VAT and corporate tax returns electronically.

The UK government has proposed to offer a discount to small businesses and individuals who file their tax returns via the internet, and who pay the tax due electronically in an effort to encourage wider uptake of internet technology. In fact, the 2002 Budget confirmed that the government would begin implementation of a three-stage process of universal electronic filing of employer returns, with incentive payments to assist and encourage smaller employers to make greater use of IT.

Going forward, employers will be able to send and receive a wide range of PAYE forms and returns via the internet. VAT-registered businesses will also be able to download and lodge their tax returns over the internet.

The discount will be linked to each of the new services offered as part of the internet lodging programme. If more than one service is used, it may be possible to qualify for more than one discount. The discounts are being made available for one year for each service although Customs and Excise is also considering a longer period in which businesses may file their VAT returns via the internet. The idea behind the discounts is that they should lead to administrative savings and enhanced customer service by offering business and taxpayers alike new ways of dealing with their tax affairs.

The budget allocation for the discounts appears to be an extra £50 for online filing for small employers paying a tax credit to their employees. The discount only applies to those who file their PAYE end of year returns over the Internet and pay any tax due electronically, and is in addition to the £50 discount for VAT and PAYE incentives. This gives a total potential discount on online filing of £150.

A business registered for VAT, which has a turnover of less than £600,000 per annum, may be entitled to a one-off payment. Receipt of the payment is upon the first lodging of the VAT return and electronic payment of any tax liabilities over the internet. The service was launched on 1 April 2001 and the incentive payments will be available for a period of one year. The payment will be automatically credited to the business's account with Customs and Excise.

The internet lodging service will be available to businesses outside office hours and will offer automatic calculation of some tax liabilities, immediate online acknowledgement of receipt and online guidance. Any outstanding earlier returns can also be sent electronically. By paying electronically, businesses will be entitled (with a few exceptions) to a seven-day extension period to lodge their tax return and to pay any tax due. Customs and Excise plan further enhancements to this service, including an online direct debit facility for payment and fuller online help and guidance.

Customs and Excise and the Inland Revenue state they are committed to tax returns being lodged via the internet. It is therefore vital that businesses going from bricks to clicks become familiar with this technology and use it to their advantage.

4.2 E-invoicing

One of the cornerstones of the VAT system is that of the VAT invoice. The issue and receipt of a correct VAT invoice is crucial to enable businesses to recover VAT and also to 'on-charge' their VAT costs. The issue in the world of e-commerce is the lack of paper or physical records in any one transaction. The question arises as to how customers are going to be able to issue and receive invoices in respect of transactions they make over the internet when there is no paper evidence of that transaction with another individual and/or his/her e-commerce business.

Customs and Excise have stated that they view the compliance obligations for e-commerce trading in the UK as the same as for any other UK VAT-registered trader.

Customs and Excise require businesses to maintain records regarding e-commerce transactions in a way that is easily and readily convertible into a reasonably legible form. Customs and Excise may require access to office computer systems to check their operation and the information stored. As part of setting up an e-business, it is necessary to be aware of the following:

1. E-commerce records or other electronic records that are encrypted will need to be decrypted and produced in a legible form upon demand.
2. Businesses which have records stored on a web server that is outside the UK are still responsible for producing them to Customs and Excise.
3. A business that uses a third party to run their e-commerce business will still be responsible for arranging for those records to be made available to Customs and Excise on request.
4. A business that currently runs an existing or physical business and then decides to enter into e-commerce should notify the VAT business advice centre in their particular area.
5. A business that uses a computer for VAT accounting should also notify the VAT business advice centre. Customs and Excise retain the power to refuse or withdraw approval for the use of computer media to store records and accounts in any individual case if Customs and Excise requirements cannot be met.

4.3 Expanding the business in the UK

What happens if a business wants to expand? It may be a bricks business wishing to move to clicks, or it may be a bricks business and an embryonic clicks business that require outside investment. It may be commercially attractive to 'hive down' the clicks business into a wholly owned UK-incorporated subsidiary to allow outside investment into that company with both an eye to a future initial public offer (IPO), and to limit the liability of that business should things not go according to plan. Do the tax rules facilitate a 'tax-free' hive-down? What about tax losses which may be made by clicks in the early years, whilst the bricks business makes profits? Are supplies of goods and services between the parent and subsidiary liable to VAT? Is it possible to obtain outside investment in a tax-efficient manner?

Hive down, losses and group supplies

If the bricks parent company hives down its clicks business into a newly formed and wholly owned subsidiary (Newco), what are the tax implications? The following example is based on the assumption that prior to the hive-down, the clicks business consists of a domain name, other intellectual property, existing contracts, computer hardware and some employees. The Newco will pay cash in consideration of the business, the amount to be left outstanding on inter-company loan account, and will receive a licence to occupy the premises owned by the bricks parent, and pay a management charge to bricks for help in running its business.

It should be possible to effect the hive down of the clicks business in most cases without giving rise to any immediate tax liability. Taking the main tax issues in turn:

- *Income*: Care needs to be taken with any transfer of trading stock, IP rights, goodwill or work in progress to ensure tax does not arise for parent company Bricks. In this regard, transfer at cost is more common.
- *Chargeable gains*: Transfers of capital assets (the domain name, other intellectual property and possibly contracts) may give rise to a liability to corporation tax for parent company (Bricks) on chargeable gains. How-ever, transfers of assets within a 75 per cent group (very broadly, a holding company and its subsidiaries, provided at least 75 per cent of the ordinary share capital is beneficially owned by the holding company and the holding company has more than 50 per cent economic ownership) generally take place on a no gain/no loss basis. In this case, Clicks is wholly owned by Bricks so forms a 75 per cent group. Clicks/Newco would inherit Brick's indexed base cost in the assets, regardless of the actual price paid. Note that any sale of Newco within six years of the hive down may trigger a tax charge for Newco.
- *Capital losses*: It is not generally possible for Bricks to transfer any capital losses made by Clicks to Newco.
- *Trading losses*: Where a business is transferred, the transferee will generally

step into the shoes of the transferor, so far as the tax position of the trade is concerned. So, Newco should inherit any trading losses, which have arisen in the Bricks trade. It should be noted that the amount of losses that may be carried forward will be restricted if Bricks retains liabilities and the amount of those liabilities is greater than the sum of the value of assets retained by Bricks and the consideration given by Newco. The carried forward losses may be used by Newco against the Clicks business. You should be aware that there are anti-avoidance provisions in this area, which may, for example, 'bite' where there is a post-acquisition reorganisation.

- *Stamp duty*: Normally, Newco would be liable to pay stamp duty at the rate of 4 per cent (subject to certificates of value being presented if the consideration were less than £500,000) on the value of any stampable assets it acquired. However, as this is a transfer of part of a business within a 75 per cent group (broadly, the test being aligned with the group relief rules), it should be possible to apply to the Inland Revenue Stamp Office for relief from stamp duty subject to the new intra-group anti-avoidance rules brought in the 2002 Budget. Once again, there are particular anti-avoidance provisions which have to be considered with great care when contemplating this relief.

- *VAT*: There should be no VAT payable on the transfer:
  - Transfers of a part of a business should generally be outside the scope of VAT as it is considered a transfer of a business as a going concern (TOGC). Special rules apply where real property is transferred as part of the TOCG, and adjustments may be required under the capital goods scheme;
  - The transfer of a business, within a VAT group, is outside the scope of VAT. If Bricks, the parent company, and Newco are not part of a VAT group, it may be appropriate to apply to Customs and Excise to VAT group them. This should also be helpful going forward, as any supplies of goods and services between Bricks and Clicks will then be outside the scope of VAT. It will be possible to register Bricks and Clicks as part of the same VAT group, as the parent company, Bricks, wholly owns Newco.

However, as always, specific advice should be sought in this regard.

4.4 Attracting outside investment in a tax-efficient manner

Are there ways to attract tax-efficient investment into the Clicks business? The UK government offers encouragement by way of tax relief under various schemes. Although the schemes are relatively simple in concept, they are extremely complex due to anti-avoidance provisions and the government believing that, in the past, investors have obtained tax relief on a 'guaranteed return'. The three main tax reliefs are as follows.

Corporate venturing scheme

The Inland Revenue has produced a booklet, IR 2000, giving details of this scheme. It is intended to encourage companies to invest in small higher risk 'trading companies' (see further our discussion of EIS and VCT relief below), and to form wider corporate venture relationships. The investee company (the company in which the investment is made) must not be a 51 per cent subsidiary of another company (so, for example, any investment would have to be into the Bricks parent company), and financial companies that invest by way of business are not eligible for relief.

If the scheme applies, then any company investing in the investee business will get 20 per cent corporation tax relief on cash subscriptions for new ordinary shares in the qualifying unquoted small company, providing the investing company has received from the investee company a certificate of compliance that the requirements for investment relief are met. The relief will be withdrawn in certain circumstances, including if the investing company disposes of the shares within three years. When the investing company disposes of the shares, tax on any chargeable gain arising may be deferred to the extent that any gain is reinvested, within prescribed periods, in another corporate venture holding. Note that the investing company must not control, for the purposes of the relief, the investee company.

Sale of substantial shareholdings

The 2002 Budget confirmed that there would be an exemption from a charge to tax, on any capital gains accruing to a company on the sale of a shareholding in another company, where that shareholding is a 'substantial holding'. This may prove particularly helpful to any potential corporate investor in the company.

The UK government took the view that increased business efficiency, and a greater ability for UK companies to compete in the world marketplace, would be achieved by relaxing the capital gains rules to remove an immediate tax charge when companies rationalise their substantial shareholdings. It is also aimed at ensuring that important decisions on corporate restructuring and reinvestment are made for commercial, rather than tax reasons.

The basic conditions for full exemption from corporation tax on chargeable gains are:

- a qualifying shareholder company; which
- has held a substantial shareholding in a qualifying company (a trading company or the holding company of a trading group) throughout a twelve-month period; and which
- realises a gain on the disposal of shares in that company.

A substantial shareholding is to be fixed at a 10 per cent shareholding level.

Venture Capital Trusts (VCTs) and Enterprise Investment Schemes (EIS)

Broadly, these enable individuals to obtain tax relief on their investment in the company when made through a VCT or through the EIS scheme.

VCTs

Individuals may invest in a quoted vehicle (VCTs are companies listed on the London Stock Exchange), which in turn invests in the debt and equity of different unquoted small companies. An individual investing through a VCT may obtain

- income tax relief on the shares subscribed for at the rate of 20 per cent on up to £100,000;
- deferral of capital gains tax on a chargeable gain from the disposal of any asset where the gain is invested in shares or which income tax relief is obtained;
- exemption from capital gains tax on the disposal of any ordinary shares;
- exemption from income tax on dividends on ordinary shares;
- deferral of capital gains tax on a chargeable gain from the disposal of any asset where the gain is invested in shares for which income tax relief is obtained.

The relief will be withdrawn if the shares are disposed of within three years, or if the VCT loses its qualifying status (note that pursuant to the 2002 Budget, VCTs will retain their status where they merge with one another or are wound up).

Gains arising on the disposal of shares that were acquired by subscription or purchase up to the £100,000 limit in any year are exempt from CGT (and any losses are not allowable). There is also a mechanism to allow individuals to defer CGT when they reinvest the gain made on the disposal of any assets in VCT shares.

The precise rules for VCTs are complex and beyond the scope of this chapter. However, the company must be a 'qualifying trading company' and the total gross assets of that company and any companies within the group must not exceed £15 million immediately before the VCT acquired its shares, or £16 million immediately afterwards.

EIS relief

EIS relief is available for individuals who make direct investments in certain unquoted companies. The EIS is designed to help small, high risk, unquoted trading companies raise start up and expansion finance by issuing full risk ordinary shares.

The money must be used for a qualifying business activity – that is the company must carry on a qualifying trade (or be preparing to do so) or research and development.

Income tax and capital gains tax relief is available to individuals investing in unconnected companies. The relief includes:

- income tax relief (at 20 per cent) on the amount invested (of up to £150,000 per tax year) and relief from capital gains tax on disposal of the shares, provided that they are held for at least three years after issue although sometimes time begins running at the time the trade for which the money was raised begins;
- relief for most allowable losses on the shares against either income or chargeable gains; and
- deferral of capital gains on a chargeable gain from the disposal of any asset where the gain is reinvested in the shares.

Deferral relief is sometimes available to people who have a past connection with the company but again, there are conditions attached which extend beyond the scope of this chapter.

There are a number of conditions that must be satisfied before individuals can access the tax concessions available under the EIS and VCT schemes. Indeed, there are also conditions governing companies seeking to obtain VCT, EIS or similar tax status. These conditions can be relatively complex.

For companies seeking status as a VCT or EIS, they must, by way of example:

- carry on a qualifying trade wholly or mainly in the UK;
- be quoted or listed if applying for VCT status;
- be unquoted or unlisted if applying for status as an EIS;
- obtain approval in writing from the Inland Revenue.

For individuals seeking income tax, and capital gains tax relief, they must establish (as an example) that they:

- have held the shares for more than three years;
- do not exceed the maximum investment threshold;
  - £100,000 for VCT;
  - £150,000 for EIS;
- be unconnected to the company in which they invest (as a broad and general rule).

Note that the criteria are complex and specific advice should be sought.

5. Expanding the business internationally

So, what is the tax position where it is proposed to expand a clicks business across EU borders or internationally? What are the international tax rules, and how will they affect the business? First, the broad international direct tax principles will be considered followed by a look at some cross-border/international VAT issues. In this section, the position of the non-UK resident entity, who may wish to transact with the clicks business, will be considered.

5.1 International direct tax principles

Broadly, the taxation of international transactions is based on concepts of residency: tax authorities have jurisdiction to tax business entities that are resident in their jurisdiction or derive income in their jurisdiction.

Double tax agreements

Double tax agreements (DTAs) generally carry the weight of legislation and constitute agreements between two countries governing the tax treatment of transactions effected between those two jurisdictions. The DTAs govern who has taxing rights over the specific transaction. DTAs also act to reduce the withholding tax obligations (generally payable on interest, dividends and royalty income) as compared with transactions outside Treaty member countries. Tax havens, such as the British Virgin Islands, do not, as a general rule, enter into DTAs with many countries and the withholding rates are higher.

Taxable presence

A company will be resident in the country in which it is registered and/or in which the management and control of that company is located. Generally, that country's taxation authorities will then be able to tax the company on its world-wide profits and gains.

If a person carrying on trade in the UK is able to do so without establishing a branch or agency (degrees of taxable presence which are determined on an analysis of the facts) in the UK, then the profits from the trade will escape UK tax.

One of the things that tax authorities will review when examining whether a branch or agency exists is where the contracts of the business are concluded (and sometimes even performed). Another test is to determine where the business operations take place and locate where the profits in substance arise.

The concept of permanent establishment is often bandied around in international transactions. In countries which have entered into DTAs with each other, business ventures are generally assessed to see whether they constitute a permanent establishment and, accordingly, are taxable in the host jurisdiction to the extent that the profit is derived in that jurisdiction. A basic definition of permanent establishment is a *'fixed place of business through which the business of an enterprise is carried on'*(Article 5 (1) OECD Model Treaty). The maintenance of storage facilities, conducting display and delivery activities or activities aimed at the collection of information do not generally constitute permanent establishment. The use of an agent can attract the status of permanent establishment; however, the use of an independent agent, acting in the ordinary course of business as an agent, will not generally constitute permanent establishment.

The problem with international e-commerce transactions is that a taxable presence can be very hard to isolate. Even e-commerce businesses transacting through companies can still (whether intentionally or not) mask transactions via the use of sophisticated technology and thereby reduce the income flowing through the UK presence, and increase income flowing through other structures (for example, a presence in a tax haven).

Transfer pricing

Broadly, a transfer pricing regime seeks to ensure that related parties who transact do so at 'arm's length' (except, generally, where the transaction is within the UK). This is something to bear in mind when setting up a company resident outside the UK as part of the move from bricks to clicks.

Under the transfer pricing rules, the business will be required to lodge corporation tax self-assessment returns on the basis that transactions are effected on an arm's length basis, and accordingly, the business will pay tax on any income derived from those transactions using those arm's length values. Conversely, losses must be accounted for in the tax returns as if they were incurred in effecting arms length transactions between related parties. The concept of related parties is broad and may catch parties holding 40 per cent of the issued share capital in one of the transacting parties.

The transfer pricing rules, from an e-commerce perspective, are currently under consideration by the Organisation for Economic Cooperation and Development (OECD). However, it is not anticipated that radical change will be needed to bring any OECD recommendations into effect in the UK.

The more pressing concerns, from an Inland Revenue perspective, are practical – such as the identification of parties, transactions, transaction values and finding similar transactions to assist in determining what constitutes 'market value' for an infinite range of transactions which may occur over the internet.

The other problem that the Inland Revenue faces is the plethora of intellectual property and intangible assets being used in internet-based transactions, especially those occurring between group members situated in and outside of the EU. This is problematic because it is difficult to trace the use of such assets (and therefore difficult to assess against arm's length rules), and may avoid the taxation net (to the extent that transactions are not at arm's length). This is discussed further below.

The application of the transfer pricing rules (an arm's length requirement) is made more difficult in an e-commerce environment because there may not be third party transactions which are referable to the transaction under examination by the Inland Revenue. In other words, in e-commerce it may prove difficult to compare non-virtual transactions (historically more of a known quantity) with those 'virtual' e-commerce transactions.

Application to e-commerce

The concepts discussed above pose a significant problem to international tax authorities. Consider the example of a web-site.

If a web-site hosted by a non-UK resident merely offers information to prospective customers (that is, it is an advertising medium), then this is unlikely to constitute trading in the UK and is unlikely to be taxed in the UK. The position is likely to be similar if a UK company with a web-site located in the UK liases with a customer resident abroad.

However, the position is less clear where the customer actually interacts with the supplier through the web-site or actually effects purchases through the web-site. Consider the following: if the only presence which a non-UK resident has in the UK is an interactive web-site that is accessible from the UK and upon which UK customers may place orders, it is likely that this is not a sufficient presence to amount to a branch or a permanent establishment in the UK (although this will not be conclusive). If the non-resident's physical operations are located outside the UK, it should therefore escape UK tax (but not necessarily the other country's taxes) on its profits, but this will ultimately depend on the facts.

Current OECD thinking seems to suggest that a web-site is nothing more than software and data and therefore it amounts to intangible property. Accordingly, it cannot constitute a place of business for the purpose of constituting a permanent establishment. It follows, therefore, if a business has a web-site accessible from the UK, but has no other presence in the UK, then its profits should escape UK tax. The same arguments should apply for a clicks business conducting activities abroad.

The position gets even more complicated when a server is introduced into the equation. If the server is operated from a location in the UK, it adds an element of tangibility, which may be enough to constitute a permanent establishment. This means that the tax authorities may have jurisdiction where the server is itself physically located in the UK. There has been no final determination as at the date of writing as to whether a server constitutes a permanent establishment, however, the OECD is trying to establish that a server together with a web-site can constitute a permanent establishment.

Compare this position to using a third party ISP. A third party ISP may be an independent agent for tax purposes (as discussed above), and the 'structure' may fall outside of being a permanent establishment.

If the server was found to be used exclusively by a non-resident in connection with trading activities then it may constitute a permanent establishment and would be taxable in that jurisdiction. Similarly, automatic equipment (operated without human intervention) can be classified as a permanent establishment where it amounts to the conduct of a business. Again, this depends on the facts in each case.

A careful analysis of the facts and an understanding of the party's intentions are vital. The degree of permanence indicated by a web-site, server location and other technological advancements is a vital consideration before embarking on a bricks to clicks enterprise, especially if international sales are anticipated, because the enterprise may find itself with tax liabilities in numerous jurisdictions that it may not have anticipated and accounted for.

5.2 Application of VAT

It is in the realm of cross-border and international e-commerce that defects are exposed in the VAT rules. It is worth distinguishing between goods and services sold over the internet (which the clicks business may start up with), and the sale of digitised products over the Internet (which the clicks business may expand into).

5.3 Goods and services sold over the internet

Here, the general rules outlined in the introduction to VAT will apply. As discussed, the sale of goods is relatively straightforward, but the supply of services is quite complex. Even so, the rules should operate to allow VAT to be charged as appropriate. However, the concern is the leakage of VAT in respect of B2C transactions as there is no 'reverse charge' mechanism and it is difficult to police services supplied from outside the EU into the EU. Various solutions have been explored, including the use of sophisticated technology and legislation placing the onus on the supplier to check the identity of the buyer.

5.4 Supplies of digitised products

A clicks business may be sophisticated enough to take goods and services and transform them into a digitised format that may be downloaded directly onto a computer. Examples of digitised products would include photographs, software updates, films, games and music. In line with international agreements, supplies of digitised products are treated as services for VAT purposes. Compare this to the original versions of these products, which have largely been treated as goods for VAT purposes.

Customs and Excise have issued guidance that the supply of music, films and games should be taxed where the supplier belongs. This creates difficulties, as the supplier will have to charge VAT, whereas those products in non-digitised forms would be zero rated when exported outside the EU. Customs and Excise believe that 'off-the-shelf' software, certain intellectual property rights, the provision of services by experts, the sale of domain names, and the provision of online information should be treated as a Schedule 5 service (i.e. where the recipient belongs). Customs and Excise have also indicated that where a package of digitised products, including domain names, Internet connecting and web hosting, are provided, those will also be treated as the provision of a Schedule 5 service. There are particular difficulties with this Customs and Excise treatment of digitised works of fiction and digitised works of fact. Digitised fiction is taxed where the supplier belongs, whereas digitised fact is taxed where the recipient belongs! This is a very complex area and it may be that zero rating for supplies of books eventually disappears.

Recently, EU Ministers agreed to issue a uniform set of rules concerning VAT invoices and digitised products. The Ministers agreed that there will be a single standard form of VAT invoice for use in all Member States, which must include the same information and will follow similar lines to the standard VAT invoice that we are used to.

The Directive requires Member States to accept digital invoices where it can be established that the origin and integrity of the data are confirmed using either electronic signatures or electronic data interchange (EDI).

The Directive will authorise businesses and taxpayers to store invoices electronically. The Directive must be implemented by 1 January 2004.

6. Applicability of government tax concessions and initiatives

The British government's stated aim is to make the UK the best environment in the world for e-commerce. As part of this plan, there are a number of government incentives and concessions which may be applicable to a bricks to clicks business.

6.1 Filing systems

As discussed, both the Inland Revenue and Customs and Excise are introducing (or have introduced) internet filing systems, which include a tax incentive for internet filed returns. This is discussed elsewhere in this chapter.

6.2 Development costs

Web-site design and development costs

Tax payers can claim a 100 per cent first year capital allowance on the costs of purchasing a ready-made web-site or other costs they incur in creating and designing a web-site. The 100 per cent first year capital allowance is available providing that the web-site is set up for the taxpayer's business. It does not matter whether the web-site is used for e-commerce or is merely a promotional site.

Taxpayers can normally claim 100 per cent first year capital allowances on the cost of acquiring their web-site name or domain name as part of setting up their web-site. Exceptionally, taxpayers may pay a significant amount to secure a particular domain name. In such a case, the cost of acquiring the domain name will not qualify for capital allowances at all and it is not an allowable expense.

Employee costs

It is common in the commercial world to supply subsidiary businesses with employees via a management or services agreement. Any income received by the parent company, in this case, the existing business (pursuant to the management agreement) will generally be income and will be taxable as such. Conversely, the costs incurred by the recipient company, in this case the Internet or e-commerce company, should be deductible as a business expense.

Creation of intellectual property, information technology and goodwill

New rules apply to the taxation of intellectual property from 1 April 2002. The new treatment will bring the tax treatment of intangible assets into line with their accounting treatment. The new rules will apply to all intangible assets including goodwill. The new rules will not generally apply to existing assets (except in the case of reinvestment relief and royalty payments). Tax relief will be available for the purchase of intangible assets in line with the depreciation used in the accounts. Profits and losses arising on the sale of intangible assets will be taxed and relieved as income as opposed to capital. For those assets not depreciated in the accounts, a straight-line deduction will be available. Reinvestment relief will be available for gains (profits) arising on the disposal of intangible assets, where the sales proceeds are invested in shares in the company which has assets within the new regime, provided that the holding is at least 75 per cent. Finally, other related party transactions will be deemed to have occurred at market value.

Specifically, regard should be had to the following points:

1. Tax relief will be available for the purchase price of intangible assets (including goodwill) and it will be available as it is written off (amortised) in the company accounts.

2. A tax deferral will be available for gains arising on the disposal of intangible assets which are reinvested in the purchase of other intangible assets.

Companies moving from bricks to clicks and seeking to rely on the new tax provision for intellectual property will need to note the following:

1. They are effective only from 1 April 2002.
2. These are complex and will require companies to adopt new record-keeping requirements.

6.3 Capital allowances

Capital allowances for existing assets

The capital allowances regime allows businesses to write off certain kinds of capital expenditure as deductions. Depending on the nature and amount of the capital expenditure, a capital allowance can be claimed immediately or over a period of years. The rules governing when an amount can be claimed immediately rather than over a period of years vary depending upon what kind of expenditure is being dealt with. Generally, the tax authorities say that the taxpayer is not entitled to exercise any choice over which method applies in particular circumstances.

Capital allowances can be claimed for capital equipment that is, broadly, purchased and used in a trade or profession or used for the maintenance or repair of business assets.

Capital allowances should be claimed in the tax return. The calculation of the allowance depends on the type of asset involved. The types of assets that Internet or e-commerce businesses may come across include:

- machinery and plant, including computer software;
- industrial buildings such as factories;
- know-how and patents;
- scientific research or research and development.

There are many conditions and requirements that taxpayers must meet before they are entitled to access the capital allowance relief provisions. By way of example, capital allowances are available to non-residents in respect of a trade to the extent that the trade is assessable in the UK, that is, subject to UK corporation and VAT tax regimes.

There are proposals for an increase in specific capital allowance incentives for technology-based investments. There will be a 100 per cent first year allowance for spending by small businesses on information and communications technology over the next three years. The types of technology covered include computer equipment, communication technology and software including software assisting in the creation of a web-site. The allowance will not be available for leasing or letting on hire transactions.

There will be an additional 40 per cent allowance for investment in machinery and plant by small and medium sized businesses. It does not apply to expenditure on information and communications technology.

A 'small business' is defined as one with a turnover of less than £2.8 million annually, assets worth not more than £1.4 million and no more than fifty employees.

Research and Development (R&D)

Where a business fulfils certain conditions, it is entitled to immediately write off the whole of its capital spending on R&D against income. To qualify, a company must spend more than £25,000 on qualifying R&D expenditure before it can obtain the relief. R&D tax credits give extra relief for certain R&D spending by small and medium sized companies (there may be a different definition of company size to that stated above). The definition of R&D expenditure is detailed but, broadly, the activities must be creative or innovative and performed in the fields of science or technology and must be undertaken with a view to extend the knowledge in that field. Commercial development without scientific or technological investigation will not satisfy the tests. However, the following are not appropriate R&D activities:

- general education and training;
- scientific and technical information services;
- general purpose data collection;
- acquisition of rights in R&D.

Where all the criteria are satisfied, there is a significant capital allowance for capital expenditure on scientific research related to a trade, incurred whilst carrying on that trade or where a person commences a trade connected with that research.

The 2002 Budget heralded a 25 per cent 'super deduction' for large companies. Taxpayers will generally be able to claim a deduction even though they may outsource their R&D activities to approved institutions such as universities.

Essentially, the Budget mirrored the R&D concession available to small and medium enterprises.

Investment Readiness Programme

You should also be aware of the investment readiness pilot project which the government announced in the 2002 Budget. The programme is aimed at helping small businesses with regard to different financing options and will also offer practical support to help small businesses become 'investment ready'.

7. The future for e-business and e-commerce

Unfortunately, the future for a business entering into e-commerce is uncertain from the point of view of its tax position. There is a plethora of draft legislation and UK and international policy reports, together with UK and international recommendations which are, at the most, flawed and inadequate to protect the revenue base and at the same time provide an efficient environment in which e-businesses may transact.

The areas or topics that are under current consideration include:

- The effect of having a web server in a country. In particular, it remains to be conclusively determined whether a web server constitutes a permanent establishment. It appears at this stage that it will.
- The effect of an in-country web-site hosting service. Again, this is an international tax issue and focuses on the effect of having 'agents' (non-resident web-sites which provide the services advertised) and whether this constitutes a permanent establishment.
- Transfer pricing rules. E-commerce may be used to facilitate companies establishing pricing arrangements with the result that income is predominantly sourced in tax havens and remains outside the UK and other OECD member states' tax nets.

From a tax perspective, the key considerations for international governments and the OECD are twofold:

1. Ensure that commercial benefits at a domestic and international level are not stifled by the taxation burden; and
2. Ensure that the revenue base is not eroded by the advent of e-commerce.

If the international governments and bodies are able to adhere to these principles then businesses may take a great deal of comfort. However, it is a case of 'let's wait and see'.

The other future consideration is changing technology. New and more advanced technologies may eventually mean that tax authorities will be able to download entire trading records from e-businesses and issue assessments for tax based on these figures.

So what can be done to plan ahead? The obvious route for businesses is to stay in touch with what is going on by checking some of the Internet sites, and keeping 'an ear to the ground' with bricks to clicks colleagues. The media are generally quite good at broadcasting the more significant news items.

Also, a business must stay as flexible as possible so that it may quickly adapt to any change that is introduced.

The Application of Competition Laws and E-commerce

Introduction

Competition law has three principal aims:

1. to prohibit anti-competitive agreements;
2. to prohibit the abuse of a dominant position; and
3. to control anti-competitive mergers.

These aims apply as much to companies active in e-commerce and the internet as they do to those in other areas of commercial activity. The EU and UK competition authorities aim to adopt a flexible approach suited to the fast-moving internet and e-commerce markets by using the established competition law framework and by relying on tried-and-tested economic principles. As there is no new body of competition law or principles to apply, analogies and examples from other sectors can be applied with equal measure to the internet and e-commerce sectors. As described below, the consequences of not considering competition law issues in relation to any proposed agreement or conduct may be very serious. Awareness of the fundamental principles of competition law is important for anyone involved in commercial negotiations or decision-making.

This chapter aims to provide:

■ a summary of EU and UK competition law;
■ guidance on what types of agreement and behaviour are acceptable and what areas must be avoided;
■ guidance on mergers in e-commerce and internet markets; and
■ examples of decisions and cases relating to e-commerce and the internet to illustrate the issues raised.

1. EU and UK competition law

This section sets out the key provisions of EU and UK competition law. In practice, many other competition law regimes exist and may be relevant to any particular agreement or conduct. Some comfort may, however, be gained from the fact that most EU member states have regimes that mirror EU law and therefore compliance with the EU regime will generally ensure EU-wide compliance. The possibility remains, however, that some non-EU regimes may be relevant.

1.1 EU competition law

The two fundamental principles of competition law are set out in Articles 81 and 82 of the EC Treaty. Article 81 prohibits anti-competitive agreements and Article 82 prohibits the abuse of a dominant position. These provisions are set out below in full for reference:

Article 81(1)
The following shall be prohibited as incompatible with the common market: all agreements between undertakings, decisions by associations of undertakings and concerted practices which may affect trade between Member States and which have as their object or effect the prevention, restriction or distortion of competition within the common market, and in particular those which –

a) directly or indirectly fix purchase or selling prices or any other trading conditions;
b) limit or control production, markets, technical development, or investment;
c) share markets or sources of supply;
d) apply dissimilar conditions to equivalent transactions with other trading parties, thereby placing them at a competitive disadvantage;
e) make the conclusion of contracts subject to acceptance by the other parties of supplementary obligations which, by their nature or according to commercial usage, have no connection with the subject of such contracts.

Article 81(2)
Any agreements or decisions prohibited pursuant to this Article shall be automatically void.

Article 81(3)
The provisions of paragraph 1 may, however, be declared inapplicable in the case of

– any agreement or category of agreements between undertakings;
– any decision or category of decisions by associations of undertakings;
– any concerted practice or category of concerted practices;

which contributes to improving the production or distribution of goods or to promoting technical or economic progress, while allowing consumers a fair share of the resulting benefit, and which does not –

a) *impose on the undertakings concerned restrictions which are not indispensable to the attainment of these objectives;*
b) *afford such undertakings the possibility of eliminating competition in respect of a substantial part of the products in question.*

Article 82
Any abuse by one or more undertakings of a dominant position within the common market or in a substantial part of it shall be prohibited as incompatible with the common market in so far as it may affect trade between Member States.
Such abuse may, in particular, consist in –

a) *directly or indirectly imposing unfair purchase or selling prices or other unfair trading conditions;*
b) *limiting production, markets or technical development to the prejudice of consumers;*
c) *applying dissimilar conditions to equivalent transactions with other trading parties, thereby placing them at a competitive disadvantage;*
d) *making the conclusion of contracts subject to acceptance by the other parties of supplementary obligations which, by their nature or according to commercial usage, have no connection with the subject of such contracts.*

It is clear that, in each case, an effect on trade between Member States is essential for an infringement to have occurred. Where no such effect is likely – for example, the agreement is made between two UK-based companies – it is necessary to consider national laws.

1.2 UK competition law

The key provisions of UK competition law are set out in sections 2 and 18 of the Competition Act 1998, and are known as the Chapter I and Chapter II prohibition respectively. They mirror almost exactly the EU provisions with the exception of the reference to trade between Member States:

The Chapter I prohibition
Agreements between undertakings, decisions by associations of undertakings or concerted practices which –

a) *may affect trade within the United Kingdom, and*

b) *have as their object or effect the prevention, restriction or distortion of competition within the United Kingdom,*

are prohibited unless they are exempt in accordance with the provisions of this Part.
Subsection (1) applies, in particular, to agreements, decisions or practices which –

a) *directly or indirectly fix purchase or selling prices or any other trading conditions;*
b) *limit or control production, markets, technical development or investment;*
c) *share markets or sources of supply;*
d) *apply dissimilar conditions to equivalent transactions with other trading parties, thereby placing them at a competitive disadvantage;*
e) *make the conclusion of contracts subject to acceptance by the other parties of supplementary obligations which, by their nature or according to commercial usage, have no connection with the subject of such contracts.*

Subsection (1) applies only if the agreement, decision or practice is, or is intended to be, implemented in the United Kingdom.
Any agreement or decision which is prohibited by subsection (1) is void.
The Director may grant an exemption from the Chapter I prohibition .... if the agreement ... contributes to (a):

improving production or distribution; or
promoting technical or economic progress,
while allowing customers a fair share of the resulting benefit; but (b) does not:

impose on the undertakings concerned restrictions which are not indispensable to the attainment of those objectives; or
afford the undertakings concerned the possibility of eliminating competition in respect of a substantial part of the products in question.

The Chapter II prohibition
Any conduct on the part of one or more undertakings which amounts to the abuse of a dominant position in a market is prohibited if it may affect trade within the United Kingdom.
Conduct may, in particular, constitute such an abuse if it consists in –

a) *directly or indirectly imposing unfair purchase or selling prices or other unfair trading conditions;*
b) *limiting production, markets or technical development to the prejudice of consumers;*

c) applying dissimilar conditions to equivalent transactions with other trading parties, thereby placing them at a competitive disadvantage;

d) making the conclusion of contracts subject to acceptance by the other parties of supplementary obligations which, by their nature or according to commercial usage, have no connection with the subject of the contracts.

Given the close similarities between EU and UK law, it is appropriate to consider Article 81 alongside Chapter I, and Article 82 alongside Chapter II.

1.3 Article 81/Chapter I

These provisions are exceptionally broadly drafted and could, in principle, prohibit any agreement entered into between two or more persons which contains any restrictions on commercial behaviour whatsoever. This is supported by briefly addressing some of the key concepts of the provisions:

Agreement

This covers any agreement, whether legally enforceable or not, and whether written or oral. There does not have to have been any meeting of the parties, and telephone calls will suffice so long as an agreement was reached. The prohibitions also apply to decisions of trade associations and to concerted practices – where there need be no formal agreement or decision to act in a certain way, merely a consensus as to some form of practical cooperation.

Undertakings

This includes any natural or legal person so long as they are capable of carrying on commercial or economic activities. A sole trader is quite capable of entering into an anti-competitive agreement.

Effect on trade

Both EU and UK competition law require there to have been some effect on trade, either between Member States or in the case of the UK legislation, within the UK. Where an agreement involves parties based in the UK, then an effect on trade within the UK is almost certain to be found. The more difficult question is to determine whether there has been an effect on trade between Member States. In practice, this term is interpreted very widely by the European Commission to include actual, as well as potential, effects on trade. As a consequence, even agreements between parties in one Member State have been found to infringe EU law where they have a potential effect on trade, for example, by making it more difficult for companies from other Member States to enter a particular market.

It follows that the scope of Article 81 and the Chapter I prohibition is very broad. Given the many millions of commercial agreements entered into each year, it is not surprising that there are a number of measures in place to ensure that only the more serious anti-competitive agreements merit the full sanctions that follow an infringement of the competition laws (see section 1.5 below).

When deciding whether a particular agreement does, in fact, infringe Article 81/Chapter I, it is necessary to consider:

- Whether the agreement has an *appreciable* effect on competition;
- Whether any *exemptions* apply to the agreement; and
- Whether the agreement is *excluded* from the prohibitions altogether.

Appreciability

An agreement will infringe Article 81/Chapter I only if it has as its object or effect an *appreciable* prevention, restriction or distortion of competition. This follows from established case law of the European Court of Justice which the Office of Fair Trading (OFT) and the UK courts are bound to follow under section 60 of the Competition Act. Any agreement not having an appreciable effect on competition is unlikely to be of interest to the competition authorities.

In the UK, the OFT takes the view that an agreement will generally have no appreciable effect on competition if the parties' combined share of the relevant market does not exceed 25 per cent. However, any agreement between undertakings which:

- directly or indirectly fixes prices or shares markets; or
- imposes minimum resale prices; or
- is one of a network of similar agreements which have a cumulative effect on the market in question;
- may be capable of having an appreciable effect on competition even where the combined market share falls below the 25 per cent threshold.

Where the parties' combined market share is higher than 25 per cent, the OFT may still find that the effect on competition is not appreciable. This will depend on other factors such as the contents of the agreement and the structure of the market affected.

The position at EU level is similar, but slightly less generous. The Commission's approach is set out in its *Guidelines on Agreements of Minor Importance*. These indicate that, in relation to horizontal agreements (i.e. those made between persons at the same level of the distribution chain), agreements between persons with a market share of less than 10 per cent are unlikely to raise competition concerns. In relation to vertical agreements – for example, agreements between suppliers and distributors – a market share of 15 per cent must be reached before there is any likelihood that the agreement will have an appreciable effect on competition.

As in the UK, certain hard-core restrictions will always be regarded as having an appreciable effect on competition at EU level – in particular price-fixing provisions and export bans. Likewise, where there is a network of similar agreements in a market, it may not be possible to rely on the above thresholds.

In practice, therefore, it is likely that the vast majority of e-commerce agreements, even those containing restrictive provisions, will not be regarded as giving rise to an appreciable effect on competition. This is especially so during any start-up period when market shares will inevitably be low, although the market share of the other party or parties involved in any agreement or concerted practice must of course be considered.

Exemptions

Even when an agreement has an appreciable effect on competition, the law recognises that many such agreements give rise to benefits to consumers and to the market in general. A classic example would be an exclusive distribution agreement, under which a distributor is granted exclusive rights to distribute a particular product in a given territory. The fact that the distributor is, in effect, ring-fenced from competition from other distributors of the same products in its territory makes it more likely that he will invest time and effort (and resources) into ensuring the effective distribution of that product. Hence consumers benefit from an agreement that, on its face, is anti-competitive.

Article 81(3) of the EC Treaty and Chapter I of the Competition Act set out detailed provisions relating to exemptions. (Notably no exemptions are available from the Article 82/Chapter II prohibitions.) These are of three kinds:

1. An individual exemption in respect of an individual agreement where the agreement can be shown to contribute to improving production or distribution, or to promoting technical or economic progress, and which allows consumers a fair share of the resulting benefit. Any restrictions contained in the agreement must be indispensable to the attainment of those objectives, and the overall agreement must not afford the possibility of eliminating competition in a substantial part of the products concerned. An agreement must be notified to the OFT or European Commission in order to receive an individual exemption.

2. Block exemptions cover particular categories of agreements that meet the exemption criteria for an individual exemption. An agreement that falls within a block exemption will be exempt automatically and does not need to be notified in order to benefit from the exemption. The key block exemptions in force at the date of publication, all of which derive from Community legislation, are those relating to:

- vertical agreements;[1]
- technology transfer agreements;[2]
- motor vehicle distribution agreements;[3]
- specialisation agreements;[4]
- research and development agreements.[5]

Other block exemptions exist in the air and marine transport sectors and a UK block exemption exists for public transport ticketing schemes.

3. UK law recognises parallel exemptions which in effect apply to agreements that benefit from individual or block exemption under Article 81(3). This exemption also covers agreements which fall within the terms of a Commission block exemption but which are not subject to Article 81 because they do not affect inter-state trade. These are automatically exempted under the Competition Act without the need for individual notification.

Exemptions are time-limited and may be granted subject to certain specified conditions or obligations. Under UK law the exemption can take effect from a date that is earlier than that on which it is granted, while under EU law backdated exemptions are only available for vertical and intellectual property agreements.

Exclusions

Under UK law, certain agreements and/or conduct are excluded from one or both of the competition prohibitions altogether. Broadly, these are as follows:

Agreements excluded from the Chapter I prohibition

1. An agreement which is subject to competition scrutiny under the Financial Services Act 1986, the Companies Act 1989, the Broadcasting Act 1990, or the Environment Act 1995.
2. An agreement which is required in order to comply with, and to the extent that it is, a planning obligation.
3. An agreement which is the subject of a direction under section 21(2) of the Restrictive Trade Practices Act 1976.
4. An agreement for the constitution of a European Economic Area regulated market, to the extent that it relates to the rules made or guidance issued by that market.
5. An agreement where it relates to production of or trade in agricultural products as defined in the EC Treaty and in Council Regulation (EEC) No. 26/62, or to farmers' cooperatives.
6. An agreement which constitutes a designated professional rule, imposes obligations arising from such a rule, or constitutes an agreement to act in accordance with such rules.

Agreements and/or conduct excluded from the Chapter I *and* the Chapter II prohibition

1. An agreement/conduct resulting in a merger or joint venture within the merger provisions of the Fair Trading Act 1973 (see the OFT's guideline 'Mergers and Ancillary Restrictions' for further detail).
2. An agreement/conduct resulting in a concentration with a Community dimension and therefore subject to the EC Merger Regulation.
3. An agreement/conduct to the extent to which it is made/engaged in to comply with a specified legal requirement.
4. An agreement/conduct which is necessary to avoid conflict with international obligations and which is also the subject of an order by the Secretary of State.
5. An agreement/conduct which is necessary for compelling reasons of public policy and which is also the subject of an order by the Secretary of State.
6. An agreement/conduct which relates to a coal or steel product within the ECSC Treaty.
7. An agreement made or conduct engaged in by an undertaking entrusted with the operation of services of general economic interest or of a revenue producing monopoly, in so far as the prohibition would obstruct the performance of those tasks.

Practical steps

Having carried out an analysis of whether an agreement is potentially caught by Article 81/Chapter I, it is necessary to consider whether the agreement has an appreciable effect on competition, whether it benefits from an exemption or indeed whether it is excluded from the prohibitions altogether. It should then be possible to reach a view as to whether the agreement in question is at risk of being found to be infringing competition law. There are three options for the parties to an infringing agreement:

1. To disregard the risks and proceed. This is a risky strategy given the consequences of infringement (see below), but may be acceptable where there are good arguments that the agreement does not fall foul of competition law and that an exemption may be available if the agreement ever became the subject of scrutiny.
2. To seek guidance or notification from the competition authorities (see 'procedure' below). This may involve some time and expense but will be the only way of obtaining legal certainty.
3. To amend the agreement so as to remove the restrictive elements or to redraft them to satisfy the relevant block exemption, etc.

1.4 Article 82/Chapter II

These provisions are both more straightforward and more complex than the

Article 81 based prohibition. In essence, there are two stages in deciding whether an infringement of Article 82/Chapter II has occurred:

1. An undertaking must enjoy a dominant position. This has been defined by the European Court of Justice as '*a position of economic strength enjoyed by an undertaking which enables it to prevent effective competition being maintained on the relevant market by affording it the power to behave to an appreciable extent independently of its competitors, customers and ultimately of consumers*' (Case 27/76 *United Brands v. EC Commission* [1978] ECR 207; I CMLR 429). This definition may not ultimately be helpful in determining whether a company is in a dominant position. The OFT and Commission have therefore indicated that a market share in the order of 50 per cent will be indicative of a dominant position. Such a finding may be rebutted if barriers to entry are low or buyer power high, such that the high market share does not in fact give rise to any real market power.

2. That undertaking must abuse its position. There is nothing unlawful about having a dominant position, but it puts the undertaking in the delicate position of having to behave in such as way as not to constrain competition in that market, and particularly not to act in such a way as to prevent existing or new competitors from challenging its position. Some of the more commonly found examples of abuse include:

   - excessive pricing;
   - discriminatory pricing;
   - refusals to supply;
   - loyalty discounts;
   - predatory pricing;
   - tie-ins;
   - full line forcing.

As stated above, a breach of Article 82/Chapter II is incapable of being exempted and will always be found to have an appreciable effect on competition. The options for any party believing it may be abusing a dominant position are therefore:

1. To continue the abusive conduct – this is a high-risk strategy given the likelihood of complaints from third parties, legal actions for damages and investigations and fines from the regulators (see below).
2. To notify the conduct to the competition authorities. This is only worth doing where there are arguments as to why the conduct should not be seen as unlawful.
3. To cease to engage in the relevant conduct so as to remove any ongoing risk of fines, damages, etc. being imposed. Alternatively to amend the conduct so that the same commercial aims are achieved but in a lawful manner.

1.5 Consequences of breach

The consequences of infringing the competition laws are serious:

1. Financial penalties of up to a maximum of 10 per cent of the turnover of an undertaking in the UK for up to three years may be imposed for an infringement of either of the UK prohibitions. Under EU law, the fines can be imposed up to a maximum of 10 per cent of world-wide turnover.
2. Any agreement or conduct which infringes competition law is void and cannot be enforced. Where an individual provision in the agreement can be severed from the remainder of the agreement, then it is possible that the remainder of the agreement will remain enforceable.
3. Third parties who have suffered loss as a result of any unlawful agreement or conduct have a claim for damages in the national courts.

Furthermore, any company found to have infringed EU or UK competition law is likely to suffer bad PR as a consequence. This may not only depress share prices in the short term, but is also likely to make relations with the relevant regulator(s) more difficult in the future.

It follows that a serious infringement of the competition laws can be an expensive mistake. The OFT's first fine under the Competition Act was £3.2 million (imposed on Napp Pharmaceuticals by the decision of 30 March 2001 [No. CA98/2/2001] for an infringement of Chapter II); the Commission meanwhile has levied a number of fines in excess of €10 million (for example, VW and Tetrapak have both received fines in excess of £50 million for competition law infringement).

1.6 Procedure

Both the Commission and the OFT have very significant powers to investigate potential infringements of competition law. Such investigations are often launched as a result of a complaint having been made by an aggrieved competitor or customer. A full description of these powers is outside the scope of this chapter. All that needs be said is that all companies are now advised to have competition compliance programmes in place to ensure they do not unwittingly find themselves the subject of a Commission/OFT investigation.

We have already referred above to the possibility of notifying agreements to the competition authorities in order to obtain some degree of comfort. Various options are available to parties seeking to pursue this route:

1. Informal guidance can be obtained at any time from the competition authorities in respect of any actual or proposed agreement or conduct. Such guidance will have no binding legal effect but can provide some useful pointers as to whether a proposal is worth pursuing;

2. Formal guidance is available from the OFT in relation to any agreement or conduct that has actually been agreed to. Such guidance will be given on the basis of careful analysis and whilst not legally binding, does give immunity from fines and the OFT will not reopen the case unless new facts come to light justifying such a step;

3. Notifications can be made to both the OFT and the Commission seeking a formal decision as to whether an agreement or conduct infringes the relevant provisions and/or seeking an individual exemption in relation to an agreement which is found to infringe Article 81/Chapter I. Many notifications at EU level are closed by issuance of a comfort letter which is not legally binding but which gives the parties comfort that the Commission's file has been closed and that it will not take further action. Where a decision is given (and this normally takes some time to obtain especially at EU level) this will be legally binding and cannot be reopened simply because, for example, a complaint has been made by a third party. Where a notification is made, third party comment will be sought prior to any decision being taken, with the views of customers generally being given more weight than those of competitors.

2. Practical guidance – Agreements and conduct likely to give rise to an infringement

The discussion so far has been on a general basis, without reference to any specific e-commerce agreement or conduct. We now turn to highlight some of the specific types of agreement and conduct, which are likely to give rise to competition concerns and which should, as a general rule, be avoided. As a general rule these observations apply equally to EU and UK law.

2.1 Agreements and concerted practices

The key focus of most competition authorities is to identify, remove and punish, cartel and cartel-like agreements. When we speak of cartels, we mean any number of agreements which have the effect of restricting competition and specifically include agreements to:

- fix prices;
- agree production or sales quotas;
- share product or geographic markets; and/or
- ban exports or imports.

Agreements that contain these kinds of provisions, or are intended to achieve the same effect, are almost certain to fall foul of competition laws and result in fines being imposed. They must therefore be avoided.

Price fixing

Agreements that directly or indirectly fix prices are likely to infringe Article 81/ Chapter I. Such agreements may take many forms, for example:

1. An agreement between two competitors that they will charge the same amount for a particular product or service, or will not charge less than a certain amount, or will stick to a particular range of prices.
2. An agreement between a supplier and a distributor or reseller or wholesaler under which the supplier dictates to the distributor/wholesaler at what price he must sell the goods or services to third parties.
3. Agreements as above, but that relate to fixing discount levels rather than the price of the product/service itself will be equally unlawful.
4. Agreements that relate to elements of the price for a particular product or service, for example transport costs, after-sales costs, credit terms etc will also be regarded as having the same anti-competitive effect as a straightforward price-fixing arrangement.
5. Agreements allowing for the exchange of price lists, or for less formal consultations on pricing levels. Any such agreements should only be entered into after having taken detailed competition law advice.

Since price is arguably the most fundamental reflection of the levels of competition on any market, the agreements discussed above are always regarded seriously by competition authorities. Accordingly, caution should be exercised when drafting any e-commerce agreement in relation to any pricing conditions, especially given the ease with which information can be shared in the context of an internet-based contractual relationship.

Agreements to share markets

Market sharing is another well-recognised form of cartel behaviour: where two or more companies agree to share out a market between them, whether that be in terms of geographic territory, product or customer. Where the parties are actual or potential competitors, such agreements are likely to be regarded as seriously anti-competitive, unless there is a clear justification for the market being divided up in this way. In the context of e-commerce and the internet, it is most likely that any agreement under which markets are shared out, will be unlawful.

Agreements to limit production or investment

An agreement to limit production, or the availability of a particular product or service, is likely to have the effect of reducing supply and thereby increasing prices. Such agreements clearly restrict and distort competition contrary to Article 81/Chapter II. In the context of the internet, such an agreement could arise where two recruitment companies agreed to limit the advertising space to be made available on their particular web-sites, as a means of driving up prices. Alternatively, two manufacturers could agree to limit their research and development budgets as a means of increasing profits and ensuring the other party does not win an advantage over the other by launching any new products. Another form of agreement limiting output can be found in agreements relating to advertising – specifically those restricting the amount, nature or form of the advertising to be used by the parties.

Collusive tendering

This is really a form of market sharing. Where two or more companies agree which one or more of them should put forward the winning bid to a particular tender, this will amount to an unlawful market sharing agreement. It is unlikely that an exemption would ever be granted for such an arrangement, although the formation of a consortium to bid for a particular project will not normally of itself be regarded as anti-competitive.

Joint buying/selling

Any agreement relating to joint buying or selling has a similar effect on the market to price fixing. If a number of competitors all obtain a raw material at the same price, this removes one element of competition from the production process and increases the likelihood that there will be less variation in the resale prices offered by those competitors. Likewise, joint selling effectively means a loss of price competition between the parties involved which is likely to have a very significant effect on competition. The Commission has also considered the issue of joint selling in the context of business-to-business (B2B) market places. To avoid the creation of buyer power or the possibility of co-ordination in a downstream market, joint purchasing is only permissible in accordance with the Commission's horizontal guidelines (see section 4.1 for a discussion of B2B market places assessed under the EU Merger Regulation).

Information-sharing agreements

This is a difficult area, but as a general rule, confidential information as to prices, terms of trade, product specifications etc. should not be shared between competitors except on an aggregated and historic basis. Where this kind of confidential information is shared between competitors there is likely to be a very significant loss of competition since any element of competitive surprise brought about by pricing decisions or new product launches will be lost. Such agreements may infringe competition law even where they relate to information that is publicly available. The fact that the agreement facilitates the exchange of information will be sufficient for an infringement to have occurred (see also the *Volbroker* decision).

These broad headings encompass the majority of the types of e-commerce agreements that are likely to give rise to competition concerns. Any agreement will be judged on its effect on competition and not its form. Therefore, it is important to ask what the parties intend to achieve by a particular agreement, rather than hoping that the avoidance of any explicitly anti-competitive provisions will mean the agreement will not fall foul of competition laws.

Examples
In a recent case, the Commission took a strict approach where it considered a company was trying to protect its traditional lines of sale from the pro-competitive effects of electronic commerce. In December 2000, the Commission opened formal proceedings against B & W Loudspeakers Ltd (European Commission press release IP/00/1418, 6 December 2000) as the company was understood to be preventing its authorised dealers from engaging in distance selling such as sales over the internet. It will be recalled that Article 81 specifically refers to agreements which 'limit or control production, markets, technical development or investment' as being unlawful. Attempts by suppliers to control the persons to whom a distributor makes available its goods are therefore likely to be unlawful.

2.2 Abusive conduct

Where a company enjoys a dominant position, a further burden is placed on that company not to infringe the Article 82/Chapter II prohibitions by abusing its position. The following courses of conduct would generally tend to be seen as abusive and should be avoided.

Excessive pricing
The most obvious means for a dominant company to seek to take advantage of its position in the market is to over-charge for its products or services. The European Court has defined excessive pricing as meaning *'charging a price which is excessive because it bears no reasonable relation to the economic value of the product* supplied' (240/96/EC Commission Regulation on the application of Article 85(3) of the Treaty to certain categories of technology transfer agreements).

In practice, there is likely to be an abuse where the dominant company seeks to charge prices that are significantly higher than those charged by its competitors, or where it seeks to charge one set of customers a price which is significantly higher than the price charged to another set of customers (see also price discrimination below). Ironically, where a company is a monopoly supplier of a particular product or service, it may be difficult for the Commission or OFT to carry out any comparisons or to ascribe a fair value to the goods or products concerned.

Apparently excessive prices (and subsequently profits) may be objectively justifiable where a company needs to recoup significant investments, or where such profits reflect a highly efficient operation where high quality products are being supplied at low cost to the supplier. Such prices/profits should be short-term features of the market following which new entry would be expected to be stimulated to compete with the incumbent supplier. Generally, the prices charged need to allow for profits significantly and persistently exceeding the cost of capital before an abuse can be found.

Price discrimination

A dominant company will abuse its position where it applies different prices (or other terms and conditions) to different customers, assuming there is no objective justification for such discrimination. Such justification may derive from the customer's position (e.g. higher prices may be merited if the customer represents a higher than normal credit risk) or where the nature of the product or service means that the volume of the order genuinely has a significant impact on the price that can be quoted.

Predatory pricing

The response of a dominant company to a new entrant is often to engage in predatory pricing. This is when a dominant company reduces its prices to such a level as to ensure that the new entrant goes out of business, following which the dominant company increases its prices to the level they enjoyed prior to the new entrant having appeared on the market. Complex economic analysis (based on the relationship between the prices charged and the costs incurred in providing the product or service) is required in practice to demonstrate that the prices being charged are indeed predatory. Furthermore, evidence of the intent of the dominant company is also often used to strengthen the argument that there has been predatory pricing.

Dominant companies are entitled to react to new entry and compete vigorously; where, however, the response suggests the dominant company is accepting short term losses in the hope of removing that competitor, then this is likely to be regarded as unlawful. For a start-up company, this area of law may well be used to attack the behaviour of an incumbent dominant operator acting in such a way as to prevent the new entrant being successful.

Tie-in sales and bundling

A dominant company will frequently seek to use its strength in its core market to leverage market share in another market. This is normally done by making customers purchase a secondary product at the same time as a primary product, regardless of whether that secondary product is required. The most high-profile example of this kind of behaviour was seen in the Microsoft investigation in the US and the EU, where Microsoft's inclusion of its Netscape browser software within the Microsoft Office package led to complaints from providers of competing browser software who were effectively precluded from making a significant number of potential sales.

Where possible, dominant companies should ensure that they allow customers to pick and mix from the products and services being offered rather than being required to take any two or more products together – unless there are objective justifications for such bundling. A variation on this abuse is 'quantity forcing' whereby a customer (often a retailer) is required to purchase a specified volume of products. This will often have the effect of ensuring that the retailer is unable to offer competing products for sale since there will be insufficient shelf/storage space for such products.

Discounting

The use of discounts must be handled with care by companies in a dominant position. A straightforward volume-based discount is unlikely to give rise to concerns, but the use of fidelity or loyalty discounts – where the customer receives discounts based on the proportion of its sales which come from the supplier, are more than likely to be regarded as an abuse since their intention is clearly to put pressure on the retailer not to sell competing products. Compare the straight volume discount, which might indirectly have the same effect but would not result in any penalty were competing products to be purchased and subsequently sold. In practice, discounts tend to be drafted in subtly different ways and a careful analysis will be needed as to the effect of that discount on competition.

This is not a comprehensive list of unlawful abuses. Any behaviour which prevents or unfairly hinders new entry, or which exploits customers may well be found to be an abuse. In practice most abuses will fall into one of the above categories or the same principles will be applicable by analogy.

3. Practical guidance – Agreements that are unlikely to raise concerns

We have so far concentrated on those agreements that are likely to give rise to competition concerns. In practice, the overwhelming majority of e-commerce and internet agreements will not give rise to any such concerns and will be fully enforceable (from this perspective at least). This section seeks to highlight those agreements where the parties can be confident that, unless particular characteristics apply, there need be no competition concerns. In addition to what is said below, reference should be made to the concepts of appreciability, exclusions and exemptions above.

The fundamental distinction made for the purposes of classifying agreements in this chapter is between horizontal and vertical agreements. Horizontal agreements being those made between two or more companies at the same levels in the market (e.g. at the same level of production or distribution), and vertical agreements being made between companies at a different level of the production or distribution chain. This is not a watertight distinction however, since a vertical agreement made between two competitors will need to be assessed as both a horizontal and vertical agreement.

3.1 Horizontal agreements

The following types of horizontal agreements:

■ cooperation between non-competitors;
■ cooperation between competing companies that cannot independently carry out the project or activity covered by the cooperation; and
■ cooperation concerning an activity which does not influence the relevant parameters of competition,

will fall within Article 81/Chapter I only if they involve companies with significant market power and they are likely to make it harder for third parties to enter one or more relevant markets.

Furthermore, the Commission has indicated that where a horizontal agreement is made between two or more competing companies it will not be likely to infringe competition law where the market shares of the parties do not exceed 10 per cent. Guidance from the OFT, puts the figure at 25 per cent for agreements which only affect trade within the UK. In both cases, competing companies will not be able to rely on these thresholds where they have included price fixing or market sharing provisions in the agreement. Therefore, many agreements entered into by smaller start-up companies are unlikely to give rise to competition law infringement.

Example

As explained above, agreements between parties with higher market shares may also be permitted where they give rise to benefits for consumers outweighing their anti-competitive effects. A good example of this was the *Covisint* joint venture (European Commission press release IP/01/1155, 31 July 2001). This was an agreement between the world's five leading car manufacturers, to establish a B2B exchange in the automotive components market through a single portal on the internet. The Commission approved the venture after being satisfied that there was no discrimination against certain classes of users leading to foreclosure of the market; adequate data protection was in place to ensure that users did not have access to market-sensitive information; and the agreement did not allow for joint purchasing between car manufacturers for automotive products. This was the first major business-to-business exchange to be examined under Article 81.

The Commission also considered the Volbroker.com joint venture (European Commission press release IP/00/896, 31 July 2000) under Article 81. This concerned the creation, by six large banks, of an electronic brokerage for the trading of foreign exchange options. Initially, the transaction was thought to restrict competition. Once again, the Commission was primarily concerned with ensuring the protection of sensitive information and the possible threat of foreclosure of the market. However, it issued a comfort letter following a host of undertakings from the parties designed to avoid the exchange of commercially sensitive information and an assurance that the parent companies would allow voice brokers, acting as principals, to participate in the venture.

3.2 Vertical agreements

Both the EU and UK competition authorities recognise that in general, vertical agreements are less likely to give rise to detrimental effects on competition. It follows that there are more generous thresholds applying to these types of agreements.

The Commission will not regard a vertical agreement as giving rise to concerns unless the market shares of the parties exceed 15 per cent, and provided it does not contain price fixing provisions or an export ban.

For agreements entered into by parties with more than a 15 per cent market share it may often be possible to rely on the Vertical Agreements Block Exemption (2790/99/EC Commission Regulation on the application of Article 81(3) of the Treaty to categories of vertical agreements and concerted practices).This exempts, from Chapter I/Article 81, vertical agreements where the supplier's market share falls below 30 per cent again subject to certain provisos, being:

- the agreement must not be between competitors, unless it is non-reciprocal and either (a) the turnover of the buyer falls below €100 million or (b) the supplier manufactures and distributes the products whereas the buyer only distributes them;
- the agreement must not contain any price fixing provisions;
- the agreement must not restrict the persons to whom the buyer can sell on the goods or services (although it is permissible to impose an active sales ban in relation to customers based in territories reserved to other distributors or the supplier). For example, where a manufacturer has appointed an exclusive distributor to act as the only outlet for its products in a particular territory, say Germany, the Commission has indicated that it is perfectly acceptable for the distributor to set up a web-site over which it

can sell the products to customers in a territory covered by another exclusive distributor, say France. This is because the distributor is engaging in passive selling, whereby it is not actively selling its product in France. If, however, the web-site specifically targeted the French market, for example if it was in French and listed contact numbers for customers based in France, this would be regarded as active selling and would not be permissible;

- the agreement must have any exclusive provisions limited to a five-year term;
- where the agreement contains an exclusive supply obligation, the relevant market share is that of the buyer – whose market share must fall below 30 per cent.

Meanwhile, in the UK, all vertical agreements are excluded from the prohibitions in the Competition Act, other than those containing price fixing provisions (See the Competition Act 1998 (Land and Vertical Agreements Exclusion) Order 2000. The Government has proposed removing the exclusion for vertical agreements. This issue should therefore be checked before relying on the Order.)

In practice, this means the vast majority of e-commerce vertical agreements (e.g. all agreements for the supply of goods or services) should be regarded as benign under EU and UK competition law so long as the hardcore restrictions, such as price fixing are avoided.

4. Merger control

The laws discussed above have referred to agreements and conduct, in other words the day-to-day commercial activities of companies in the e-commerce and internet sector. Merger control laws apply where an agreement gives rise to a change of control of an undertaking and certain specified turnover, asset value or market share thresholds are met. There are many examples of co-operation in the e-commerce and internet sector which have given rise to merger situations requiring the clearance of one of more merger control authorities.

Almost 100 countries world-wide now have merger control laws in place. This text refers only to the EU and UK regimes. One key point to note in respect of merger control laws, is that whilst notification of agreements is voluntary in respect of Article 81 and Chapter I, most merger control regimes impose a mandatory filing requirement. Thus, the first question to be asked in assessing any agreement is (a) is this a merger; if so (b) does it fall within any one or more merger control regimes; and, if so (c) are there any mandatory filing requirements.

4.1 EU merger control

Merger Regulation 4064/89 (the Regulation) requires that certain large-scale mergers ('concentrations having a Community dimension') must be notified to the Commission for clearance and, subject to certain very limited exceptions, cannot be the subject of parallel merger inquiries under the domestic merger control provisions of EEA (that is EU and EFTA) Member States. (The EFTA Member States are Norway, Iceland and Liechtenstein).

'Concentration'

The concept of a concentration includes full and partial mergers, some joint ventures and acquisitions of control.

Control is defined by the Regulation as the ability to exercise *decisive influence* over an undertaking by, in particular, the ownership or right to use all or part of its assets or the existence of rights or contracts conferring decisive influence on the composition, voting or other commercial decisions of the undertaking. For example, an undertaking can acquire control over another when it holds 50 per cent or less of the other's voting shares, but nevertheless has the de facto ability to affect strategic decisions of that undertaking. Where a minority stake gives rise to decisive influence, the acquisition of such an interest may result in the creation of joint control whereby two or more undertakings are able to exercise decisive influence jointly and thereby share control. This is normally the situation in a joint venture.

'Community dimension'

A concentration will have a Community dimension if:

a) the combined aggregate worldwide turnover of all the undertakings concerned is more than €5 billion (around £3,089 million; exchange rate as at 7 November 2001); and

b) the aggregate Community/EFTA-wide turnover of each of at least two of the undertakings concerned is more than €250 million (£154 million);

unless each of the undertakings concerned achieves more than two-thirds of its aggregate Community-wide turnover within one and the same Member State. (Only concentrations with a Community dimension are referred to in the remainder of this section.)

A concentration also has a Community dimension if:

a) the combined aggregate world-wide turnover of all the undertakings concerned is more than €2.5billion (around £1,544 million; exchange rate as at 7 November 2001);

b) the aggregate Community-wide turnover of each of at least two of the undertakings concerned is more than €100 million (around £61 million);

c) in each of at least three EU Member States the combined aggregate turnover of all of the undertakings concerned is more than €100 million (around £61 million); and

d) in each of at least three of these Member States the aggregate turnover of each of at least two of the undertakings concerned is more than €25 million (around £15 million);

unless each of the undertakings concerned achieves more than two-thirds of its Community-wide turnover within one and the same Member State.

There are complex rules setting out how turnover should be calculated.

Joint ventures

The creation of a joint venture performing on a lasting basis all the functions of an autonomous economic entity (i.e. a 'full-function' joint venture) constitutes a concentration for the purposes of the Regulation. Accordingly, full-function joint ventures which satisfy the turnover thresholds are subject to the Regulation.

Joint ventures which are not full-function are subject to Articles 81 and 82 of the EC Treaty and possibly also to national merger control laws. Full-function joint ventures which do not satisfy the turnover thresholds and which have as their object or effect the coordination of the competitive behaviour of undertakings that remain independent will also be subject to Articles 81 and 82 and possibly also to national merger laws. Full-function joint ventures which do not satisfy the turnover thresholds but which also do not have this object or effect will fall subject only to national merger laws (where they apply).

Procedure

Any concentration with a Community dimension must be notified (on Form CO) to the Commission, at the latest, one week after the earliest of the conclusion of the agreement, the announcement of the bid or the acquisition of control.

The concentration may not be put into effect before notification and is automatically suspended until a decision of compatibility with the common market (see below), unless the Commission has waived the suspensory requirement.

In straightforward cases, a concentration will be cleared within a month, or six weeks where undertakings are negotiated. In difficult cases raising competition issues, the Commission's timetable may extend to five months in total.

Will the whole transaction be covered by the Regulation?

A clearance of a concentration under the Regulation will by implication include clearance of all 'ancillary restrictions'. These are contractual terms or arrangements which might restrict competition but which are 'directly related and necessary to the implementation of the concentration'.

The difficulty lies in the Commission's construction of the words 'directly related' and 'necessary'. Restrictive arrangements not considered to be ancillary to the concentration will need to be assessed separately under Articles 81 and 82.

The approval process

In assessing a concentration, the Commission will determine whether it creates or strengthens a dominant position in the relevant market with the consequence that effective competition in the common market or a substantial part of it would be significantly impeded. If this is the case, the concentration must be declared incompatible with the common market. Unlike EU law on dominant positions (Article 82 EC Treaty), there is no requirement for abusive conduct; the mere creation of a dominant position with foreseeable competition risks will by itself be sufficient. In making this assessment, the combined market share of the merged undertakings within the relevant product and geographical markets will be an important factor, as will the magnitude of barriers to entry and expansion, procurement patterns and the existence of any vertical links between the parties.

The Regulation contains provisions allowing the Commission to attach conditions to the clearance of a merger, either after the initial period of inquiry or following a full investigation. Such requirements could include commitments on the part of the acquirers to divest certain parts of the target undertaking with a view, for example, to reducing market share or eliminating other competition concerns.

Third party comments

The procedures under the Regulation make full accommodation for third party comments. Competitors and customers will be sent questionnaires by the Commission, and a notice will be published in the Official Journal seeking any additional third party comment. Finally, it would be open to a party that could establish a legitimate interest to appeal a Commission decision to the European Court of Justice.

Examples

The dominance test as set out in the Regulation has provided an effective means of examining the impact of mergers in many hi-tech sectors such as telecommunications, the internet and the media. Generally speaking, the Commission aims to develop an environment, which allows an open and competitive internet market to flourish.

The Commission has addressed competition concerns in cases where it has considered that access to networks is essential for the provision of other services leading to the so-called Gatekeeper effect, where the dominant party is able to dictate the conditions in the market. Many of the cases concern potential dominance in the infrastructure used for electronic commerce or the control of upstream content.

The prohibited MCI Worldcom/Sprint merger (Case No. COMP/M.1741 MCI Worldcom/Sprint, 28 June 2000) was an example of a case where the Gatekeeper effect was produced by a horizontal overlap (i.e. the combination of two operators' networks). The Commission was primarily concerned that the concentration would create an entity with such a strong lead in the market for top-level connectivity providers that its competitors and consumers would be unable to exert any competitive constraint upon it. The Commission was equally concerned that control over such an important infrastructure could be used to leverage the parties' positions into related markets.

The same theme arose in the case of Vodafone/Mannesmann (Case No. COMP/M.1795 – Vodafone Airtouch/Mannesmann, 12 April 2000). The parties intended to merge their national mobile networks to form a pan-European network. The Commission was concerned that the accumulation of the various networks would create a company of such magnitude in the market for the delivery of pan-European services that it would have an anti-competitive effect. The Commission allowed the concentration but required the entity to open up its integrated network to its competitors for three years. This ensured that the company's strong position in one market could not be used to strengthen its position in the related service market. The time limit recognised the fact that competitors were likely to try to build an alternative infrastructure in the future.

The Gatekeeper effect has also arisen in the context of vertical integration (i.e. the combination of services at different levels of the supply chain). A clear example is the AOL/Time Warner case (Case No. COMP/M.1845 – AOL/Time Warner, 11 October 2000) in which the Commission considered that the concentration would result in the vertical integration of AOL's service provision with the media and entertainment content of Time Warner and Bertelsmann. The new entity would probably be dominant in the online music delivery market by becoming a Gatekeeper and being allowed to dictate the terms for the distribution of music over the internet. The Commission eventually cleared the merger on the basis that AOL / Time Warner would divest itself of Bertelsmann.

Vertical integration concerns also emerged in the proposed Vizzavi joint venture between Vodafone, owner of the Mannesmann group, and Vivendi, owner of Canal + (Case NO COMP/JV.48 – Vodafone/Vivendi/Canal+). The parties intended to create an internet portal service designed to group together information and transactional services on one convenient site accessible via computers, televisions and mobile phones. However, the Commission was concerned that the parties' existing strong positions in the infrastructures of pay television and mobile networks could be leveraged into the internet portals market. To remedy this, the Commission's approval was conditional upon the parties granting third parties the same access to their facilities as the joint venture would enjoy.

The emergence of popular web-based B2B trading and B2B electronic marketplaces promises to create a more transparent, cost-effective and efficient means of conducting business. Essentially, buyers and sellers of similar products are able to carry out procurement activities using computer systems. The Commission has cleared a large number of electronic market-places in a variety of industries. For example, the Commission gave the green light to MyAircraft.com (Case No. COMP/M.1696 – UTC/Honeywell/12/ MYAIRCRAFT.COM, 8 August 2000), a joint venture between UTC and Honeywell for the one-stop provision of shopping and supply management functions to all aerospace participants. The Commission found there were no competition concerns as alternative modes of conducting business were available to third parties and it was likely that the venture would face competition from other existing or planned B2B market places in the same sector.

Similarly, the Commission approved the Emaro joint venture between Deutsche Bank and SAP, providers of software (press release IP/00/783, 14 July 2000. 7. Press release IP/00/1775, 10 December 2001). Emaro is an electronic trading platform allowing suppliers of office equipment to conduct business online with their suppliers. The Commission was satisfied that there was no overlap between the parent companies' activities in any of the markets relevant to the concentration.

More recently, the Commission cleared the creation of Eutilia and Endorsia electronic marketplaces. Eutilia is a joint venture between eleven European electricity utilities to provide B2B services in the area of procurement of goods and services to utilities in the electricity sector, including auctions, buy/ sell enquiries and supplier database services. Endorsia is owned by five manufacturers of machines and industry components. It is designed to support the buying and selling requirements of manufacturers, distributors and end-users for branded industrial goods and services by acting as an electronic interface between individual sellers and their customers. In both cases, the Commission found that the internet portals would be open to all potential users on a non-discriminatory basis without forcing exchange members to use the portal as their only means of conducting business. There was also sufficient protection to avoid commercially sensitive data from being disclosed between competitors.

A number of useful lessons can be learnt from the Commission's assessment of B2B marketplaces so far. Any companies wishing to establish an e-marketplace without infringing EU competition rules should consider the following guidelines if they wish to avoid the potential pitfalls that the Commission has identified in the past:

1. Ensure secure data protection and put in place safeguards against the exchange of information to protect against the exchange of sensitive information between competitors.
2. Joint purchasing is only permissible in conjunction with the Commission's horizontal guidelines so as to avoid the creation of buyer power or the possibility of coordination on the downstream market.
3. Ensure open and non-discriminatory access to the exchange from all interested parties in order to reduce potential market foreclosure concerns and ensure open access to the marketplace.
4. Ensure separation between the exchange venture and its parents supported by a Chinese Wall structure to address the problem of only a handful of privileged market participants having access to certain information due to their status as market owners;
5. Ensure that no attempts are made to lock users into the proposed exchange. This safeguards against the threat of market dominance by one exchange.

4.2 UK merger control

UK merger control legislation is primarily contained in the Fair Trading Act 1973 (FTA). The FTA applies to actual or proposed mergers where:

a) two or more 'enterprises' (at least one of which is carried on in the UK or by or under the control of a company incorporated in the UK) cease to be distinct (i.e. are brought under common control or ownership); and
b) either one or both of the following criteria is satisfied:
   - as a result of the merger a market share of 25 per cent or more of the supply or consumption of goods or services of a particular description in the UK is created or extended ('the market share test'); or
   - the gross value of the worldwide assets taken over exceeds £70 million ('the assets test'). 'Gross value of worldwide assets' means the gross book value of all assets less depreciation, renewals or diminution in value but without deducting liabilities of any kind. All assets 'employed in, or appropriated to, the enterprises which cease to be distinct enterprises' are included, except any enterprise which remains under the same ownership or control. In the context of a standard corporate acquisition this will therefore focus on the assets of the acquired enterprise.

The target company will be 'brought under common control or ownership' in the following circumstances:

a) when one party acquires a controlling interest in the other party (legal control); or
b) when one party acquires the ability to control the policy of the other (*de facto* control); or
c) when one party acquires the ability materially to influence the policy of the other. (Such an ability may arise from a shareholding as low as 15 per cent, and even in the absence of any shareholding, the existence of significant contractual relations between the parties may exceptionally give rise to such an ability.)

Procedure in dealing with the OFT – guidance and filings

Unlike other jurisdictions where prior clearance is mandatory, there is no obligation under the FTA to seek prior clearance of a merger which is subject to the FTA ('a qualifying merger') from the authorities either before or after the merger takes place.

The Director General is, however, obliged to keep himself informed about mergers which may qualify for investigation, and may seek information from the parties to any such qualifying merger.

There are two possible procedures for obtaining a 'clearance' (i.e. a decision by the Secretary of State that he will not refer a qualifying merger to the Competition Commission (CC)) and two methods of seeking guidance from the Secretary of State (through the OFT) before a proposed transaction is formalised.

Seeking confidential guidance

Confidential guidance may only be sought before a proposed acquisition becomes public knowledge. It is particularly useful in acquisitions where public disclosure of the parties' proposals would raise sensitive commercial issues.

Confidential guidance may be sought informally from the OFT. This will normally involve a meeting with the OFT preceded by a briefing paper and can be arranged at relatively short notice.

A formal application for guidance, which is given by the Secretary of State through the OFT, will require a fuller submission to be sent to the OFT which will then evaluate the merger as if it were a published case.

Under both procedures, the OFT is precluded from seeking the views of the interested third parties and is entirely dependant on published information or information supplied to it by the applicant. Consequently, in certain cases the Secretary of State or the OFT may feel unable to give confidential guidance.

Seeking clearance using a Merger Notice

There is no obligation under UK law to seek clearance for a merger. However, two means exist for doing so. The first is the statutory Merger Notice under which a merger is pre-notified to the OFT on a standard form following which the merger will (subject to the possibility of extension) be deemed to have been cleared by the Secretary of State twenty working days after submission of the Notice unless at or before that time it has been referred to the CC. The OFT may request further information and may seek one extension of time of fifteen working days.

Seeking clearance without a Merger Notice

The 'traditional', non-statutory way of seeking clearance from the Secretary of State (through the OFT) exists alongside the statutory procedure. This is the submission, in a bespoke format, of relevant information and market analysis, together with a request for clearance.

This route remains most appropriate for difficult or controversial cases (e.g. contested takeovers or mergers with significant market overlaps where the statutory timetable may not give the OFT time to reach a view).

The OFT aims to provide clearance from the Secretary of State within 45 working days from the receipt of a satisfactory submission in 90 per cent of cases.

Fees for merger clearance

Fees are payable for obtaining clearance. The amount of the fee depends on the value of the assets to be acquired.

Reference to the CC

The Secretary of State will refer a qualifying merger to the CC for further investigation when he considers that it is likely to operate against public interest.

Remedies

There is a statutory procedure for avoiding a reference to the CC under which the acquiror agrees to enforceable undertakings to the Secretary of State. Such undertakings are typically to dispose of the part of a business which gives rise to competition concerns, but can also relate to conduct.

If the CC concludes that a merger may be expected to operate against the public interest, the Secretary of State may prohibit the merger or allow it to proceed subject to conditions. He may also allow the merger to proceed unconditionally despite an adverse CC finding.

If the CC concludes that a merger may not be expected to operate against the public interest, the Secretary of State may not intervene.

To date there have been no detailed analyses in the UK of mergers in the e-commerce and internet sectors. The approval of the Commission in relation to ECMR cases is likely to be of some influence on the UK authorities when such a case is brought before them.

At the time of writing, the government has proposed significant reform of UK Merger Control in the Enterprise Bill. It was proposed that the assets test will be replaced with a turnover test of £45 million and the public interest will be replaced with a new test of 'substantial lessening of competition'.

5. Summary – what the risks are and how to be compliant

Competition law seeks to encourage commercial activity and not to stifle it. Large corporations with market power are expected to act more carefully in ensuring their agreements and conduct do not harm or restrict competition. However, a newly-formed company will not need to concern itself with whether it has abused a dominant position, nor will merger control laws generally apply to any small acquisitions it makes. All companies do, however, regardless of their size, need to ensure they do not enter into agreements which fix prices, share markets or which create actual barriers to trade across EU Member States' boundaries. Such restrictions regardless of the size of the parties will be unenforceable and may result in fines being imposed, or damages being sought by third parties.

Many companies, of all sizes, seek to limit their exposure to competition law by putting in place competition law compliance programmes, which are effectively audits of a company's agreements and practices coupled with training for senior management so as to ensure both past and future agreements and conduct reflect an awareness of competition law. Both the OFT and Commission have publicly stated that the existence of a compliance programme, along with evidence that it was observed and taken seriously, will be a factor in assessing the size of any fine to be imposed, should an infringement come to light. Such an awareness within the company will also help senior management to identify where competitors, suppliers or even customers are acting unlawfully and where it may be possible to make a complaint to the OFT or Commission or even to bring an action for damages, where loss has been suffered.

Notes

1. 2790/99/EC Commission Regulation on the application of Article 81(3) of the Treaty to categories of vertical agreements and concerted practices.
2. 240/96/EC Commission Regulation on the application of Article 85(3) of the Treaty to certain categories of technology transfer agreements.

3. 1475/95/EC Commission Regulation on the application of Article 85(3) of the Treaty to certain categories of motor vehicle distribution and servicing agreements.
4. 2658/2000/EC Commission Regulation on the application of Article 81(3) of the Treaty to categories of specialisation agreements.
5. 2659/2000/EC Commission Regulation on the application of Article 81(3) of the Treaty to categories of research and development agreements.

Appendix:
Useful Sources
of Information

Entity	Internet address
Chapter 1	
OFTEL (for unfair contract terms)	www.oftel.gov.uk
International Chamber of Commerce	www.iccwbo.org
European Commission	www.europa.eu.int
Chapter 2	
Whois domain name searches	www.whois.net
ICANN (registration of domain names)	www.icann.org
Nominet UK (domain name services)	www.nic.uk
Internet Service Providers Association	www.ispa.org.uk
Royal National Institute of the Blind's 'See It Right' campaign	www.rnib.org.uk/digital
The National Computing Centre (Escrow services)	www.ncc.co.uk
Chapter 3	
Information Commissioner's Office	http://www.dataprotection.gov.uk/
E-mail Preference Service (site includes preference service facilities for fax, e-mail, telephone and SMS)	http://www.emailpreferenceservice.co.uk/
Direct Marketing Association	www.dma.org.uk
	Http://www.dma.org.uk/shared/lgl_code.asp
DMA Codes of Practice	Http://www.dma.org.uk/shared/lgl code.asp
Financial Services Authority	www.fsa.gov.uk
Marketing Law web-site	www.marketinglaw.co.uk
Chapter 4	
European Commission	www.europa.eu.int/comm/index_en.htm
UK Trade Marks Agency	www.patent.gov.uk/tm

Entity	Internet address
Chapter 4 *continued*	
Office of Harmonisation in the Internal Market (OHIM)	www.oami.eu.int/en
Financial Services Authority	www.fsa.gov.uk
Council of Europe's Cybercrime Convention	www.conventions.coe.int/Treaty/EN/cadreprincipal
Internet Services Providers Association	www.ispa.org.uk
Chapter 5	
National Outsourcing Association	www.noa.co.uk
Chapter 6	
British Codes of Advertising and Sales Promotion	www.cap.org.uk – select 'The Codes' option on list of options.
Advertising Standards Authority (ASA)	www.asa.org.uk
The Interactive Advertising Bureau UK	www.iabuk.net
Admark scheme	www.admark.org.uk
Patents Office	www.patent.gov.uk
Office of Fair Trading	www.oft.gov.uk
Federal Trade Commission	www.ftc.gov
Cigarette Code (on ASA site)	http://www.asa.org.uk/index.asp?bhjs=1&bhsw=1024&bhsh=768&bhswi=1004&bhshi=602&bhflver=4&bhdir=1&bhje=1&bhcold=24&bhrl=-1&bhqt=-1&bhmp=-1&bhab=-1&bhmpex=&bhflex=4,0,28,0&bhdirex=8,0,0,206&bhcont=lan
Email Preference Service	www.emailpreferenceservice.co.uk
Direct Marketing Association	www.dma.org.uk
Marketinglaw.co.uk	www.marketinglaw.co.uk
Department of Trade & Industry	www.dti.gov.uk
Federal Trade Commission	www.ftc.gov
UK Intellectual Property	www.intellectual-property.gov.uk
Chapter 7	
The Internet Assigned Numbers Authority (IANA)	www.iana.org
The Internet Corporation for Assigned Names and Numbers (ICANN)	www.icann.org
VeriSign	www.verisign.com
Nominet	www.nic.uk

Entity	Internet address
Chapter 7 *continued*	
World Intellectual Property Organisation (WIPO)	www.wipo.int
National Arbitration Forum	www.arb-forum.com
CPR Institute for Dispute Resolution	www.cpradr.org
Eresolution Consortium	www.eresolution.ca
Chapter 8	
European Court of Human Rights	www.echr.coe.int
Information Commissioner	www.dataprotection.gov.uk
Chapter 9	
Business Link	www.businesslink.org.uk
Customs and Excise (e-commerce)	www.hmce.gov.uk/bus/vat/e-comm.htm
Customs and Excise (generally)	www.hmce.gov.uk
Inland Revenue (e-commerce)	www.inlandrevenue.gov.uk/ecommerce/index.htm
Inland Revenue (e-business)	www.inlandrevenue.gov.uk/ebu/index.htm
Inland Revenue (generally)	www.inlandrevenue.co.uk
Inland Revenue Information Centre	www.inlandrevenue.gov.uk/enq/index.htm
Office of the e-Envoy (Part of Cabinet)	www.e-nvoy.gov.uk/ecommerce_index.htm
Small Business Link	www.sbs.gov.uk
UK Online for Business	Www.ukonlineforbusiness.gov.uk
Chapter 10	
Competition Commission	www.competition-commission.gov.uk
Office of Fair Trading	www.oft.gov.uk
Europe Online	www.europa.int
Sources of information from the author	www.osborneclarke.com
	www.ocalliance.com
	www.marketinglaw.co.uk
	www.gamesbiz.net

Osborne Clarke

Osborne Clarke is a firm of solicitors with offices in London; Bristol; Thames Valley; Palo Alto (California); Cologne; Frankfurt and Copenhagen; and associated offices in: Paris, Brussels, Rotterdam, Barcelona, Madrid, Helsinki, Tallinn and St Petersburg.

Any enquiries should be directed to Simon Rendell, Head of the Technology, Media and Telecommunications Department at the London office or on his email at:
simon.rendell@osborneclarke.com

OSBORNE CLARKE UK OFFICES:

Osborne Clarke
London
Hillgate House
26 Old Bailey
London
EC4M 7HW

Tel: 020 7809 1000
Fax: 020 7809 1005

Osborne Clarke
Thames Valley
Apex Plaza
Forbury Road
Reading RG1 1AX

Tel: 0118 925 2000
Fax: 0118 925 0038

Osborne Clarke
Bristol
50 Queen Charlotte Street
Bristol BS1 4HE

Tel: 0117 917 3000
Fax: 0117 917 3005

Web-site: http://www.osborneclarke.com

Index